VIOLENCE

A Writer's Guide

Books by Rory Miller

Meditations on Violence
Facing Violence
Force Decisions
Violence: A Writer's Guide
Talking Them Through

Edited by Rory Miller

Leading the Way by Tim Bown
Campfire Tales from Hell

Co-Authored

Scaling Force, with Lawrence Kane

Writing as R. A. Ellis

Horrible Stories I Told My Children

VIOLENCE

A Writer's Guide

RORY MILLER

WYRD GOAT PRESS

Cover and interior book design by Kamila Miller

ISBN-13: 978-1481921466
ISBN-10: 1481921460

CreateSpace First Print Edition
Also available as an ebook from Smashwords, Amazon, Barnes and Noble and other retailers. This book and other fiction and non-fiction books can be purchased from the Wyrd Goat Press website.

ACKNOWLEDGMENTS

First and foremost: More than anything I have ever written VAWG was driven and directed by students. This second edition is a compilation of two on-line classes originally sponsored by Savvy Authors http://www.savvyauthors.com/vb/content.php. So, to the people on the forums at Savvy Authors and the e-mail lists at RWA Kiss of Death, Lowcountry RWA, and the FF&P chapters, and the in-person panels and workshops at the South Coast writer's Conference and Orycon—Thanks. It means more than you can know.

Jayel, Bart Kemper, Mike Moscoe, the deadly and insightful Krista, charming Wendy Wagner, intelligent and hilarious Jason V. Brock, brilliant and experienced Pat MacEwen and the Steves (Steve Barnes and Steve Perry) and dozens, maybe, of other co-panelists were all fun and educational.

The heroes and heroines in my life have been full and deep. They've bled and cried and buried friends, sometimes more friends than they can count except for one day a year that is just for that. And they've tossed babies in the air to hear them giggle. The big lessons came in blood and a lot of people have paid the price. Most can't be listed by name. Teammates and criminals; good friends and honorable enemies; even the many dishonorable enemies did more than merely inform this book. They made me. How do you thank someone for that?

Thanks to Steve Perry for graciously agreeing to do the foreword and to Sara Mueller, Kaila Lee, Guy Letourneau, and Lawrence Kane for looking over the manuscript. I owe you all lunch.

And lastly K. The keel on my ship, the smile on my face, the moon in my sky. Keeper of my sanity. Purpose for it all.

TABLE OF CONTENTS

FOREWORD

Real violence is seldom as it appears in movies, on TV, or in books. The classic squared-off duels, barehanded or with sharp things rarely ever happen in the real world. The guy who can nail flies in the air with a handgun he just picked up for the first time is as much a fantasy character as Mickey's dog Pluto. The fellow who trains for a few weeks and then goes on to defeat a horde of armed attackers with years of practice? The tiny woman who cleans out the biker bar in her spike heels? No, sorry. Things don't really work that way.

The hero who gets shot, or clonked on the head with a tire iron, or otherwise injured but who shakes it off as nothing and proceeds to kick ass is mostly a character of fiction. Yes, there are people who have done this, but they are less the rule than the exception.

Serious injury and illness can bring out the best and the worst in people, but it almost always does something that needs to be considered. A lot of people have been stabbed and didn't notice it until later. Some have been shot and didn't feel it.

Others have been batted by an open handed slap, or punched in the chest, and fallen over dead.

If you are writing about your intrepid spy or ninja, you need to know about physiology, weapons, and things hormonal that go back to the veldt and the caves. If you don't, you run the risk of losing readers who might know these things.

Schweitzer's Rule of Writing: If you don't know it, don't say it. Because as surely as you do and get it wrong, somebody out there will notice and call you on it. As soon as you snick that Glock's external safety on, you lose the gun nuts who know that there's no such thing.

I first became aware of Rory Miller six or seven years ago, which began a lively series of discussions about things martial, both on-line and over coffee. I have read all of his books, said good things about them in public, and developed a lot of respect for his abilities when push comes to shove. I've also gained respect for his abilities to tell people about the subject of push-comes-to-shove, both in person, and on the page.

These are distinct and different things, and because you can do one does not mean you can do the other. If you can do both, you have something to offer.

Which brings us to the current book at hand, the second edition of Violence: A Writer's Guide. The title is self-explanatory, and what the book offers is exactly that, based on Rory's experiences with real-world violence.

He'd rather I not talk about him much, but you need to understand what qualifications he brings, which include time in the military, as a deputy sheriff, and a stint as a civilian contractor in the militarily-active Middle East.

Hands-on experience counts in a lot of areas, and it matters here.

(Please note that Rory and I don't agree about everything he has to say, but since, with this title, we skew toward my realm, me being mostly a fiction writer, where we differ is more to the end of dramatic license than to reality.)

So why would a fiction writer need a how-to-write book by somebody who is not a fiction writer? Isn't that like the Pope talking about birth control?

Not quite.

If you are offering a tale, the ability to convince readers who know about a thing that you have a passing acquaintance with will go a long way to keep them turning pages. A lot of readers have great built-in bullshit detectors, and when it goes off, they stop reading. And even for those who don't know, the ring of truth will sometimes resound loudly enough to sell a story to a reader. They don't know for sure if it is true, but it sounds true, and they will go with it.

There is a caveat. The needs of fiction writers follow the classic dictum: Truth alone is no defense. A thing may be absolutely true, but useless in a story for a couple of reasons: 1) Even though it is true, it is boring, and 2) even though it is true, readers still won't believe it.

Violate either of these rules and you lose your readers.

You can fix this. You can figure out ways to make something that doesn't seem all that interesting more exciting. And you can make a thing sound true, even if it isn't.

Anybody here ever been to another planet via spaceship? No? But there are all kinds of stories that people will happily follow along wherein the writers have made that seem real enough so readers will suspend their disbelief.

Vampires? Zombies? Wizards?

I could offer a bunch of examples, but if you are adept enough to have read this far, you can think of plenty of your own. When you lead readers into make-believe, they will go along, if you know how to move carefully enough so you don't lose them.

Writer George Turner said, in *A Pursuit of Miracles*, "A thing can be told simply if the teller understands it properly." What Rory Miller does in this book is offer writers more understanding about violence and how it works. And since he understands it properly, he can do it in a straightforward and simple fashion.

In writing, as in life, you don't have to follow the rules all the time, but it really helps if you know what they are, and, when you break them, that it is intentional and not by accident. You need to know that just the right bit of lore dropped into just the right spot will do wonders for believability.

This book has a lot of that kind of lore. It's a gold mine for writers.

Herein is a wide swath of material, ranging from physical to physiological to psychological. Nuts-and-bolts stuff, links to articles, pictures, videos, and what is real versus what is not. This is good material, and some of it is hard to watch, and apt to disturb you, especially if you have never witnessed real world violence; but–you need to know. Both as a writer and as a citizen of our society. Because knowing is better than not-knowing.

If this is your first introduction to Rory Miller's writing, it's a good one. I offer that if you are a writer, you should consider further research among his other books.

Steve Perry
New York Times Bestselling Author of *The Man Who Never Missed*
Beaverton, Oregon, December, 2012

INTRODUCTION

I should explain myself, and also give an introduction to what you will get in this little book.

My name is Rory Miller, but I've been called "Sarge" in a jail, "sensei" in a dojo and "abu Orion" in Baghdad. Rory is fine.

I don't write fiction. I do write fight scenes. I have written some of the most realistic fight scenes ever ... because they have to stand up in court. Conflict is the core of drama and much of my adult life has centered around conflict. The good side is that I know a lot about real violence. One of the many downsides is that I know enough that most fiction is infuriating to read.

What follows won't teach writing techniques. If you are a good writer or at least learning to be a good writer, you know more about the nuances of plot and point of view and voice than I do.

What I will try to do here is introduce you to the world of violence. To the parts that people don't understand. The parts that books and movies get wrong. Not just the mechanics, but how people who live in a violent world think and feel about what they do and what they see done. The psychological, physical, and spiritual reality.

Once upon a time, I was sitting on a panel, "Bashing Your Way Through: Writing Realistic Fight Scenes" at the Oregon Science Fiction Convention. The moderator, a very nice lady named Jayel Gibson, opened the panel by declaring, "NO ONE engages in violence except out of great fear, great anger, or great desperation."

"I do it for money," I said.

Jayel almost choked, but we became good friends.

In what follows, we're going to go over weapons, how they are used, the mindset of someone who uses a weapon and the effects.

The effects will be the weakest part. I've had bones (especially fingers) broken with blunt objects and been concussed. People have tried, but I've never been successfully stabbed or shot. Shot at? Yes. Hit? No. So there are some details that would be hearsay if I went too deep, and that's not why you are here. If I go outside of my experience, I'll try to let you know.

There will be links in many of these chapters. Some will go to pictures or video. They will be graphic. Put that 'graphic' in bold and italic. Watch at your own risk, but there is really no way to just dip your toes in. You will either see a body that has been chopped up with machetes or you won't. There's no 'sort of' way to see it. And that is one of the things that your characters should grasp very well. Fiction, for the readers and most of the authors is the ultimate 'sort of' experience. The reader gets the vicarious thrills of a fight without the pain or the smells or the screams or the consequences. And maybe the author gets that too ... but the characters absolutely can't. You and your readers can thrill over two swordsmen weaving a net of impenetrable steel until a feint, a cut and the hero stands over the villain he has vanquished. Your hero though, watched the seizure-like activity as the villain died, watched the twitches and the feet kicking against the ground. Probably, if it wasn't quick, saw the thirst and heard the villain scream ... and the hero knows damn well he would scream just the same if he had been a little less lucky. And the hero heard that final rattling (like an aborted snore) breath and heard the bowels let loose before he smelled it. Safely reading or writing a book, violence can be consequence free. If it is ever consequence free for the characters you have missed ... everything.

... 1 ...

ESTABLISHING A BASELINE

Violence in our culture is treated like a taboo or at least an aberration. Stylized violence is everywhere, but real information is rare and actively discouraged. In a lot of ways, most modern Americans and Europeans know as much about violence as they learned about sex in junior high school locker rooms.

So here are some myths and platitudes and how professionals feel about them:

"Violence never solved anything." This platitude is so patently and obviously false that it takes some pretty special mental gymnastics to say it, much less believe it. The fact is that some things, especially dangerous things happening very fast, can ONLY be solved by violence. This adage frequently infuriates professionals because sometimes the problem they have solved with violence was their own survival or the survival of someone they loved. Survival is pretty hard to devalue.

"Violence is the last resort of the ignorant" only shows the ignorance of the person stating it. It would be an ideal truth in a homogenous society of wealthy people with equal education. It is one of those ideas that only works if everyone involved chooses to believe it ... and the first person to reject the idea will dominate, kill or enslave the others. It is especially funny because many people who deal professionally with violence are pretty well educated and worldly. To hear such a pronouncement from someone who chooses to be ignorant about violence ... sigh. Maybe "Unthinking platitudes are the first refuge of the ignorant."

"Violence begets violence." Sort of. But that's kind of like saying "Sickness begets medicine." Here's the deal, and it's one of the basic truths. Violence is dangerous and it hurts and there is no guaranteed win, but an act of force is the only thing that can stop an act of violence. If a crowbar is coming at your head, there is no form of negotiation that can help in time. If part of the other guy's definition of a win is to enjoy you broken and begging, there is no win-win. You must understand that not only are there people who enjoy debasing others, they have been very common throughout history and they are still the norm in certain cultures.

Because we live in a society where hunger is rare and there is a rule of law and invading armies or bandits stealing food and raping are unheard of, we forget that this level of violence was the norm for most of human history. Pockets of it exist in even the most affluent society. And it can erupt when things start to break down.

There are other myths and 'common knowledge' which may not be so:

"Never bring a knife to a gun fight." The wisdom of this depends on many, many things. At extremely close range the knife is far more versatile than a gun. The gun does damage in one direction and in one vector (barring powder burns and concussion waves, which you can get in enclosed places.) If you can get the muzzle away from you, you won't take damage. The knife does damage in, out, and sideways.

One of the critical differences is whether the weapon is in hand. In reaction time tests, I've managed to draw my duty weapon from a level 3 holster and fire in 7/10 of a second. If the knife is already out, that's enough time to cover at least five feet and begin slashing or, if the knifer is already at close range, to stab me at least four times. Probably more.

And that brings us to another concept that is rarely true: "A killer is a killer." Not really. Knife and gun are extremely different skills. Not just physically, but emotionally. Shooting can be done at a distance, clinically. Sniping is basically a problem in applied mathematics. Setting aside the stalking aspect, shooting sometimes doesn't feel as real or immediate as knife work.

Knife is different. It is close and personal and messy and very much a thing of horrible smells and sounds—shit and urine and partially digested food and the metallic smell of blood and screams and wheezes and sometimes splats. All that happens with gunfire, too, but you might not be close enough for it to register.

Anyway, if your character is the most cold-blooded pistolero or fighter pilot in the world, it doesn't mean or even imply that he can handle himself, physically or emotionally, with a knife or unarmed. Most knifers can shoot (maybe not well, but emotionally it is easier). Shooters may or may not be able to cut.

"Weapons are used to win fights." Absolutely not, and this is something that martial artists and people who watch too much television trip over all the time. Weapons are not used to win fights. They are used to kill people. Outside of macho bullshit posturing, fights don't happen in the professional world.

No intelligent person will square off or give you a chance. They won't take you from the front unless they can trick you. Only an amateur, and a stupid one at that, will let it turn into a fight. If it is serious enough to use a weapon, I am going to walk up as casually as possible and shoot you in the head. If I'm out of practice and don't think you are armed, I'll shoot you in the chest—twice—and then move on, to another victim or to go through your pockets or to leave. If it is a knife, you might feel a hand over your mouth but the real reason is to pull up against the base of your nose with a slight twist (it takes you off balance, puts you on your toes and twists your spine so that your core strength is completely gone) and then the knife will slam into your kidneys like a sewing machine or drop behind the collar bone going for the heart and the ascending aorta... a quick sharp pain and then eyes fade in tunnel vision.

"Good training will prepare you to face a weapon." Maybe. If the training was extraordinary and you are lucky. Over 90% of the martial arts knife defenses I've seen are against the long-range lunge, an attack that almost never happens. Very few instructors (I can count the ones I know on my fingers) teach defenses to the common attacks—the prison yard rush, the grab-n-stab, the handshake assassination or the military methods. Most weapon defense training is little more than a talisman that makes you feel safe.

There are some drills that often blow holes in common beliefs.

The Tueller Drill. You may have heard of the "21-foot Rule." In 1983 Dennis Tueller published an article in SWAT magazine, "How Close is Too Close?" Dennis experimented and found that a man with a knife could consistently close a distance of seven yards and stab or slash faster than an officer could draw his firearm. This means that within seven yards, a knife is an immediate deadly threat. Note that this was in 1983. Many agencies have switched to triple-retention holsters since then. That makes officers even slower on the draw.

The Manson Drill is the brainchild of Tony Blauer, (http://www.tonyblauer.com/) one of the top instructors in police and civilian self-defense in the nation. The threat ("Threat' is the law enforcement term for an individual who may require force–it sounds more professional than saying 'the bad guy') is given a rubber knife and then meditates to put himself into a mindset of implacable savagery. The students then try to defend themselves not against a partner but against an enraged butcher. All of their nifty, skilled martial techniques fail.

The Reception Line Drill is mine. One of the students is selected and told that he has been elected to high office, that it is time right now for the big victory banquet where he or she will thank supporters ... but that security believes someone may attempt an assassination. The student must go through a line shaking hands, hugging, being nice and chattering all the while looking for an assassin. Usually, one of the people in line has been given a rubber knife and absolute freedom in when and how to use it.

Not only does the Reception Line drill showcase how hard it is to flip the switch, it also showcases the stilted body language of the person expecting trouble and illustrates how hard it is to survive an assassination. There are other lessons in the drill. The first is that people tend to try to find martial or physical solutions to survival problems. No one uses mirrors to check out potential threats or calls for help or even warns others about the knife. No one, so far, has accessed a weapon of their own. And no one has looked at it as a strategic rather than a tactical problem. No one has simply said, "I love you all but I've picked up a flu bug and won't be able to socialize today." Or in some other way changed the dynamic.

The Action/Reaction Drill. Beating someone to the draw is a myth. Even if it was possible, other than a shot to the brainstem, there is nothing a bullet can do that can stop another person from pulling a trigger for several seconds. Heart blows up? You have about ten seconds to take the bastard with you.

To demonstrate this, using sim guns (real weapons modified to shoot a marking round) I will let two officers point their weapons at my chest, fingers on the trigger. I have a weapon at my side. They are to give their commands (e.g. "Drop the weapon"). If I comply, fine. If I make a move to become a lethal threat, they shoot.

Remember, they are on target with fingers on the trigger. My weapon is at my side.

Consistently, I get off three rounds (all hits, I practice this) before either can react and simply twitch a trigger finger. Further, if I side step when I shoot, they will both miss, aiming at where I was.

Understand that there have been fast draw experts, like Bill Jordan and Jelly Bryce. There have been Japanese swordmasters with incredible draws. But in order to make it work an extremely efficient motion has to be coupled with a conditioned reflex. There is no decision making in this process and, hence, no hesitation whatsoever.

Decisions are almost always telegraphed. Fast draw or punch, there are a variety of 'tells' that let you know the attack is coming. A narrowing of the eyes. A sharp inhalation. The shoulder drops. The hand draws back. For your protagonist's reactions to consistently beat an antagonist's action, the antagonist must telegraph and the protagonist must have one, simple action (not a variety for different situations) trained to reflex. A reaction can't beat an action...but the right flinch triggered by a telegraph might.

Confrontation Simulations. This is the sim gun stuff. Very few civilians will ever experience this but it is catching on with cops. It is equipment-intensive and expensive. Basically, everyone wears armor, especially eye protection, and has safe training versions of what they carry normally (expandable baton, pepperspray, Taser, handgun, whatever). They go into situations with minimal information, just like real life, and have to use judgment as well as skills. All the rules (force law and/or policy) are in effect.

You find out real quick that in the chaos of life, your pretty range skills don't work real damn well. Over time, you do develop the skills to make good shots and good decisions under stress. You remember to use your physical skills. But the first few are wild ugly chaos. It's an eye-opener.

Why do people use violence? Because it works. Violence ***works***. Characters may need tortured reasons and justifications for their depredations. Real criminals (and I'm talking low-level street hustlers, not some psychopathic super-criminal) don't need rationalizations. It just works.

The following link leads to a video can be hard to watch. It is a Russian video of a crack addict attacking a fifteen year-old girl for her purse. She died after some time in a coma.

RUSSIAN MUGGING http://static.fontanka.ru/monstr.html

You can choose not to watch the mugging if you don't want this sort of thing in your head. Many people don't. But it may be harder for you to understand this book, and real violence, if you close your eyes to it.

You may have worked your whole life to get your credit rating and savings. A crook can get your ATM card and your PIN with a few minutes of judicious beating. Don't lose sight of this fact, not in your fiction and not in your real life: people use violence because it works ... and the less people are prepared for it, the better it works. The more peaceful a group, the easier they are to victimize.

What follows talks about levels of violence. You can apply it to your characters, but I want you to think of it in terms of your life. It's important to understand the levels because people (including authors) can rarely imagine upwards. In other words, if you live at a low level of violence, the motivations and beliefs of someone who functions at a higher level may be completely alien to you.

Most groups (offices, associations, gym classes, schools) are made up mostly of good people who avoid conflict. *Nice* people. They are the backbone of society and people generally seem to believe that this attitude is what humans should aspire to.

Nice people are easy victims for ***manipulators***. Manipulation is an extremely low level of violence, but it is violence. Gossip, subtle bullying, understated threats, chilling someone out and forming alliances are all types of coercion.

Truly nice people don't understand manipulators or really get "why people can be so mean." Manipulators, on the other hand, see nothing wrong with what they do. They are just 'getting things done' and 'aren't hurting anybody'.

The manipulator will walk all over nice people, until they run into someone *assertive*. The assertive person will be the one to stand up and say, "I know what you're doing. Knock it off or I will stop you." The assertive person sets boundaries and backs them up, usually not physically but by resorting to policy or not being afraid to talk to others and gather allies.

Assertive people are rare because direct confrontation is discouraged in our society. Until you get used to it, being assertive can feel very uncomfortable ... but assertive people, just like manipulators, don't think they are doing anything wrong.

Manipulators, on the other hand, think assertive people are bullies. Even if the manipulator is self-aware enough to grasp their own manipulation, they will say, "But I never got in anyone's face. That assertive person is rude!" Even nice people will feel uncomfortable around an assertive person and consider her pushy or bossy.

Notice this pattern repeats. At each level, the people who use the level feel fully justified ... and they universally characterize the people below them as 'weak' and the people above them as 'bad.'

The *aggressive* person stops the assertive in her tracks. When someone barges into the office screaming threats and swearing, most assertive people crumble. The aggressive person, again, doesn't see anything wrong. That was just self-expression. The assertive person (and the nice people and manipulators) feels the aggressive person was completely out of control.

Take a break here and think about these levels. This is as far as most people have any real experience. Whatever level you are at is the one where you can reasonably talk about your own motivations and is the level you are comfortable dealing with.

Most (almost all) people are *completely unprepared* for the next level higher. The level each person is on is the one that they have justified. That level is good. The next level up is 'bad'. People tend to define violence as the level above the level they are willing to use. The strategies for dealing with any given level do not work and often backfire when attempted on a higher level of conflict.

This is important, because if you are trying to extrapolate the mindset of someone comfortable with high-level violence from your experience with a merely manipulative office bully you will miss a ton. It will not only read false, but it will read as (weak? Watered-down? Tenuous? Unconvincing? Shallow? Impotent? Trite?)

Two more levels:

The aggressive person may feel like a big boss, screaming and insulting and making everyone cower. When some one hauls off and slaps the aggressive person, the aggressor has no idea what to do. Assault trumps aggression. Sometimes ***assaultive*** is angry, sometimes it is cold. Emotional intensity matters less than the fact that an assaultive person is comfortable using physical violence as a tool. Again, the assaulter will feel completely justified ("She shouldn't have made me angry" or "He had it coming"). The aggressive bully will feel violated and self-righteous ("I may be a little loud but I don't go around hitting people!")

And, finally, the assaultive person, whether a barroom brawler or a wife beater, is completely unprepared when he crosses a woman who is willing to slit his throat. ***Murderous*** (again, cold or hot) is a completely different animal, an undiscovered country.

Nice-Manipulative-Assertive-Aggressive-Assaultive-Murderous

This model has a few implications for you. First and foremost, beware of extrapolating from your experience at low levels to high levels. Second, no matter how well your protagonist functions at one level it takes a special circumstance or motivation to get them to go a level higher, much less two ... and even a professional will have no idea what to do there. Not just the physical mechanics, but the emotional and spiritual barriers. I had well over three hundred unarmed fights (unarmed on my end, anyway) with inmates before I ever shot someone. It was an entirely different feeling.

It has some implications for your fiction. If your character spends a lot of time at the higher levels of this model, most of what happens at the lower levels seems petty. When you transition from a job where people are trying to kill you to a job where office politics are high drama, the politics aren't that interesting. For people to whom the politics are everything, the professional strikes them as odd, maybe crazy.

This can be compounded by the way the professional considers options from much higher on the violence hierarchy than have never occurred to others in the office: "If he's such a bad boss, we could just kill him." Sometimes it's humorous, usually, but the undercurrent is there.

In relationships, there are things that seem obvious to us, to violence professionals. When our spouses are complaining about the office gossip or a bad boss, we suggest being assertive: "Honey, get in his face and tell him to back off. He'll back down." It seems obvious to us. Hell, it might be two steps below where we would solve the problem. We don't realize that we are asking a good person to jump two steps into behaviors they think are bad or aggressive.

There is 'friction' inherent in this model as well. Any given society will also have a comfort level. We may fantasize about gunslingers and pay actors staggering sums of money to portray fighters, but when a store clerk draws a gun on a robber actively trying to kill him, he is far more likely to be fired than to get a medal. Even when an act of assaultive or murderous violence is completely justified, even necessary, society is likely to react and punish those who are capable. This is something your effective protagonists will have to live with.

Direct and indirect violence rewards

Most people play at or study violence (martial arts) for indirect rewards. They want to be seen as tough, or feel less afraid or get the trophy. Professionals execute violence for a direct goal—to stop the threat or to subdue the victim.

There are profound differences in motivation, attitude and how professionals move and act. A professional does not fight you, doesn't even think about fighting you. He takes you out.

This is easier to see and teach in person than to write about and is most apparent in how weapons are used. A sword fighter may hear about an opponent who uses a combination: face thrust feint, disengage, slash behind the extended knee (the coup de Jarnac, for anyone with a historical bent). A fencer, duelist or sword fighter's reaction to hearing of this will be to come up with a counter combination, a cross body parry and drop to a low line parry, then riposte on a low line to the gut ...

This is dancer/game/amateur thinking. A professional's first choice would be to take the person out using surprise before the duel; his second would be to use a superior weapon first—shoot the threat before he even begins his combination. Third choice would be to use equal weapons first. The fourth is to disregard the combination and kill.

The duelist is interested in winning, in maintaining honor. The professional is interested in killing, as quickly and efficiently as possible. Maintaining honor and winning are *indirect* goals. Killing is a *direct* goal. Working towards direct goals peels a lot of bullshit off of your tactics.

It can take years to learn how to fight with a sword. If you have the right heart, the right mindset, learning to kill ruthlessly and efficiently with a sword takes about twenty minutes. If he or she has the right mindset, the killer will beat the fighter almost every time.

Then, of course, when you find the killer with the discipline to train, you have a god of battle.

✧✦✧✦✧

HOMEWORK:

On the scale of nice-manipulative-assertive-aggressive-assaultive-murderous, what is your level? If you say it is anything above assertive, go be rude to a stranger. That shouldn't be a problem for you. It's a quick way to check your self-assessment.

Write a one-page profile of a good person who is one, two or three levels above you on that list. Write why she is a good person and why she is fine with that level of coercion.

Now for the writing assignment: Write, from this person's point of view, a one page description of YOU. Write what this protagonist thinks of your choice to function at your level.

TO RECAP:

- ✧ This is a lot to cover, but the big point of this is to try to establish a line between what you actually know about violence and what you have been told
- ✧ People use violence because it works
- ✧ There are levels of violence and the level you are comfortable with does not read as violence to you
- ✧ Going down levels is easy, going up levels is difficult
- ✧ Violence has both direct and indirect goals
- ✧ Professionals focus on the direct goals, amateurs on the indirect

DISCUSSION – The Russian mugging

The video shows a man, identified by Russian news sources as a crack addict, closely following a small woman into an elevator lobby. In the grainy film, the man looks tall and skinny and wears glasses. The woman is small. She walks to the far corner of the lobby. The man follows. He stands very close. The woman does not look at him, just stares at the bank of elevators. The man grabs her by the head, one hand covering her mouth and pulls/lifts/twists so that she hits the ground face up. He begins stomping on her head.

I counted the takedown and eleven stomps in seven seconds, but the film is grainy. There could have been more stomps. He then bends down and either tries to take her purse or go through her pockets. He stands up and begins stomping her head again. According to news reports, this was because she wouldn't stop screaming.

This dynamic, search and stomp, is repeated. When the elevator arrives, he drags her limp body into the elevator. One of my students was Russian and followed the case in the news. She says that the girl, 15 years of age, was in a coma for months and then died, and that the perpetrator was caught because of the video.

This is a good example because it is not special. It is a simple attack, a typical mugging.

Addiction is huge in crimes like these because it is one of the few things that we experience in the modern era that imitates survival violence. Whatever you might do for food or water on the edge of death is what an addict will do to feed his addiction. There are some other mental gymnastics that beginners have to go through to justify that level of violence, but it becomes easier over time until with an experienced violent criminal there is NO psychological fall-out. If it is reinforced quickly enough with cravings satisfied, it becomes soothing.

When you go back in history (or even folklore) people would do this and worse for food (Hansel and Gretel, anyone, as a cautionary tale to avoid cannibals?)

This is not special!!!! He kept stomping her head because she wouldn't quit screaming. Not because he was afraid of being identified, not because he had rage issues, not because of psychosis or dementia brought on by his addiction. She was screaming. It bothered him. Head trauma shuts people up.

Psychopath? Maybe. It doesn't take any mystical evil or Hollywood-style mental disorder to make people act this way. It only took a form of simple math: "I want X and don't care about you. What is the fastest way for me to get X?"

This isn't a super-criminal. This is a skinny Russian crackhead. This is very much the way an average assault goes down. Look at the victim choice, the range, the choice of technique, the victim's body language ("There's something wrong here," she thinks, "but if I just don't make eye contact or antagonize him, it will be all right.") which was exactly what the threat was looking for.

Psychopath and Sociopath have both been removed from the DSM-IV and are considered extreme Anti-Social Personality Disorder (APD). The terms psychopath and sociopath never had distinct definitions. There used to be a test that distinguished a true sociopath from an APD, but for whatever reason the APA (American Psychological Association) no longer recognizes it.

The essence of a true sociopath (and mimicked to varying degrees by APDs) is that the world seems unreal. People are just pictures. The only real things are personal pain and personal pleasure and both of those are fleeting. Most are quite stupid, because by their nature they can't learn from others. They can be very good, even brilliant in a narrow field, but they learn largely through trial and error. That's why the character of Hannibal Lector rang so false. He was a good bogeyman, but a terrible depiction.

A real Dexter (to name another great character that rings false to me) would casually rape his sister if the thought occurred to him and he had the urge. He would shut her up through fear, blackmail or violence–whichever he thought would work with the least complications. And he wouldn't feel anything about it one way or the other the next morning.

Once upon a time I had to read a child molester's journal to determine if it was evidence. It was. He was shocked and disturbed. His victim, after all, was his daughter. How is that different than his shoes? He could do what he wanted with his shoes. How was this different? Isn't that what 'his' means?

No matter how disturbing you found this video, I have to remind you that you can't hear it and you can't smell it. The smells stay with you forever.

✧✦✧✦✧

... 2 ...

CONTEXT

There are seven things that surround any act of self-defense and almost any fight or use of force. If you want a fight scene to appear real or to seem like it happened in a living, breathing world, these seven things are the context that you must understand. A professional will have a working understanding of all of these aspects. An amateur, a character who is not a veteran of a violent world, will be completely unprepared for most of what follows.

1) **Legal and ethical issues.** Self-defense law is a specialty, and it is something that can screw up a character with the wrong training. It is also one of those things that can make the novel read wrong. Killings and beatings, justified or not, don't happen in a vacuum. Cops show up. Lawyers get involved. Families of the deceased start suing. The tension is unbelievable. You will hear the deceased, no matter how violent and despicable a criminal (or how terrified your protagonist) described as a, "Good boy. He would never hurt anybody. He was just depressed. I don't know why she called the police at all instead of an ambulance..."

The legal stuff is very complex. I did a short sidebar on it in "Meditations on Violence" and Loren Christensen put a chapter in

"Fighter's Fact Book 2: The Street". There is extensive information in "Facing Violence" (YMAA 2011).

The basic things you must understand: First of all, self-defense is an ***affirmative defense***. This means that the defendant is admitting to the underlying crime (say, taking a life) and is claiming it is justified. It shifts the burden of proof largely to the defense. The defendant must prove that she had no choice.

The second basic is that the criminal and civil courts and processes are not the same. You can be found "not guilty" or "justified" in a criminal court and still be sued and lose in a civil court.

Self-defense laws are usually written into state statutes. Most of the state statutes are available on line. Do a search in the on-line statutes for "justification". If self-defense has not been written into state law as a justification (as in Massachusetts) or the statutes are unclear you may have to search for "jury instructions" and "self-defense." Rhode Island is the only state I've found with nothing on line.

Always check local statutes, but generally:

A 'deadly weapon' is anything designed to kill or cause serious physical injury, like a knife or a gun. (One implication of this is that if you use a closed pocketknife on a pressure point or pistol-whip someone, you still may need to justify deadly force.)

A 'dangerous weapon' is something that can cause death or serious physical injury but is not intended to do so, like a hammer.

In some jurisdictions, if you hold a bottle of beer the normal way, with the opening on the thumb side of your hand and the body on the little finger side, it is a bottle of beer, possibly a dangerous weapon. But if you reverse the grip, it is legally considered a deadly weapon. And that can be the difference between a murder or a manslaughter prosecution.

If your villain or protagonist is a pro, they will know things like this. Most will know the local self-defense laws (disregard if you are writing a historical or fantasy: self-defense or most kinds of law enforcement are relatively recent concepts). They will also know, for instance, that baseball bats are iffy—sometimes they break bones and sometimes they don't, relatively random. But axe handles reliably break bones if you use the thin edge and reliably don't if you use the wide edge, in case you just want to send a message.

"Use a axe handle. Trouble with baseball bats is sometimes you break his legs and sometimes you don't. You break legs on a stevedore, he can't go to work, he can't earn any money and your boss don't get paid. Use a axe handle and if you want to break a leg, you hit with the thin edge and you don't want to break a leg, you hit with the flat side."

The ethical issues make for interesting character development. Everyone has issues with using force on a human. (Even some of the most extreme criminals will have lines they will not cross—not because of feelings, in some cases, but to protect a self-image.) No one, until they do it, knows exactly where that line is. Many can't kill. Some can't bring themselves to hurt. Some will protect their self-image even at great cost. Long ago a friend told me that she would never hurt a human being, even to save her own life or the life of a child. Would she cling to that image, to her own death?

Warning: the article in the following link is pretty disturbing. Ms. Davis writes with remarkable courage about her rape. I recommend it, but be prepared.

"Betrayed by the Angel"

http://www.utne.com/2005-01-01/betrayed-by-the-angel.aspx

Many professionals have work-arounds. It is easier to do dangerous jobs if you don't have much of a survival instinct. That gives you the detachment to go in. To get back out, you need to find your survival motivation. My motivation is my kids. I will die someday. I accept that. I will, however, do everything in my power to keep my kids from being orphaned. Works for me.

2) Violence dynamics. There are social and asocial types of violence. Social violence is for status, territory, or the good of the group. Asocial is hunting, and the victim is not seen as a person at all.

Social violence breaks down into the Monkey Dance (MD), Group Monkey Dance (GMD), Educational Beat Down (EBD) and Status Seeking Show (SSS).

The ***Monkey Dance*** is a status ritual almost always between young men. The basic pattern is a hard stare, followed by a verbal challenge ("What you lookin' at?") followed by an approach, often trying to look bigger and tougher, then contact, either a two-handed push on the chest or a finger poke, then a punch, usually a wild, looping overhand swing.

Both people play. The stares, verbal challenges and chest pushing are often mutual. Sometimes the punches are tentative and followed by a step back.

The ideal is for friends to step in and separate the 'fighters' so that they have established a reputation for being willing to fight without actually getting hurt. Hitting the head with a fist is far more likely to damage the fist than the head. Other then the medial metacarpal breaking (called a "boxer's fracture") if someone gets hurt in this scenario it is because he fell and hit his head. Like bighorn sheep butting heads, it's a safe way to establish dominance in a group, and is probably biologically determined.

The *Group Monkey Dance* establishes boundaries and loyalties. The low level is when an outsider tries to interfere in a group's activities and the group turns on the outsider. This happens frequently when people try to break up fights and the audience turns on the person trying to help or when police show up to a domestic violence call and the victim turns on the officers.

The second level is about bonding. Committing violence together, whether hunting a mammoth or doing a drive-by, is intensely bonding. Nothing makes a group as tight as adrenaline and shedding blood together. The bodies dragged through Fallujah, the wildings in Central Park or the gang roving Seattle randomly attacking people are all examples. But so are the deep ties between soldiers who have been on combat patrols together and SWAT teams.

The highest level of the GMD is when an outsider or an insider believed to have betrayed the group is savagely beaten, tortured and/or murdered by the group. It turns into a contest of proving loyalty by doing damage.

The *Educational Beat Down* is simply enforcing the rules of the group. It's a spanking for adults. In both redneck and some inner-city cultures, a thwack on the back of the head (always from a higher status to lower status member) is a reminder to watch manners. In some societies, the EBD can be relatively savage. Many people honestly feel that beating a spouse or child is teaching. It is not a euphemism or an excuse. It is what they believe.

In dysfunctional groups or groups with an insecure leader, the EBDs can be extreme, e.g. Al Capone murdering his lieutenant at the dinner table with a baseball bat. It wasn't intended to teach the dead guy, it was to send a message.

The *Status Seeking Show* is what happens when someone decides to get a reputation for being 'hard' or 'crazy'. Such a reputation is a very valuable thing in certain circles. An SSS is one or more acts of extreme public violence—shooting a stranger, picking a fight and beating someone to a pulp (ignoring the stops built into the Monkey Dance,) using a weapon in a Monkey Dance, etc. Ambushing a cop is a great way to get a reputation.

In asocial, or predatory violence, the threat has already put the victim into a "non-human" category and there are no internal limits on the force the threat can use. The limits are imposed externally—chance of getting caught, chance to do prison time, amount of prison time (with very experienced violent criminals sentencing minimums do act as a deterrent).

There are two types of predatory violence: ***resource*** and ***process***.

A ***Resource Predator*** wants something tangible and the victim is merely a source: usually money or something that can be turned into money, sometimes a car. He will use the level of violence that has the best pay-off-to-risk ratio. Merely threatening violence works most of the time. Aggressive panhandling is one of the lowest levels of implied aggression, but it often works.

If the threat judges that violence is his best option, it will be fast, hard and from surprise. The entire goal is that the victim has no time to respond and will be frozen, trying to figure out what is happening. This tactic is almost always successful.

(When a former bad guy read "Meditations on Violence" he said I got one thing wrong: "You gave 'em too much hope, Sarge. I used to come up on 'em just like that and none of 'em ever had a chance.")

A ***Process Predator*** enjoys the act of the crime. The pain and dominance are the fun part. Rapists. Serial killers and torture murderers. People who get addicted to the Status-Seeking Show.

Want to get into their heads? Are you sure about that? Here goes: Do you have something in life that defines who you are? A hobby? Writing? Martial arts? Something where the world makes sense, something that makes you feel totally alive. Something that defines who you are. For some reason, there are a handful of people who feel this way about hurting others. About rape or about killing. The way that you feel when you finish a story or find the perfect phrase is the way that they feel when they make someone beg.

Predators use two types of tactics, charm and blitz. Read Gavin DeBecker's "The Gift of Fear" for the best list I've ever seen of the specific tactics that charm predators use to get close to you or even to get access to your living space. Once they have established privacy, the predator will go to work.

Charm predators are masters at making friends quickly, at manufacturing a relationship that didn't exist seconds ago. And then they presume on this relationship to get their victims to a private place.

A blitz predator attacks with overwhelming force from surprise. A charm approach is often followed by a blitz assault.

3) **The third basic of violence is prevention.** Avoidance is merely staying out of places where bad things happen. Staying away from three kinds of places (where people get their minds altered by drugs, alcohol or ritual; where young men gather in groups; where territory is in dispute) will reduce the chance of encountering violence to almost zero.

A professional knows this and avoids those places. If she can't avoid them or needs something there, she is aware of the situation and takes precautions–stays alert, brings a weapon and back-up if possible.

Escape and Evasion is the habit of constantly revising a plan for how to get out of here now. Pros often walk the perimeter of a new building before going in, noticing traffic flow and exits. They keep track of ways to leave a room and what routes are concealed (a bad guy couldn't see you) or covered (something between you and the bad guy that could stop a bullet.) Beginners look at doors and stairwells. Some remember to look at windows they could break. A few are experienced or concerned enough to check which walls are drywall and could be smashed in a few seconds or minutes. Sub ceilings are sometimes an option, but they won't cross the load-bearing walls, are fragile and tend to make a mess of dust when lifted.

The one time I actually found an air-duct big enough for an adult, it sucked pretty bad. They are screwed together and have the sharp ends of the screws protruding inside everywhere. I was cut to ribbons.

The third element of avoidance is de-escalation. Sometimes mere presence can do it. People are usually quick to stop being bad when a cop shows up. The presence of witnesses will also discourage most criminals.

Usually, de-escalation refers to talking someone down. This is one of the things that authors and screenwriters get really, really wrong.

The psychologist Abraham Maslow postulated that there are five levels of need that all humans have. These needs must be addressed in order. In other words, if you are being eaten by a lion you don't worry about getting stores for the winter or whether your faction will be running the tribe.

The quick run down:

People need to live: they need food and water and must avoid being killed or freezing to death. Survival is the base level of Maslow's pyramid.

Only if the previous level is taken care of do people start to worry about security: Having enough food for tomorrow; building a barrier to keep the tigers out of the cave. Security is the second level.

If the first two are stable, humans want to be in a group. They want to belong. For the third level, Maslow coined the incredibly awkward word, 'belongingness.'

Once they belong, they want to be established, to have a place in the group and maybe a little love. The 'Esteem' level.

Once they achieve stability within a group, they can pursue their dreams, become what Maslow called "self actualized."

In our society, very few people have ever experienced deprivation of the first two levels. Physical security was taken care of by our ancestors long ago, to the extent that the normal way to deal with the possibility of hunger (and that itself is a far cry from starvation) involves paperwork and not snares or spears.

We have been conditioned to believe that self-actualization is a good thing, that it allows those who achieve it the security to act on their altruistic impulses.

This means that almost all of the conflict that most modern people experience has been driven by problems at the 3rd and 4th levels, the social levels. So citizens, including authors and counselors and teachers and specialists, draw from their experience with social conflict to write scenes of criminal violence. It comes out with very nice, poignant dialogues where someone touches the inner pain in the violent criminal and turns things around ... poignant dialogues that in real life would leave the criminal laughing and the speaker bleeding.

People using violence for Maslow's level 1 are in a survival mindset. This is where a lot of incidents with the mentally ill or excited delirium go bad. No one is going to make a connection with your inner child when you are panicked and drowning in a raging sea (not a metaphor–drowning is one of the few times a citizen will encounter this. The most mild-mannered person in the world will drown a rescuer by trying to climb up on the rescuer to get another breath of air.)

People using violence for Maslow's level 2 are very common. These are usually junkies trying to get money for drugs. It may not seem like a survival issue to your logical brain, but it feels like one to an addict. They need money. They need it before withdrawals kick in. If your talking gets them the money, fine. Just be quick about it. If it doesn't, they will shut you up, fast and hard. Their need outweighs your humanity. Their tortured past is not even on their minds compared to their present pain. You can make a connection here, but it is not easy and I haven't seen it done well in fiction or cinema.

An addict will be willing to do whatever you would do to keep yourself or your family from starving. That is how strong the drive is, and one way that you can, slightly, understand an addict's worldview. Conversely, if something (like talking about your childhood) would fail to dissuade you from feeding your children, it won't work on the addict either.

Lastly, Process Predators are about as self-actualized as they can be. They are being who they are and doing what they love, maybe the only thing that makes them feel alive. Trying to make a deep connection only amuses them. Some will play along, because the look of betrayal when the victim realizes that she has just wasted a bunch of time instead of fighting is pretty delicious ....

For de-escalation to work, you must know what kind of threat you are dealing with.

The next three aspects (4-6) cover an actual attack, and we'll do those in the next chapter. For now, I'd like to skip ahead.

7) **The last element of conflict is the Aftermath.** Any time you use force there is the potential for criminal or civil legal entanglements, medical complications and psychological issues.

The better you understood force law going in, the better you will do with the legal aftermath. The better your character understood her own internal ethics, the easier the psychological aftermath will be.

There are also medical implications. Even winning is rarely free. In the rush of adrenaline you may not know if or how badly you were injured. I had an inmate who didn't realize he had shattered his hand until a half-hour after the attack. (He was the attacker, but he kept hitting his victim in the head with his fist even after several bones broke.) A friend didn't know he was stabbed in the ass until he felt his shoe squishing when he was trying to unlock his car.

A good blow to the head may not affect you at all until the swelling starts to squeeze your brain and you pass out (and potentially die) hours later.

Even if all goes well immediately, there is a potential for blood-borne pathogens. Many of the people who initiate violence, especially for drugs, do not live extremely hygienic lives. Just being involved in a brawl can put you at risk for HIV and Hepatitis C. In "Campfire Tales From Hell" Eddie Gilbert wrote about living for a year under a 75% likelihood of death after he contracted hepatitis from a fight he doesn't even remember. He passed away of liver failure a month ago, as I write this.

The psychological aftermath is getting a lot of lip-service in fiction now, but often without depth. Here's the deal.

We all have stories of who we are. This is our identity, and it is about as real and consistent as a wisp of smoke. Like all good works of fiction, this story is heavily based on conflict. Fortunately (or not) real conflict is vanishingly rare in most people's lives. Ergo, much of our internal story, our identity, isn't really based on anything.

When someone is exposed to violence for the first time, who they thought they were rarely survives. The big tough guy may crumble and usually freezes. People who always thought they had dignity beg. People who have studied yoga and meditation for years to keep negative energy out of their lives find out it was all a lie. Martial artists find out that their black belts only cover two inches and if they want to cover the rest of their asses, they need to do it themselves ... and most can't.

So, there's the first big issue. In a big episode of violence, identity tends to be shattered. What happens next, internally, is that the person starts writing a new story. Creating a new identity. It is hard because much has been proved false and no new truths have stepped in to replace it. Susan Brison in "Aftermath" describes her own process of this. It isn't a book that I recommend for survivors. Many of her decisions afterwards were disempowering but she chose to see them as empowering and fragile readers may not notice that. But I heartily recommend the book to people who deal with survivors, or write about them.

The second big issue is the sense of isolation. Most people today have never experienced serious violence and aren't sure what to do or think. Friends want to ask, but are afraid of bringing up memories or causing damage or seeming like vultures, so they stay silent. The survivor sees the look followed by the silence and reads it as condemnation or fear.

Simultaneously, strangers with no boundaries may butt in and ask. Some physically lick their lips when they do it. They are vultures. I can't speak for everyone, but knowing that there is a subset of young women who hit on me because they believe that I am extremely violent is pretty damn disturbing. A different personality type would exploit that.

PTSD (Post Traumatic Stress Disorder) doesn't just come from the event. It comes as well from a sense of being betrayed or treated unfairly. People who came from hard lives, the "children of adversity" who thrive in the special operations world are far more resistant to PTSD because they didn't expect life to be fair, easy or good.

People who have had one ugly violent encounter are at risk for PTSD because their basic beliefs about how the world works were betrayed.

People who have repeated encounters with violence do better than those who only have one (Exception: there is a victim personality that either jumps from abusive relationship to abusive relationship or is serially victimized by different predators or both).

And this is my bias, here, because of the people I have known with multiple violent encounters, most prevailed. I can't speak with authority about the trauma of losing or being victimized repeatedly.

The first violent encounter you find out what was false. After that, you start learning things that are true. You also find out that some of what you thought you learned (OMG I froze! I'm a coward!) aren't really true, either. Most times, people freeze because they can't figure out what was going on. That's not the same as fear. No cowardice involved.

But it takes multiple encounters to figure out what is going on and where you fit in the Looking-Glass world of violence.

Multiple encounters ease the first problem—shattered identity—but can compound the second problem, isolation. Sort of, and this is an aside. Processing does take time. Multiple events coming too close together can overwhelm even the toughest and most adaptable character's coping skills. Dealing with an injury is one thing. Dealing with failure another. Illness of a family member. Suicide of a friend. All in the space of two days? You'll get some cracks.

Remember that PTSD is specific. Hypervigilance, intrusive memories and flashbacks and avoidance behaviors. That's PTSD. There are lots of other ways to have psychological impact that don't fit neatly in that box. Dreams. Sleep dysfunction. Obsessions. Guilt–and guilt is a completely different animal than PTSD and may or may not be justified. And some people are okay with it. And some people have faith that they will become okay with it, and those people are almost always right.

An act of violence will change you. You will never be the same. That does not mean you are broken.

Dealing with violence demands a different thought process and often results in a very clear ordering of priorities. It winnows internal bullshit like nothing else.

Many of the angsty things that drive drama have no meaning for me. Everyone that I love knows it. To love someone and not tell them, not give that tiny gift when I might die tomorrow is stupid. And I don't care if they love me back. The world is not about me, and I'm not going to live through it anyway. I don't love to get something in exchange. It is just a fact. "I'm in love" is very similar to "I'm bleeding." Just an observation about my state, which may have some obligations attached. The world doesn't owe an attachment to me.

Few enough people look at the world this way (including immature violence professionals) that it can be hard to spend time with other people and hard for them to spend time around us. That increases the isolation.

There is a persistent myth in the martial arts that young men went to the temple to study fighting and achieve enlightenment. They believed this because of all of the very wise monks who lived there, men who could puncture certainty with a koan or could love without attachment.

None of those old monks achieved enlightenment in the temple. At that time, the temple was the one place where an old warrior could peacefully retire. What they learned of truth and enlightenment (which is not the presence of wisdom but the absence of bullshit) they learned on the edge of death.

✧✦✧✦✧

HOMEWORK:

Look up your state's criminal codes. Look for self-defense but also look at the legal definitions of each of the violent crimes. Then dissect the last fight scene you wrote and list the crimes.

TO RECAP:

Violence happens in a context that includes:

- The legalities of the world
- The personal ethics (conscious or unconscious) of the people involved
- Predictable patterns and types of violence
- Opportunities to prevent or de-escalate violence
- Potential medical, legal and psychological aftermath

... 3 ...

MECHANICS OF A PHYSICAL 'FIGHT'

We have to define a couple of things. I put 'fight' in the title because I really don't have a better word. That said, fights are generally stupid and I don't do them.

This may mess with your writing, but you need to know something. Fights aren't dramatic. Professionals, whether a SWAT team or a mugger, do everything in their power to keep fights from being dramatic. One side gets the advantage early and keeps it. That's the goal.

Most people think of fighting in the context of martial arts (almost always based on a dueling paradigm) or from fistfights they have seen. The fistfights are incredibly predictable. Both sides, usually young men, follow a script:

Hard stare (the other usually locks eyes or starts the next step)

Verbal challenge e.g. "What you lookin' at?" (witty repartee follows)

The approach, both trying to look bigger and tougher (and everything about the body posture—bouncing on the toes, squared up, muscles clenching and bulging—are designed to make him look bigger, like a cat puffing out fur. And every last bit of that is bad body mechanics for fighting)

A push to the chest or finger poke (sometimes push back, sometimes next step)

An overhand looping punch. The fight is now on. It will usually involve a few ineffective punches before the two tangle up and one trips and they wind up rolling on the floor and throwing wild punches.

This is called the Monkey Dance. It is stupid. Professionals do not play this game. Good guy or bad guy, if we can't handle it verbally (downcast eyes and apology works; as does raising the stakes "Son, I'm on parole. If this fight is going to cost me two years in prison, believe that I will make it worth the time") we jump steps. Take him out before he gets to the chest push stage. By jumping steps a professional almost always get surprise.

The Monkey Dance appears to be biological, just like the way domestic goats butt heads. It is also designed not to do serious injury.

For too many people, this is what they think of as a fight. It is not serious, not dangerous and never self-defense. There are too many opportunities in the Monkey Dance to just leave to call it self-defense.

Most professionals do not 'fight' people. They take them out. They put them down. They do everything in their power to prevent the target from fighting back.

Of the seven stages mentioned in the last section, we skipped the three that compose the fight. Here they are:

4) **The ambush.** Good guy or bad guy, the person initiating the attack works to get an effective move in right away, and keep up the pressure so that the victim never recovers. In a military ambush, this is the initial coordinated fire with, say, small arms and RPGs (Rocket-Propelled Grenades). In an entry (like when a warrant service team goes into a house expecting armed resistance) flashbangs, shouting and constant movement usually work to freeze the threats' minds, which usually allow the officers to do something very dangerous without killing anyone. A flurry of hits from behind with a brick works for a mugger.

On the receiving end, things will get bad here. The appropriate response is to have one thing trained to reflex that works on all the things you are likely to encounter. The military trains soldiers to charge the ambush, firing (this is US, some other countries must radio for instructions under fire. Our system gets fewer people killed.)

It's hard for cops to train one thing because they can be attacked at different ranges. What they need to do for a sniper or taking gunfire is radically different than the best response when someone lunges at an officer with a knife or grabs for the officer's gun from behind.

Martial artists train for reflex response in some cases, but they tend to train many responses to many different attacks. If the attack is one of the ones they have trained against and the training has either been very long term or is really fresh, they'll do fine on the first attack ... if they saw it coming.

5) **The next step is the freeze.** Everyone freezes when attacked. Some only freeze for a fraction of a second, some stay frozen until the assault is over, sometimes until they die.

There's lots going on and lots of different elements to a freeze, even different types of freezes.

At the minimum, when you are ambushed, you have to switch from your day-to-day mind to your fighting mind. Even soldiers on patrol must switch from watch-walk-listen to SHOOT. With experience, this can get really fast, too fast for most people to notice.

One of the worst freezes, and the one that cripples people who are not used to violence, is *thinking*. Thinking takes time and under assault time is damage. To think, "I need a plan" while taking damage will not help you. By the time you come up with a plan, you will have taken too much damage.

Completely untrained people hit four times a second. Trained and experienced people can more than triple that. If every second of thought is four solid hits to the head, by the time you think your way out of it you may not be physically capable to execute the plan.

Worse than this, even, are the people who freeze on, "Why is this happening?" It has all the drawbacks of the planning freeze but with the added problem that getting the answer wouldn't help in any way.

When you are taking damage and scared, a bunch of neurotransmitters dump into your system. They can freeze you like a deer in the headlights or make you go limp and lose bladder and bowel control. You have probably heard of this as the fight or flight reflex. Biologists call it the Fight-Flight-Freeze reflex and freezing is the most common in the wild. Freezing doesn't draw the predator's eye and, if the attack is already on, the predator may become bored with a limp catch if the predator isn't that hungry.

Freezing often feels pretty nice. There's a warm kind of floaty feeling and everything looks crystal clear. There is often a roaring in your ears like the ocean. You feel comfortable. The words in your head are so clear that you *must* be thinking logically: "Wow, is that my blood? It's so red."

A professional will likely, but not always, recognize this feeling as a freeze. An amateur rarely will. It takes an extreme act of will to break out of it. The primitive part of your brain wants you frozen—its millennia of experience says frozen animals are less likely to be eaten than moving ones and all this newfangled training is a pipe dream.

There is also (later in the fight) a possibility of freezing in motion. Sometimes very scared people repeat the same act or say the same things over and over again even when it clearly isn't working. One officer repeated over and over again, "Drop the rifle, drop the rifle" instead of shooting. He locked into that verbal loop until he was shot. This can be a hard one to watch. My personal copy has the dialogue subtitled. Links change. If the link below is broken, go to a video sharing site and search for "Dinkheller."

The murder of Kyle Dinkheller:
http://www.youtube.com/watch?v=k8-ycSkoYfc

6) **The fight.** If your protagonist survives the ambush and breaks the freeze, the fight is on. Ideally, if he or she had a good counter-ambush response, the bad guy will have frozen as well and leveled the playing field.

At this point, most of the things you think of as fighting (fisticuffs, martial arts, sword play, shooting) apply. With some caveats:

- The threat is not automatically in front of you and you will have to deal with that before you can deal with the threat.
- Fights are dynamic affairs. One of the reasons that shooting at the range is so different than gun fighting is that gun fighting involves a lot of running and ducking. Taking time to aim makes your head a good target. Martial arts defenses against grabs often ignore the fact that grabs are rarely used to hold people in place but to yank them into the air and force movement. It is much harder to hit someone with power when you are both moving than it is to hit a heavy bag.

✧ Fights happen in places. There are doors and walls and obstacles to trip over and improvised weapons everywhere. A lot of techniques that work great in training work less well in a toilet stall, but on the other hand, misdirecting someone's head into a pipe does more damage than a fist.

✧ Fights are stressful. Under the stress hormones you may not feel pain, but you may not feel your fingers either, or be able to find the safety on your weapon. You might not be able to hear anything, even gunfire or words of warning. Tunnel vision is common. So is remembering everything in slow motion. Basically, if you have not been exposed to enough fights to get some control of the adrenaline, you will be clumsy (fine and complex motor skills are hampered) partially deaf and blind; and not thinking very well.

There are also two things that your experienced protagonists may experience in the fight.

The first is hitting the zone. It's been described as an optimum level of adrenalization. Senses, thought process, and coordination are all at peak. You can tell what a threat is about to do. Tachypsychia (the sensation that everything is happening in slow motion) kicks in, but you can use it. You're in slow motion as well, but you can use the time to be supremely efficient and weigh options. In the zone, you can use all of your training and all of your instincts. You can pull off things that seem impossible. There's a section on that coming up, but one example from my blog:

Character Flaw 12Feb2007

Good training, especially good scenario training, can uncover holes in your skill sets and a myriad of bad habits. Sometimes what you learn is so heavy that it can only be described as a character flaw–sometimes it's not what you know or what you did, it is who you are.

Second day of the training and we are practicing witness transport and protection. Drive, stay alert, arrive at drop, bail and set up a hasty perimeter, scan for safety or clear as necessary and touch base with the receiving unit, then remove the protectee from the vehicle and escort inside.

First scenario and we took fire. I hear the 'pop, pop, pop' of sim fire from across the street. I turn and engage, closing. I fire three shots from 25 yards to 20 and the threat turns and runs (odd, we are taught and practice even in a scenario to stay in the fight no matter what). Doesn't matter–another threat to my left and I sprint, tactical reload, sprint to the dead space behind the building that threat is using for cover. He's still firing at my team, tunnel-visioned and I pop around the wall at his knee level and fire three rounds into his belly just below the vest, all angled upward. I turn and scan 360, looking for a third threat and my team is screaming, waving me over. While I've gone off on this little murdering hunt they've kept one vehicle in the kill zone waiting to extract me. I sprint, dive in the window and we tear off.

That's it, my character flaw. One of 'em, anyway. When attacked, I counter-attack. Normally, that's a good response. Not here. The mission, the team, are my responsibilities as a team leader. All those things disappear and the thing that comes out is what it is–implacable and predatory–just not part of the team.

The goal, now, is to consciously take control. To remember the mission even when this deep button is pushed. To trust my men on the perimeter to do the killing if killing needs to be done. To force myself to look at the big picture. That's going to be hard.

BTW–the guy ran because I shot him right on the tip of the nose. Those suckers can hurt.

Since this is on the edge of true confession time–also at this training I did the most egregious friendly fire kill ever. We were ambushed again and everyone fell back in good order to the hardened (solid cover–a concrete building) drop. The instructor (sneaky bastard, JJ, but I'll never again back into an unknown or take a safe zone on faith) had put one more threat inside the safe house. We backed into a deadlier ambush. One of my team peeled, trying to find a way down a corridor to flank the room the threat was firing from. The rookie put his weapon and light on the door. I button-hooked through into the connecting room. The threat was silent, suckering us into crossing the threshold into another kill zone. I signaled the rookie to kill his light and saw the shadow of the threat on the floor. I dove, sliding on my side and fired four shots into the threat's groin and lower stomach at an upward angle (may be seeing a pattern here). It wasn't the threat. The threat had run to the basement. It was the officer who had run down the corridor to flank. Not only had I shot my own man, but I stalked him and assassinated him.

Lots of things would or could have changed this–threats and officers wore the same armor, officer watching the door instead of the stairs ... but those are incidentals. This is the purpose of training at this level–to find holes, to get better.This was great training.

The second is battle joy. There is a second when you know that the fight will happen and there is no way out of it and suddenly all bullshit falls away. You are you, the best body, mind and spirit all together, everything you have and are and it is all on the table to live or die. It is a feeling like your soul is just behind your ears and it is singing.

I have hit that battlejoy and gotten a manic grin that shut down a whole room of prisoners. Whatever signal it sends, when you touch that, people can feel it. Not to get too spiritual on you but ... On the inside you are not human but a force of nature. You know you can be killed, but you feel you can't be stopped, at least by any human.

Attacking: The Offensive Point of View

The paradigm I used in "Meditations on Violence" is that attacks happen close, hard, fast, and from surprise.

Close, because the threat wants you in a position where he can do maximum damage (next time you hit a heavy bag, notice how close you stand. That's where a bad guy will initiate from. Nothing like sparring distance, huh?)

Harder than you expect from training because most people in training either pull their strikes or use safety equipment. A threat doesn't want to impress you, he wants you out of action.

Faster. Most martial artists are used to sparring timing: feint, play for position, strike, maybe a combination, block and counter. A threat uses a flurry of attack with no thought of defense. Why defend when he knows he is hitting his victim so fast and hard that the victim will be obsessed with his or her own defense? Almost everyone freezes under a flurry of blows. Even if the blows are pulled, the information locks the person into the OODA loop.

From the blog:

OODA Introduction 25JAN2006

This might be a little technical, but I'll try to catch you up quick. The OODA loop has become the standard nomenclature for combative decision making. In essence, each person must Observe what is happening; Orient to the observations–basically interpret the sensory input; Decide what to do about it; and Act.

This isn't new–I remember one martial arts instructor from long ago who had the "Four P's": Percieve, Present, Plan, Perform. My sensei taught it as the elements of speed–perceptual speed, interpretation by experience, the decision tree and then neuromuscular speed. It isn't new or even fresh, but OODA has become standard.

Clarifying example:

O: You see a fist suddenly growing larger (observe)

O: Hey, that must mean it is getting closer! I'm being punched! (orient)

D: What should I do about it? Block or duck? Duck! (decide)

A: Duck! (act)

I was taught these as the elements of speed with the caution that reactive moves, such as blocking, rarely work because the bad guy is on step four when his action triggers your step one. His "act" is the first thing you "observe".

Time is most critically lost in the two middle steps. In the orientation step, inexperienced people try to gather too much or too little information. In combat or self-defense, the usual problem is to try to get too much information. I need to know where his good targets are and my available weapons. That is all. Martial artists tend to also want to know how he reacted to their last attack and what he is likely to do next. That's chess thinking, not brawl thinking–predicting what the threat will do in four moves is useless if the intervening three moves are stabs. The most fatal orient decision in an ambush is the "why" question–"Why are they doing this?" "What does this mean?" You won't get an answer and if you did get an answer it won't help you. But many, many victims freeze right here, with the 'why'.

Decide is the second time waster. There's a thing called Hick's Law which states that the more options you have, the longer it takes to choose one. Makes sense. I call this the Brown Belt syndrome. It's what happens when you have too many cool ways to win and you get your ass kicked while you are weighing options. The way to grow past this is something I call "meta-strategy". Again, this is something I've back engineered from the people that consistently make it work, not something I'm reasoning out.

The people I know who consistently do well in ambushes or have often beaten the maxim that action is faster than reaction have one thing in common. They have a group of techniques that form the core of their strategy that they DO NOT SEE AS SEPARATE TECHNIQUES. Mac has hundreds of disarms and counter-attacks, but when he is surprised he "de-fangs the snake". He can and will do it in a hundred different ways, but in his mind it's just one thing. James "does damage". Again, hundreds of techniques that are all one thing in his brain. I "take the center".

Operant conditioning is critical in self-defense because it is possible, in certain situations including surprise attacks, to cut out the middle two step and develop an automatic, reflex-level response.

Two or more people in conflict have their OODA loops activated and they feed off of each other. My actions are your observations. When what you observe changes, you must re-orient. If I can conclude my loop faster, I not only act faster and get more damage in, but I also throw you off your loop. If you start to swing and I hit you in the face, most people will stop their swing to re-orient.

The closer the events reflect previous experience, the less time it takes to orient. If the event is completely new, such as a judoka experiencing his first leg lock, it is effectively invisible–there is nothing in the past to orient to (which explains the effectiveness of judo in 1888; jujutsu in America in the 1920's, karate in the 50's and BJJ in the 90's). This is also the purpose of cognitive interrupts or context shifting: doing something, such as blowing a kiss or drooling, that doesn't compute as a fight. In short, you can attack the OODA loop as well as attacking the body.

Completely untrained people hit four times a second. A decent boxer or martial artist can easily double or even triple that.

Becoming a predator is most common in our society with serious addiction. You need drugs. In order to get drugs you need a lot of money (IIRC, the last number I heard was $400 a day. Every day. Just to keep the withdrawals at bay.)

Most people can't do serious violence because they recognize the humanity of others, even animals. When society is or becomes marginal, that is a luxury. If there is not enough food for your family, compassion for others goes down. If someone in the village starves every year, feeding a prisoner instead of executing him condemns innocents to die. If the only way you can feed your babies is to raid another village and kill to take their food, you'll find a way to do it or you and your babies will die. Most of us can't relate to the power of addiction, but might be able to imagine what we would be capable of if starving (Read Elie Wiesel's "Night" for an amazing description of what desperation will do to ordinary people.)

Beginning violent criminals have to *learn* to dehumanize their prey. First crimes are usually sloppy because of the emotional blocks. They learn harder/faster/closer/surprise either through trial and error, having experienced it themselves, or being mentored.

✧✦✧✦✧

HOMEWORK

Dissect your last fight scene. For each character write down what his or her goal was (survive, escape, world domination, send a message...) and the parameters. Parameters are the things the character cannot let happen, like dying or going to jail or looking bad in front of an audience or... If you know your characters, this should be easy.

Now analyze the fight. Given those parameters and goals, is this the kind of fight that each would have engaged in? Pay special attention to whoever initiated the violence. Did this act of violence efficiently and safely work to satisfy her needs?

TO RECAP:

- The first element of the fight is the ambush
- The goal is to make sure it never develops into a fight
- People freeze. They freeze to different degrees and for different reasons, but people freeze
- Fights are dynamic, happen in environments
- The body has certain reactions to stress
- Attackers like it hard, fast, close and from surprise

… 4 …

SURVIVAL STRESS RESPONSE (SSR)

We've touched on this a number of times. Here is a fuller explanation.

The survival stress response is a fancy term for the effects of extreme fear. When your body and hindbrain perceive an immediate threat, hormones are pumped into your system that change your mind, body and senses. I'll use the phrases 'adrenaline' and 'adrenalized' but adrenaline is just one of a cocktail of chemicals involved.

Changes to perception:
I've been told that the eye physically changes shape. I don't know if that's true. But most people experience "tunnel vision" – a sharp focus on things right ahead and a complete blindness to anything even a little bit to the sides. I've used this to get close to people fighting and break them up. Approaching about 30 degrees from the front, I was totally invisible.

Things in that focused area can seem unnaturally clear. Dr. Alexis Arwohl writes about an officer who was reading his partner's brass as the expended cartridges flew through the air. This clarity can make things seem bigger and closer than they actually were, and sometimes results in people seeing a bad guy as very close who was actually quite some distance away.

I was playing the bad guy for a carjacking scenario. The student was very much into self-protection and had simulators on him for two guns, two knives and a canister of pepperspray. That was his "every day carry." As I ordered him out of the vehicle with my gun in his ear, I expected him to use the door opening to mask his draw. Nope. He stepped away, hands up, facing me.

I had my weapon (simulator) pointed at his face and kept screaming, "Walk away! Just walk away!"

He backed away until he was about twelve feet away. Then a strange expression flashed across his face and suddenly, but slowly, he moved, taking one step closer and slapping his hands together. I was confused.

In the debrief, the student said that he saw the barrel of my gun as if it was right in his face. His tunnel vision had made me appear ten feet closer than I was. He was trying to disarm me.

"Auditory exclusion" is the name for the deafness of combat. I've been within 20 yards of a gunfight and just heard a pop-pop-pop that I couldn't identify as gunfire. Have read of people who thought their weapons malfunctioned because they never heard the bullet fire. And at the same time, I've been engaged with threats and all I could hear was his breathing, and it was deafening. And sometimes all you hear is the rushing in your ears.

Between the tunnel vision and auditory exclusion, normal people never hear or see a third party joining the fight from the front or flank. Most don't even register when a friend shouts a warning.

Blood is pulled to the center of the body, an ancient mechanism to keep you alive as long as possible when an animal is chewing on your arms and legs. You lose feeling in the extremities, a godsend when you are being eaten by a tiger, a disaster when you are trying to work a safety catch or load a single bullet. This makes your hands and feet very insensitive. It is difficult, even if you remember, to feel textures or the ground beneath you.

Physical Changes:

Your body changes, and many of these changes are reflected in the perceptions. Your insensitive hands and feet, for instance, are also clumsy. You drop things. Stumble.

Some people develop great short-term power, and that's good. But it is clumsy and exhausting and a few injure themselves, pulling muscles and straining joints, and don't notice until later.

Coordination is impaired. At lower levels, fine skills like writing are disrupted. Things slip through your fingers. You can't dial a phone or pick up a coin. Working a key or any fine manipulation (like carefully aiming a gun) become difficult. This is why lighting a cigarette could be so iconic in old films. It was a very pointed way to show that the protagonist's hands were not shaking, not even a bit. Some bouncers (where smoking is still allowed) ostentatiously light cigarettes to show how calm they are and head off a potential fight.

At higher levels of fear, you can't work your hands and feet together. All of your martial arts training seems to be forgotten. A notch worse and all you are capable of is a stumbling run or swinging your dominant hand over and over like you are trying to club someone with a branch. At the highest level, you just freeze and your bladder and bowels let go and you don't even notice.

The more adrenalized you get, the worse the physical effects are.

There is a zone where everything is working beyond normal: senses are at peak acuteness, coordination is spot on and the brain is working fast and subconsciously. Few people reach this stage. I have never heard a reliable account of anyone achieving this in the first fight.

Mental Effects:

It is sometimes hard to distinguish perception and cognition. Did the officer read his partner's brass? Or did he merely remember that he read it? Your character under stress may be the ultimate unreliable narrator, or may be experiencing things that people who live in a comfortable, safe world simply can't imagine.

Thoughts can seem crystal clear, but irrelevant. You may notice time going slowly but instead of using the time, you spend the slow motion time wondering why you aren't using the time. When things seem to go in slow motion, you're going in slow motion as well, otherwise it would be a superpower. Some people get hooked on the slow motion and start thinking, "That's weird, everything is so slooooowww ...." A very few can use the opportunity to choose more efficient actions.

Your brain will do dumb things a lot under the SSR. Really strange and irrelevant thoughts will float through your head ... or completely relevant thought that cries for action and you stand there frozen, not really distinguishing between thinking about things and doing them: "Is that my blood? Should I be doing something about that?" Or worrying about missing work when you see your hand being carried away by a dog.

Random, irrelevant thoughts may wander across your brain and seem very important at the time, "What color was my first girlfriend's eyes? Wouldn't it be horrible to die and not remember ...." People often get stupid–making a bad plan–and then get stubborn about it. Something that is common in other forms of shock as well. And everything makes perfect sense at the time.

The slow motion feeling is called tachypsychia. Sometimes there is another state. Especially when you survive an ambush and do really well, you will have no memory of it at all or just a blur.

At these levels of fear, your kick-ass martial artist's skills will have evaporated entirely.

NYPD statistics from 1994-2000 show a hit percentage at 0-2 yards of 38%. Trained officers at contact range to six feet miss 62% of the time. At the range, it would be almost unheard of to miss at six feet. At 3-7 yards, they missed 83% of the time.

That's how badly skills degenerate. The average trained officer under stress shoots worse than the average beginner not under stress. There's more going on, of course. It's not just adrenaline. There are also the differences between the range (good footing, good lighting, prepared, time, no fear, little movement) and real life. But skills degenerate. For a good example (primarily for males) compare your regular conversation skills with your verbal skills the first time you asked someone on a date. Yeah.

All of these effects are mitigated by experience. An experienced fighter can usually bring himself to the zone with just a little warning, and some snap into it when attacked with just the tiniest freeze as they switch gears. When a professional sets up the attack, he can use specific calming behaviors (rituals, stretches or breathing exercises) to get to the zone prior to the attack.

However, if the type of fight is novel, the warrior returns to square one. I had enough hand-to-hand fights in the jail that at one point I realized I was bored and planning the paperwork while taking down a convict/boxer. Shortly after that I shot someone as part of a tactical operation and afterwards had all of the adrenaline responses just like I was a rookie.

The veteran of a hundred gunfights will not be psychologically prepared for the up-close messiness of his first knife encounter. Stuff like that keeps the world fresh and exciting.

Hitting the Zone

This all sounds pretty horrible. But there is a good side.

I have hit 'the zone' in training with handguns, knives and sword. In real life I have only hit it unarmed.

Some will tell you that 'the zone' is a perfect level of adrenaline, where your efficiency is amped but you don't get the stupidity or clumsiness usually associated with adrenaline. Maybe.

There are other models. Maybe it is spiritual. Maybe you can train to it (but I have never once seen anyone hit the zone from training alone). I like to think it is what happens when your monkeymind shuts the hell up and lets the rest of your brain and body unload. Maybe that is what the Japanese arts mean when they talk of '*mushin*' or 'no mind.'

It is the exact opposite of choking. We all know what choking is. You are going to do something you are really good at, something you have practiced a thousand times. It is simple … and when you do it in front of an audience or when it really matters and you start thinking and worrying and screw it up.

In the zone you are absolutely aware of the audience, the stakes, all of that, but you don't care. You are the action. Precise as a machine but fluid as a leopard. And you feel utterly unstoppable. You can be killed, but you can't be stopped.

One from training:

Perfect Predator Moment 13February2007

One last story from the training. This is the other side of my character flaw.

Our turn to play bad guys. We're in position, one changing a tire, unarmed. One hidden in the trunk of his car, ready to pop the latch. He's very much armed. One guy on long cover, watching from inside a building. His firing will be the signal (but he's a rookie and has fired prematurely in every scenario so far). I'm waiting behind a door. This time we aren't going to hit the witness on the way in, but on the way out.

I watch from the shadows through a crack in a window. They drive in, wary of the guy changing his tire. They set up a perimeter, move the witness in and fall back to a tight inner perimeter on the 'clinic'. In a few minutes they come out. Someone sees the rookie and the officers respond professionally, firing back, moving to cover, preparing to roll their vehicles out of the death zone, pulling the witness back to the hard cover of the clinic. The ambush is blown.

I step out. One officer is responsible for my sector–he's in the rear seat of the car with a rifle. He's looking right at me but I fire three shots to his face before he is consciously aware that I am there. The team leader is scrambling to get into the car, the passenger seat on my side. Three more shots, two to the back of the head and one to the neck, then I fire two over his shoulder into his driver's head and turn towards the clinic. Someone is firing his weapon out the door at my long shooter across the street. I put two sim rounds on his hand and he falls back, cursing. I feel my slide lock back and change magazines without looking. I hear the officers inside. One takes command, "We need to get to the truck!" They file out, witness in a protective sandwich between them. Weapons at the ready, eyes darting. They walk out the door directly in front of me like I am invisible on their left flank. Three shots on each blamblamblam, blamblamblam, blamblamblam. Pastel colors explode, all shots in tight groups at the edge of the arm holes in their body armor.

I'm untouched. It was only sims, only a game, but the cold precision of it is settled in my belly. Nineteen rounds, nineteen hits. There's a round in the chamber left and an empty mag in the weapon. I can feel it. The world is huge and fills my senses and at the same time it is exactly the size of the very tip of my front sight.

The zone is pretty cool, but I have never met anyone who could stay there until they'd had several fights. Even those that can, start over at square one when the type of violence changes. So your gunfighter protagonist will turn into a jellyfish in his first knife fight. And probably have nightmares, too.

Given time, you can adjust your hormone level. When we try to raise it to the zone, we call that getting psyched up. When we are too excited, the advice is to "take a deep breath and calm down." You probably recognize these from your own life. The people who have this time, generally, are the bad guys. They pick place and time. An attacker can have rituals to psych himself up. Almost universally, the victim is denied the advantage of time.

✧✦✧✦✧

HOMEWORK

Do something in the next 24 hours that scares you. Go to a climbing gym. Go to a gun range. Sing karaoke. Ask the person you've been thinking about on a date.

For that matter, if you want to have an awesome life, do something that scares you every chance you get. Shoot for once a day.

TO RECAP:

- Under extreme stress, hormones are pumped into your system
- These hormones affect your perception, cognition and motor skills
- You can become inured to specific stresses

DISCUSSION: The Murder of Deputy Kyle Dinkheller

The video was taken from the dashboard camera of Deputy Dinkheller. He has pulled over a man for driving erratically. The man gets out of his pickup and begins doing a dance, singing, "Shoot me! Shoot my fuckin' ass! Shoot me!"

The deputy tries to calm the threat down and orders him to approach. The threat shouts "I am a goddamned Vietnam combat veteran and I am not taking orders from you."

Deputy Dinkheller calls in that he has someone acting strangely.

The threat (Threat is the typical cop euphemism for someone who requires force) rushes Kyle, shouting, "Who you callin' motherfucker?"

The next part happens off camera, but it sounds like Kyle draws his expandable baton. Likely he ground it against the threat's sternum, using pain to drive him back. The threat returns to his pick-up and begins loading a .30 caliber semiautomatic assault carbine.

The deputy has been getting more agitated. His voice increases in pitch, rate and volume. He starts to become less coherent on the radio. Early in the encounter, Deputy Dinkheller tells Brannon repeatedly, "Get back!" as Brannon approaches, meaning, 'Stay away, keep your distance.' When Brannon returns to the truck and starts loading the carbine, Kyle keeps saying, "Get back!" but now he means almost the opposite thing.

Kyle begins repeating himself, over and over, "Put down the rifle! Put down the rifle!" When you show this video to a room full of cops, they start shifting nervously. They know Kyle needs to shoot. Some will say it out loud. Kyle doesn't, at first.

The threat closes, firing. Kyle returns fire, but the threat has the superior weapon, mobility, and tactical training and experience. The threat closes, bobbing and weaving. Kyle screams when he is shot. He is still trying to scream for help into the radio. He is back in the fight, but it is too late. He is shot again and screams.

The threat has either a jam or needs to reload. As he turns away Dep. Dinkheller, who is not yet dead, shoots again. The threat turns, flanks the deputy and kills him. The last shot, according to reports, hits Kyle in the eye.

The threat drives away.

It is chilling the way a good horror/suspense movie is chilling. The camera is not pointing at the point of action and so you do not see anyone get shot or die. But you hear it, and it is real.

This video is important. By all accounts, Kyle Dinkheller was a good man. He was a good shot and considered a good officer. There is nothing in my history or his to indicate I am the better man.

That means if he can freeze, so can I.

If he can get caught in a loop, so can I.

... 5 ...

BAD GUYS AND VIOLENCE

As already stated, bad guys use violence because it works. They want something. Violence is a quick and often a safe and efficient way to get it. If it looks like it won't be safe or won't be efficient, the criminal gives the whole situation a pass.

That's criminals. We'll get back to them, but let's talk about some other potentially violent people.

Altered states of consciousness. Mentally ill people are not more criminal than others. People with altered states of consciousness, whether caused by mental illness, drugs, or extreme emotion can be dangerous and unpredictable.

With schizophrenia, the person may be responding to a world that only they can see. They may be told what to do by voices that wear them down. They may see some connections that make no sense to us—that high-pitched noises come from the devil and therefore babies cry because they are possessed and the only way to save the babies is to remove their voices ....

The man was driving his head into a concrete wall. Again and again, he would stand, back up to the limits of his ten by twelve foot cell and run, driving his head into the concrete wall. He said he was trying to "knock myself to heaven. I want to see my grandfather." The challenge was to use a type of force that would stop him without increasing his head trauma. A Taser saved his life.

Most fights with the mentally ill happen because the mentally ill person is terrified. They may not be able to interpret that someone is trying to help, and the fight often turns into a frenzied, frantic flailing. Lots of thrashing and biting.

Follow the dynamic. If someone who is not acting 'right' (your protagonist is unlikely to be able to tell at first glance if the person is drugged or mentally ill or in a severe emotional state) does something dangerous either to others (like breaking down a door and demanding honey) or to themselves (like running into traffic) they need to be stopped. The nature of the altered state of consciousness is that they cannot be expected to stop or control themselves. So someone intervenes.

The person in the altered mental state sees the intervention but is unlikely to see it as help and quite often sees it as an attack. They fight, in a panic. When they start to lose, it doesn't occur to them to surrender, they fight harder. More force is used.

(Non-mental illness, like a diabetic reaction, can also trigger erratic and violent behavior. Graham V Connor, one of the cornerstones of police force law, was a US Supreme Court decision about a police use of force stemming from a diabetic crisis).

In some cases emotionally disturbed people have fought to heart failure. Just like a horse can be run to death.

This brings up a point that affects a lot of officers but doesn't get a lot of play. The truth is that force is used to stop force. But we all want force to be used 'justly'. If someone dies after a use of force, we want it to be a bad guy, not a poor disturbed kid who panicked. That can be really hard on good people who had to use force.

Here's the deal. Hardened, experienced criminals know how to surrender. They know how much fight they can give without being hurt. They talk tough knowing that as long as they keep their hands in plain sight, they are safe. Some (many, actually) actively try to provoke the officer into an act of unjustified force. They might be able to sue or put pressure on to get charges dropped. We rarely use force, and rarely much force, on serious criminals. Serious criminals know how to behave when the police show up.

Regular citizens don't know how to behave. Some fight when they have no hope of winning or even when it will be a crime to do so. Many stand on rights they do not have or demand to be treated in a way that the officer won't or maybe can't (by law or policy) accommodate. If you go to jail, the officers will take your wedding ring because if you are housed with someone who is willing to bite your finger off for something shiny, the officers will be responsible. The officers will take the ring even if the arrestee is willing to fight for it. So force is more likely to be used on a regular citizen in a bad situation than on a serious criminal. In the book, "The Code of the Street" Elijah Anderson makes a similar observation from the other side–people who live in the inner city rarely get injured in robberies because they know the etiquette of being mugged.

The EDP (emotionally disturbed person) is the worst case, as described above. And the least deserving of pain or injury. But, to repeat, force is not about justice. It is about stopping people.

Back to criminals. Like anyone else, a bad guy uses violence socially or asocially.

Social violence, as already described, is for the (perceived) good of the group. It is used to establish a hierarchy, to enforce the rules and norms of a group, to establish boundaries of membership or to strengthen bonds.

If it is for the good of the group, are these actions bad? It depends.

Sometimes, cultural differences will make it seem that way.

You, your readers and your point of view character may see things that are heinous crimes in your culture that are completely acceptable in another society. Cutting off a hand for stealing. Clitorectomy. But don't get smug–wouldn't some modern forms of body art be considered mutilations in other places and times? Is the hijab the sign of a repressive paternalistic society? Or is the bikini, something a sex slave might be forced to wear in a hijab culture, the sign of a paternalistic society? And is choosing either better or worse than being forced to wear them?

(Think that through–which is more horrific, a child abuse victim who is targeted and attacked or the one who seeks it out because she has been groomed to believe that true love involves physical violence?

Grooming victims is beyond the scope of this book–for now–but it is just one of many horrible sides of this world.)

Sometimes, a person will attempt to use social violence and do so ineptly, like a bullied child over-reacting and inadvertently causing death. An attempt to set boundaries can go tragically wrong: "I said NO!" and a push and person falls down the stairs and will never walk again ....

And sometimes it is very dark. A predator will hide his intentions in a social pattern, such as a premeditated date-rape. Some will use social reasons to justify bad actions. Almost every case of domestic abuse I can think of, the perpetrator stated he was 'teaching a lesson.' And sometimes the threats' intention is to send a very clear message e.g. lynching.

Asocial violence is what happens when a person is able to completely or partially dehumanize a victim. It changes a fight to a hunt. I'm not sure I can put this in words. Most people can fight another human. An asocial predator can hunt one. We kill animals for food efficiently–whether hunting with a high-powered rifle or the quick throat-cutting of a *halal* butcher.

A predator, someone who is in the asocial mode, can apply this efficiency to another human.

This is rare. Most people can't do it. Some can fake it and some, with intense training can act like it for short periods of time (a war or a battle), but the humanity of their victims tends to bubble up and they pay the price later–in nightmares, separation from others and, all too often, addictions or suicide.

For those who can flip the switch violence is a completely different experience than most of us imagine it. It is a tool. With proper planning, it is an efficient and safe tool. It often makes a truly asocial bad guy feel like a god (or asocial good guy, for that matter). When something very bad and violent happens to a group of people, most run around like screaming monkeys. They cannot just shift to survival mode but cling to each other and try to figure out what it all means. Humans mix their physical survival mentality with their social survival mentality.

To be asocial, whether naturally or trained or inured over time, is to walk into that situation without hesitation. When everyone else is spraying fire in an attempt to make others duck and not get shot, the predator is methodical … aiming, firing, murdering.

Some people, the process predators, use violence for its own sake. They enjoy the feelings of control and domination in a beating, a rape or a murder. They may fantasize about torture-murders and work to live out their fantasies. These guys are rare. The risks are high and the rewards are generally intangible.

Most predators use a subconscious (or even conscious) risk-reward analysis. Aggressive panhandling for a dollar is low payoff, but it is very nearly zero risk. Showing a weapon and ordering a potential victim to obey (if you have analyzed the victim) is lower risk than using force (sometimes people panic and fight when hit; in any case using force influences prosecutors to be more vigorous).

I mentioned early on that in some cases the death penalty or minimum sentencing standards are deterrents. It is in these cases. The more professional and experienced a criminal is, the more likely sentencing possibilities are on their mind when planning or conducting an assault. Two examples from my local criminals:

"Normally after I beat him down I would have gone through his pockets, but that would turn it into robbery and that's a measure eleven charge." (Measure 11 is Oregon's mandatory minimum sentencing statute for violent crimes.)

And:

"I held his head with my other hand so it wouldn't hit the wall. I know how you guys trump up charges …."

No one is merely their criminal acts. Hard core violent criminals don't have a lot of friends and most addicts have ripped off family so much that family doesn't trust them … but their moms still love them and so, up to a certain age even with horrific abuse, do their children.

Part of it is that parents and children are conditioned to love. Part of it is that in the attempt to make sense and normalize life, people can go through amazing justifications for a family member or friend.

The number of times that a local criminal well known by us to be a brutal pimp, drug dealer and extremely violent finally met his end (usually at the hands of another pimp or dealer) and his family came out of the woodwork to say that "He was a good boy" "Very gentle" "He had some trouble when he was younger but was turning his life around" and the like leaves me cold.

I always wondered if they really believed it. In a few cases I know the family members were terrified of the subject and had sworn out Restraining Orders ... but they sounded sincere. They were genuinely grieving.

I used to remind rookies that each of our inmates was three people—the one who did the crimes; the one the family knew; and the one we saw in jail. Some of the most violent criminals were good inmates. They knew the system, knew how little they could get away with and tried to do the time quietly. Some whiny little low-level hustlers tried to play big guy in jail. It never ended well, but some never learned. And at visiting every week, you would see a four-year-old on his crack-addicted prostitute mother's knee looking through the plexiglass and talking into the phone saying, "I love you daddy. When are you coming home?"

✧✦✧✦✧

HOMEWORK:

Two assignments for this one.

#1: Sorry about this, I'm going to push your buttons. Remember the earlier question about whether choosing or being forced is darker? Envision two characters. One is an eleven-year-old girl who has been abducted and held by a violent sexual sadist for four weeks. She is chained in a basement. The other is an eleven-year-old girl who has been raised from the time she was six to believe that her duty as a daughter is to satisfy her father's brutal sexual urges. Dark enough?

Write a one-page diary entry from the point of view of each of these little girls.

#2 Getting into the head of a resource predator.

There is a very real possibility that your children will starve. No one will help you. List what you are willing to do. Don't be vague. 'Anything it takes' is not an acceptable answer. Will you steal? Rob? (You should know the difference if you did the Chapter Two homework.) Murder? Prostitution? Would you sell or prostitute one of your children to feed the others? It happens all over the world...

Further questions: As an adaptable human being, how long would it take you to convince yourself that what you do isn't really wrong? That you are the good one, your victims in some way deserve this? They are the bad guys? Would you band with others in your same position? (And would you trust those others? How much?)

And if this situation was never going to change, would you teach these values to your children?

If you want a good ballpark of what people would do for drugs, think what you would do to feed your children.

TO RECAP:

- Social violence is used to establish place in a hierarchy; to set the boundaries of in and outside the group or to enforce the social rules
- Asocial violence depends on an ability to 'other'
- Asocial violence is for a specific goal- to get stuff or to enjoy the process
- The humanity of the victim does not enter into asocial violence
- Experienced criminals/predators use a risk/reward analysis
- Violent people have lives beyond their violence

... 6 ...

GOOD GUYS AND VIOLENCE

There are different kinds of good guy protagonists. Professionals (cops, soldiers, PIs, etc.) Reformed Bad Guys, and the Ordinary Person in Extraordinary Circumstances (OPIEC). They each have different problems and look at the world in different ways.

Humans are incredibly adaptable. Which means we can get used to anything. Which means that things that seem paranormal level to outsiders is simply doing a job.

One of my friends once wrote that he wasn't a 'real cop' like me, because I spent eight hours a day with violent criminals, he wasn't sure he could handle that. He called himself a 'glorified investigator.' The guy who said this was a former undercover working narcotics, a SWAT sniper and was leading a homicide task force. You can't get more cop than that. In my mind, he was the real cop, I was just a glorified babysitter. I don't even work enforcement ....

Mechanics do things that seem magical to me. So do accountants. I can't even understand higher physics. IT geeks are gods ... all because it is outside my understanding.

The thing with violence is that it has more 'mythic weight.' Because fewer people have any experience and because so much of drama is based on conflict, people think it is special and important. That's attributed, and not something healthy insiders feel.

Professional Good Guys

Some good guys get involved in violence as professionals. Police, soldiers, bouncers, maybe private investigators, bodyguards.

Except for those glorious rookie months where they know lots of facts and understand almost nothing, professionals do not think or feel about violence like citizens do.

Professionals approach violence differently. First and foremost, it is not some separate mysterious thing that only happens in a world turned upside down. Violence is natural. Force is a form of communication–for a good guy the most emphatic way possible of saying "No" "Stop!" or "I am not going to let that happen." (For bad guys force is usually just a way to say "Gimme!") Force works regardless of language barrier or altered states of consciousness or how dedicated the bad guy is. Sometimes it takes more force than others, but with enough force the behavior stops.

Professionals use force to stop or prevent behaviors. Amateurs use force to establish dominance quite often. That's important and leads to one of the questions an author must answer before a fight scene:

Assuming the character knows anything about fighting, he needs a damn good reason to go hands-on. In almost every action movie there is an early scene to establish how bad-assed the protagonist is. He walks into an armed robbery about to go down and clears out the whole gang or breaks up a street fight and uses his mad martial arts skillz to take out a gang. It's probably exciting for the audience. From professionals watching you get muffled gags and mutterings like, "Fuckin' wannabe."

In almost all of those scenes, the protagonist could leave. He could apologize. He could stay out of the situation and call for police or, if he is an officer, back-up. The only reason not to do these things is an ego so grotesque coupled with intelligence so low that there is no chance the guy would have survived being a rookie.

Get this–fighting is dangerous. Pros know this. All moderately intelligent people know this. It is much safer if you do it from ambush. It is much safer if you have friends, especially well-armed and trained friends.

Fighting also has consequences. Your protagonist beats up six gang-bangers who are hassling an elderly lady. Congratulations. He now has six people who will support each other's story that he attacked them from ambush and they were trying to calm *him* down. He couldn't have beaten six if they were fighting, so *they* must have been the peacekeepers. The protagonist will be lucky not to face criminal charges. Even if he does, he will face, and lose, a civil court case that will take all of his money and possessions and garnish his wages for life.

And if he is a cop, he will lose his badge and be labeled dirty, because any good cop would have known better and would have called for back-up. The very fact that he didn't make the call, in real life, would be a solid sign that he was acting criminally.

Wait! There's more! He needs an even better reason to go face to face. Why he let it become anything resembling a fair fight. You do not only need to explain why the protagonist was fighting, but why he was fighting like an idiot. Like an amateur. *Like a character in a bad novel.*

Pros spend a lot of energy and attention on averting violence.

The primary skill is an ability to see violence coming. They need to be able to read terrain, read the dynamic and read people.

Reading Terrain

In any given area there are positions of power. Corners of the room limit the number of directions you can be approached, and hence the number of directions you need to watch. Hence the cliché of action adventure heroes not sitting with their backs to doors, trying for the corner table. (It's sometimes fun to watch cops go out to lunch together.) If you aren't in the power position, always notice the people who are.

There's more, though. There are places in a given room where you have advantages in visibility–you don't need to be facing the room if there's a mirror above the bar. If the sun is setting behind you, you will see the shadows of anyone trying to approach from the rear. Almost all elevators have a handrail that is shiny enough you can see the reflection of anyone trying to hide to the side of the door. In certain venues I throw my sunglasses on the table upside down. It's a casual thing, no one notices ... but upside down puts the lenses at a better angle to see what is behind me in the reflection.

Your protagonist will also look for freedom of action for himself, "funnels of death" and escape routes.

It's not enough to be sitting in the corner if your weapon hand is pressed up against the wall. Being *pinned* in a corner is no advantage. Fights, especially gunfights, are very mobile affairs. What are the three critical skills for small unit operations? Move, shoot and communicate. Movement is critical.

The "funnel of death" is any small space that a person must come through, like a door or a hallway. It is easy to concentrate firepower in such a small area and the longer you are in one, the more likely you are to be killed. Violence professionals rarely stop in the doorway to scan a room. They scan what they can from outside and then step in quickly and get to one side of the door.

Scanning for escape routes also becomes habit. Things don't always go well. Good guys don't always win. If you have a plan, you can usually get out. If you don't, you will be cut down while you are trying to think of a plan.

✧✦✧✦✧

HOMEWORK:

Start cataloging, from this moment forward, the positions of power in each area you are in. Pay special attention to shadows and reflective surfaces. Start looking for escape routes, hiding places, areas that provide cover and alternate ways into buildings and rooms. Be creative–can you break a window or hide in the subfloor of a computer room?

✧✦✧✦✧

Reading Dynamics

People are social animals and violence is usually a social thing. An experienced protagonist can often read the people around him as a group and see danger signs well in advance. It's a good habit for writers, too.

Look at the flow of movement. People give more room to things that scare them and many people are remarkably intuitive. On public transportation or in any crowded area, who gets more personal space than others? Who gives them that space? Is it a crowd of regulars who know the local players? Or is it a group of strangers working on instinct?

The clothing–is it the norm for people to have untucked shirts or collared shirts with open fronts worn loose over t-shirts? Then the signal is that being armed is normal here.

See a group of guys with short hair, maybe goatees, wearing almost no accessories beyond a watch and a wedding ring, with loose jackets or fannypacks across their bellies? That's a group of cops.

See two guys standing close and looking over each other's shoulders as they talk? Probably extremely fit and with primarily greenish-black tats? That's a pair of cons who haven't been out long enough for their addictions to destroy the bodies they built on the weight pile in the yard.

✧✦✧✦✧

HOMEWORK:

Next time you are in a crowd, practice looking at things from different magnifications. Find a high place and look at the crowd like it was water–where does it go, what does it avoid? Then look at small groups that you can identify–how does a family move through a mall? How does a group of teenagers hanging out interact or ignore the people around them? Skip looking at an individual for now, instead just look at hands, just look at eyes and just look at shoes. Personally, I look at pockets and count clip-on knives, but that's me.

✧✦✧✦✧

Reading People

There is an old police saying, "The eyes may be the window to the soul, but people kill you with their hands." Always watch the hands. Your pro will get very nervous if he can't see someone's hands, especially someone who 'pinged' his 'radar'.

Pros tend to recognize other pros, good or bad. They scan a room the same way, often dress similarly (movement and weapon concealment are very important) position themselves the same way. People who have trained to fight move slightly differently than others. (Though sometimes dancers move very similarly they rarely watch the world the same way.) We call this 'pinging the radar'.

A story from Northern Iraq:

The first time I saw him, my initial reaction was to label him as an extreme danger, probably an assassin. This is a place where that word isn't bandied about. I mean it very literally. It took me almost two days to be sure that he was part of our security detail. 'Slim' is insanely alert, moves silently, rarely talks. There is a museum dedicated to the atrocities that Saddam Hussein perpetrated against Slim's hometown. He has been fighting for a very long time.

Things are quieter now–he makes his living as a bodyguard–but what kept him alive for so long, the zanshen, is very close to the surface.

Slim and I pinged each other's radar pretty good that first day. I read him as a professional killer and he read me as something, too. He attached himself to me after that and we watched each other with wary respect (at least on my end).

The general invites us to dinner. He has fought for a long time, too. Now we dine and drink eighteen-year-old scotch in a fine restaurant. The food is wonderful. A woman sings Kurdish songs in a dialect that no one at our table understands. Everyone is armed. The general's PSD is at the table behind us, ours is at the table near the door. Slim is with ours.

I am at relatively high alert throughout the dinner. The general is possibly the highest-value target in the region. The things that make it secure can seem like a set-up aimed at us. I don't drink much and sit so that my weapon is cleared for a draw. The general keeps piling food on my plate.

Things relax a bit when the general excuses himself and leaves. Not right away. Loyalties here can be Byzantine and probably all of us entertain the possibility that the host leaving early from a meeting place and time of his choice could potentially be a very bad thing. We disperse around the room and stay watchful. Then most relax a bit.

Mike tries to take a picture of Slim and fails. He curses his luck.

"Mike," I say, "You can't take a picture of a really good bodyguard." He and Slim both nod in agreement and the flash goes off in the camera held in my right hand, way away from my body, "But I can." The picture is pretty good, Slim in profile. Were crosshairs drawn on it they would meet just behind his eyes.

Slim is not happy, but he nods approval. I have somehow just confirmed his assessment of me, whatever that was.

Later I see that Slim has his back to me and I slip the camera out of my pouch, planning to drift around a pillar ... as soon as the thought is formed he snaps around, staring at me. He could sense me go into the hunter's mind.

That's the point of this story, really. There are things that happen to your senses on the pointy end of the spear. You become something a little different than your garden-variety human. People who haven't experienced this edge tend to either gasp with shiny eyes and think 'magic' or discount it as bullshit. But it's there, and sometimes you can only share it with others who have gone even deeper.

Pros will watch how people move; how they dress; whether they are nervous; what they watch; what they try to hide (hands, emotions...). Most people will show adrenaline indicators before they escalate to violence. A pro will not. He will show specific self-calming behaviors, such as consciously controlling breathing (autogenic or 'warrior breathing'– slow in to a count of four, hold to a count of four, exhale to a count of four, hold empty to a count of four, repeat); subtly stretch, especially the neck and spine; or check details of weapons and equipment.

Except for an extreme pro who has consciously trained against it, both pros and amateurs, when armed, have a tendency to subconsciously touch their weapons when tensions go up even slightly. Possibly just making sure they haven't shifted.

Common adrenaline indicators:

- Changes in coloration (flush or pallor)
- Breathing (rapid and shallow)
- Thirst (frequent drinking or licking lips)
- Gross Motor Activity (GMA) pacing, flexing, swinging arms
- Loss of Fine Motor Activity (FMA) shaking, dropping small items
- Unfocused gaze ("Thousand Yard Stare")
- Repetitive, rhythmic or ritual behavior- tapping, humming or bouncing. Almost never whistling, the mouth is too dry.

Violence professionals are rarely the "lone wolf" type. Most can operate solo and many prefer to, but they still work and live in social networks.

Professionals require a logistical support network. In modern times, they need to get weapons and ammunition and SBA (Soft Body Armor) from somebody. They don't make their own food and clothing, communications equipment, or transportation. Someone supplied all of that. Someone taught them to use it. Someone keeps the technology current and keeps the batteries charged.

Intelligence networks are just as critical. You can't know all the details of all the underworld strata in every city of the world. There is a common tattoo among American criminals–three dots on the web of the thumb that has a very definite meaning. It stands for "*mi vida loca*" "my crazy life." I saw the same tattoo on the Iran/Iraq border. It took me almost two months to find out what it meant there. (Sorry, can't share that.)

Getting entry into criminal circles in unfamiliar places is hard. These guys are paranoid and don't really care if they use a little too much violence or kill the wrong guy. It is also hard to stay unknown in the places you are familiar with.

Your protagonist gets information from somewhere. Often the people who gather information have the more dangerous and challenging job. When the "Mission: Impossible" team (the old TV show, I'm ignoring the movies) read their little dossiers to find out that the smuggling family had two brothers who were rivals or that Crime Boss X's wife had a drinking problem ... someone found that out. Your kick-ass tactical operator is helpless, literally working blind, if he doesn't have good intel from the guy on the ground. And being a good operator and a good intel guy are both full time jobs and require very different training and with a few exceptions, very different personalities.

Operators and Intel

There are different kinds of operators, of course, but one of the big differences is that operators (trigger pullers) need to be able to 'other' people quickly and thoroughly. They think about position and tactical advantage. Unless they are working to control it, a lot of people feel a vague disquiet in their presence, like they are being hunted.

People who gather intel need to be people persons and the best I've met are extraordinarily friendly and out-going, without ever actually volunteering information themselves. There has to be a coldness as well, but hidden. One colleague described the job of a Hostage Negotiator (usually called a crisis negotiator today): "You have to be able to make friends in a few minutes with some really nasty people and sometimes some really troubled people. Some of these kids have real problems and you need to be able to care and to reach them. And then you need to be able to talk them into coming closer to the window so that someone can shoot your new friend in the head. And you need to be okay with that."

Most trigger pullers have trouble shooting someone they have come to know. That's one of the reasons that snipers (snipers are not the same as sharp shooters or 'target interdiction specialists'–I'm talking specifically about people who go out hunting for specific high-value targets) have such a reputation for being different. They study their kills before they shoot. Most people who study the kills couldn't shoot. I don't know if most snipers would feel comfortable talking and making friends and still shoot. I doubt if many would have the skill to do both.

Tactical operators also are obsessed with maintaining control, knowing the options and planning for their own safety. Undercover work is dangerous as hell and a lot of the basic safety precautions are out the window. Back up can't be in sight and in deep cover may not be close. Armor will give you away and weapons might ....

An experienced professional also has a social network. That social network is what keeps him sane. Dealing with violence has some serious emotional repercussions. Some are immediate and obvious: you see a head split open and watch and smell the brains drip out, you lose the ability to keep death an abstraction. You know someone who took a bullet in the face, someone who was as good as you or better–well-trained and equipped and smart and cautious, just unlucky–and you realize how much you existence depends, each second, on luck.

You risk your life to save a life and you look at the person you saved probably a drug addicted loser with a long history of violent felonies just as bad as the person you saved him from–and you have to question why. Is it just a job? Is it the right thing to do? Duty? Paycheck? Or habit? It is what you know how to do and most people can't and it needs to be done.

Less immediate and obvious is the double-edged sword of simultaneously trying to live a normal life. The first edge of that sword is that it is easy for a professional to forget that he works with extremes. If you spend 80% of your waking hours with dangerous, bad people it is easy to start to believe that 80% of the world is bad and dangerous. It's stressful not only because you spend too much time in a state of hypervigilance (adrenaline-fueled, jumpy alertness) but you also feel that the people you care about are in constant danger, and they seem unable to see it.

That's the second edge of the sword. People without a professional's experience are both incredibly naïve and ill-informed about even the most basic aspects of violence ... yet they are very sure about right and wrong and swift to judge. They believe that they know more than they do. Talking about violence with non-professionals is as rewarding, illuminating and accurate as talking with first-graders about sex.

A lot has been written about the divorce rate among cops and soldiers and emergency services personnel. It's something of a cliché. Here's the deal—even a lot of professionals don't deal with the stresses of the job well. If they are drowning, it will come out in their families. If they try to keep stuff inside, to protect their families by silence ("there is some stuff in my head that no one else needs to know"), the strain will come out in the family.

And if the family can't handle it, if they need to deny the reality of what the professional deals with every day, that will come out in divorce as well.

Early in my career, I was given two pieces of advice.

The first was from a burned-out former cop. "Whatever any liberal bleeding heart wants to tell you, three percent of the world is scum. Trouble is, if you spend ninety percent of your time with that three percent, you start to believe the world is ninety percent scum. It isn't. Make sure you know good, normal people too."

The second was from one of my first supervisors. "Don't over-react when your kids are bad. You're going to see them be cruel and break things and lie and be selfish and you'll think, 'Oh my God, my kid is turning into a criminal.' That's not it. The kid isn't behaving like a criminal. Criminals behave like two-year-olds. Rehabilitation isn't the problem, most were never habilitated in the first place. You will be tempted to treat your kids like a criminal who is acting out. Don't. Just be a good parent and the kid will learn just like you did."

And, for what it's worth, the advice I would give rookies on how to do the job with out burning out: "You can take yourself seriously or the job seriously but never, ever at the same time. If you aren't laughing at something, either yourself or the world, you're doing it wrong."

There is a solid core of professionals who do the job well, long term, with great restraint and professionalism. Consistently, in this group you will find very deep, committed, long-term relationships. Nothing is hidden (including limits–once in nineteen years has my wife said, "I don't want to hear any more. This is bad." On only one subject.)

I don't know whether the high-end professional chooses or creates the relationship that allows him or her to decompress and focus on real life and function or if the good relationship allows the high-end professional to keep going.

A professional will bring different physical and emotional skills to an episode of violence as well as a completely different mindset than a non-professional. An amateur wonders if he can beat Chuck Norris. A professional wonders *how* he will beat Chuck Norris.

Physical skills will come from training and then be tempered and refined from experience. A lot of training, especially at the introductory stages, is not at all the same skill that needs to be applied in the field. A prime example is shooting on the range–static, good footing, good lighting, ear and eye protection, safety monitors, unlimited time.

A real gunfight is almost exactly the opposite in every particular. Not because the basic skills are wrong, but because they are incomplete. That goes for almost all training—martial arts and even police academy and BCT (Basic Combat Training, military "basic".)

High-Level Skills + Intensity 14August 2009

He is an up-and-coming lieutenant in a foreign service. He heard a story about something I did the week before and so he tracked me down to ask about some one-on-one training time. He wanted close-quarters handgun. (Or knife throwing. Sigh.) We went with the handgun. Four count draw, dry fire, firing from retention, moving and shooting, scanning. Because he was a leader we also went into how to train: faults to watch for, what would happen if his men ever needed to shoot as a team.

At one point he threw up his hands and said, "I am so angry. Everything they taught us was wrong!"

What he had learned at his basic training were the fundamentals of pistol marksmanship.

They weren't wrong, they were just incomplete. Beginners need to learn safety. It's stupid to accidentally kill yourself. They need to get some feeling for success and how the weapons work, so they become a stable platform. They learn grip and sight alignment and sight picture and breath control and trigger press.

They learn these fundamentals in a context that makes it easy for the instructor to monitor and easy for the student to correct–good lighting, good footing, hearing and eye protection, safety monitors and not moving.

Those environmental basics are rare as hell in real life. Gunfire is loud and muzzle flash can be blinding in low light. Often not only is the footing bad, but it may be too dark to tell how bad. And you'd better damn well be moving unless you already have good cover. If you do have good cover, think about moving anyway because the threat should try to flank you. And cover geometry can be counterintuitive–cover is often better the farther you are away from it. Said it was counter-intuitive.

There are details that came at a price–when and how to fire from retention; why the weapon should be canted out when at retention. Details that aren't on the beginning syllabus.

Combat shooting, whether raiding or counter-ambush, is a whole different animal than range training. Honestly, range training is probably closest to assassination skills, which aren't that useful for good guys.

And there are things that work very well on the range that are ineffective in real life. I was a Weaver shooter for decades, trained that way from a pup. But there are three significant flaws in the Weaver–it is almost impossible to maintain while moving. It points the biggest hole in your body armor (armpit) right at the threat. Most damning is that according to research no one has been able to pull it off in a firefight. An assassination maybe

But that doesn't make range training wrong. I go to the range. I practice my dry-fire and failure-to-fire drills. Nothing is wrong, but it is incomplete. So when I practice my dry fire, I know what I will see when the projectile hits flesh and I know what it will do to my mind and body–because I have experienced it. Once.

So I practice the pieces with as much awareness as I can of the totality, and the absolute certainty that there is a lot of that totality I haven't seen yet and I will inevitably fail and have to improvise.

You need to know what your protagonist has been trained to do. Too many characters seem to be trained in 'everything' or the authors hand wave as if Special Forces or S.E.A.L. training included everything.

Emotional skills are another matter. Dealing with stress is both a talent and a skill. Some people are wired differently. I found out early that fighting is not something I take home. Even after my one shooting, no bad dreams, no shakes or flashbacks. But I had a much harder time with whining. I did, for a while, have a recurring dream of an infinitely long hallway with cell doors every four paces and a different criminal in every cell whining, begging or demanding something, "Officer, what time is it?" "Officer, what's my release date?" "Officer, will you sharpen my pencil?" "Officer, my baby needs heroin." That last—pregnant junkies would often beg for drugs, and always say, "it's for my baby." That always bothered me.

Humor, especially dark humor, is one of the most common and most disturbing (to outsiders) ways to stay sane. As one friend put it, "You're either going to laugh or cry. If I start crying I don't think I'll ever stop." Humor has to be controlled—as necessary as it can be for the professionals, when families or reporters overhear it can destroy careers.

Many professionals rely on faith. Not necessarily a particular faith. They deal far too often with a fact that almost all of society is designed to deny:

We are all going to die. There is no way around it and no way, other than suicide, to even control it.

That's a hard truth to wrap your head around, and if it seems easy you don't understand it yet.

At one level of faith, a belief in an afterlife or that there is a plan is a huge comfort. It makes a harsh, bleak truth less harsh, maybe less bleak. Maybe it's not true.

At another level of faith, professionals take comfort in tangible things–their training, their experience or their team–so that they can believe that they won't die *this time*. It gives them the courage to go in, the belief that, sooner or later, they will be rescued if captured.

There is also a level of faith, what may be the definition of faith itself, unique to the men and women who deal with the possibility of death as a profession. How much information and preparation would it take for you to risk your life? To the professional, the answer is obvious: "As much as we have time for, and then we go."

You will never have enough training, information or skill to be perfectly safe. The operation, the mission, will have a definite window of opportunity. The ability to go in, without the possibility of knowing the outcome, defines, to me, faith. It is the hallmark of the professional.

From my blog:

What Do You Think You're Doing? 25June2007

What is worth killing for? What is worth dying for?

Believe it or not, those are the easy questions. The kindergarten version of this particular meditation. Whenever you think of self-defense or think of fighting, those questions are part of the equation. They have to be, because trying to work out your moral and ethical issues when someone else is trying to expose your inner workings to the cold air is ... inefficient.

Those questions are easy to ask and easy to answer. Too easy, because they are asked and answered from ignorance and comfort.

First thing, there are no absolutes, no trade-offs, nothing clear. It is never, "I will die to save ten children." The world doesn't work like that. It becomes, "I will risk dying for the chance of saving, maybe, some or all of the ten children." Risk and chance. You might not die. You might not save anybody. Or you might die and save nobody (an aside to the professionals–dead people don't save anybody.)

But it's not even that. That's still too clean. Because it might not be dying. When you think, "What would I risk dying for?" Take time to ask, to substitute paralysis and blindness for dying. Waking up in the same prison cell every day for the rest of your life. Waking up screaming from the same nightmare periodically, forever. Remember that dying also includes orphaning your children.

(And that's the other side, what got me thinking about this today. When you pull the trigger you may shift a human being from being to not-being, turn a person into a corpse, erase a history and turn it into meat–but you are also creating orphans and widows, who will become what they become in response to your action which may be decided and finished in the space of a breath.)

If those are off the table and it goes well for you then civil suits and legal entanglements and blood-borne disease are all out there. Or the face of someone who flashes before your eyes periodically, clutching his throat and trying to scream. Memories.

Even dying isn't what we think, not what we've been told. Some give up, sure. But the noble and heroic death, the manly eyes slowly fading as light passes and a look of satisfaction passes to the cold pallid lips ....

There's pain and fear and thirst and screaming. But that's not the worst. The worst is being beaten–you gave all you had, everything you were and it wasn't enough. As your body slips closer to death, whether bleeding out or under blows you are helpless, utterly helpless. The warrior who wanted to take his stand against the world is mewling, begging and bargaining with god for one more breath of air or one less drop of pain. As helpless as a baby. In that instant, everything you thought you knew, the story in your head of who you are, is shattered.

This just barely scratches the surface. As you train, as you teach–what do you think you are doing? What are you training for? Living and dying? If only it were that clean.

The Reformed Bad Guy

In my experience, when people change their lives it is almost always an act of will because it is the smart thing to do. "If I stay here, doing this, I will die or go to prison."

There is a lot of potential drama in that decision.

I know one man who could make his current annual salary in a few weeks just by returning to a former life and doing a few jobs, but he desperately wants to live up to his wife's desire to see him as a good guy and doesn't want the kinds of people he used to associate with anywhere near his daughter.

Another who said, "The hardest part is learning how to be angry like a white man." That's his words and perspective. In his early world if you got angry you smiled, made sure everyone was relaxed and went and got a weapon. The idea of expressing anger struck him as tactical suicide. The idea of feeling anger and not acting on it with extreme force was beyond his comprehension.

He mentally labeled this as 'white' anger.

Both these men, and many others (including me, most days) miss this life. Most could flip a switch and go back to it in a heart beat, but something else, often children, gives a motivation not to ... and all are supremely confident that if they had no choice, all the old skills would be in full play.

Getting out of the life is hard. That's what they call it, 'the life.' When you are successful, it is money and drugs and women and excitement. Status and power. That's a heavy attraction and a powerful reward. At the same time, the life is dangerous. All around you, friends will die or go to prison. When the stakes are that high, the hindbrain is always whispering about how dangerous any change can be. Fear and pleasure combine to make any change hard.

And then there is context. Frequently an inmate at release would tell me that he had made his decision, set things in motion and he would not return to jail. Most did return. No matter how dedicated to change, very few of us could go back to the same friends, the same environment, and not return to the same behaviors. Especially when those behaviors imply that there is something wrong. If all of your friends are criminals and you try to go straight, they will hassle, bully and ridicule you to keep you in the fold. Like crabs pulling a potential escapee back into the pot.

Leaving the life is an immense act of will. I only know a few who have done it successfully. All are very strong internally. All had good, even powerful reputations within their criminal communities. All left their old environment and friends. And there were only two motivations.

About half had a dark moment, usually losing a friend, mentor or family member and came face to face with the realization that they would die, soon and inevitably, unless something drastic changed.

The other half had a child. Usually a daughter. One said he was holding his baby girl and realized that some of his closest friends, leg-breakers like himself, didn't have a problem with being paid to rape a woman to send a message to her husband. He didn't want them around his daughter. He didn't want his daughter to even know that such a world existed.

Caring for children is not universal. I've known one pimp who fathered over thirty children. I believe that I have deeper connections to my dogs than he does to any of his children. But if there is an emotional connection with the baby and the mother ....

Sources

A very important point when considering your sources is that a paid professional DOES NOT mean the person has any real world experience. A rookie newly assigned to the team can put SWAT on his resume. A cook who has completed jump school and been assigned to a ranger battalion can put "Ranger" on his resume. For that matter, officers (in the military sense, not the police sense) assigned to special operations groups are officers first and operators second–many, probably most, are not required to complete the specialized training required of an enlisted man for membership.

Since the advent of the wars in Iraq and Afghanistan this is less of an issue, but in the long stretch of relative peace between Vietnam and the Kuwaiti war there were many special operations soldiers who were trained and certified but never actually deployed. Always check your sources. If something smells wrong, check deeper.

Be even more careful when you use criminals as sources. Whether they have been published as non-fiction or not, the average criminal is the ultimate unreliable narrator.

You will sometimes hear the phrase, "He had no reason to lie." That is the default in the civilized world. Lying is stressful, keeping track of lies is hard and people don't trust liars and people who don't trust you make life harder. For all of these reasons, most people need a reason to lie.

This is not true for people who were raised in a criminal subculture or adapted to one. In this environment, one lies as a default setting. If you are around people who kill, they will have no problem stealing. Or lying. The person selling drugs to your daughter will not hesitate to steal money. Mistrust and danger are the natural elements of this world, and in this world you never give up power. And knowledge is power.

In this subculture, you need a damn good reason to tell the truth. Otherwise, you lie. It's not a moral weakness or an ethical conundrum. It is simply smart, an adaptation to the environment. And, if you are a criminal who has been lying your whole life, you have gotten pretty good at it. And, if you get a chance to write a book...

Be careful with your sources.

The OPIEC Character

The OPIEC (Ordinary Person in Extraordinary Circumstances) character is a common trope and a good choice in a lot of ways. More readers will be able to relate to an ordinary person than someone who deals professionally with violence. Extraordinary circumstances allow readers to suspend their squeamishness over issues of force and violence.

The ordinary person thrust into extraordinary situations is a staple of fiction. Honestly, in real life, it doesn't work very well. In medieval times, an armed and armored knight was a match for an entire village. A handful of armored men with steel weapons were able to stand against and defeat an army of thousands in the Andes. (182 conquistadors against an army of 7000, the Incan king's elite guards, routed them at a cost of five dead Spaniards and over 2000 dead Incans).

There is a lot of power for the author if you can present an authentic and immediate experience of violence and the issues that will arise for your OPIEC.

These are the deficits the amateurs have to overcome:

- Without training or experience, the protagonist has no idea what to do
- Without experience or a very unusual personality, the amateur freezes
- The amateur tends to follow social scripts- they default to Monkey Dance tactics and don't injure the bad guy
- The amateur tends to test the waters when they do act—most people hit half force the first time they hit, and then pause to see if it worked
- Trained amateurs often have fantasy concepts— they are often shocked and freeze when the fight isn't like sparring
- Trained amateurs may be shocked by success or failure—failure is obvious, but sometimes well-trained people are devastated when everything works fine, and they hear bones or tendons snap and see a big man screaming
- Amateurs are completely unaware of the context and the aftermath (See Chapter Two)

Everything on this list are things that predatory criminals rely on in their victims. These are the reasons that violence works so well.

What To Do?

How you handle this as a writer will depend a lot on your protagonist and the situation. The most critical aspect of the situation is how much time is available.

If your protagonist is under a realistic assault it will be at close range, very fast, very powerful and with maximum surprise. That means that the protagonist will not have time to plan. Survival here will be due to instinct or skills trained to reflex. The most common survivor's mindset is when the fear, panic and surprise somehow turn into a righteous rage "I will make him pay!" and the victim, willing to take damage to give damage, turns into a whirlwind of ferocity.

If the situation is slower to develop, such as a hostage situation or a school shooting, your protagonist will have seconds to hours to think and come up with a plan. How well the plan works will depend on how well the bad guys have anticipated the possibility.

It is really, really easy, in the comfort of home to say what you will do. It doesn't work out like that. Until you or your character has reached that level, it is a dice roll what will happen. I haven't seen anything that is an indicator. One of the biggest cowards I ever worked with was a 6'4" former Marine. The guy I use as an example of people that always freeze is a gun nut, a martial arts champion and a Tactical Team member. This is why we always watch rookies so closely: until the first big fight you don't know if their instinct is to run away or run towards the fight. Neither do they.

Fighting Personalities

A lot of the bad writing is from thinking there is one certain way. Fights are idiosyncratic and very personal. Everyone has a fighting personality. One possible example:

I'm going to take this guy down. He has a reputation, possibly a weapon, and I want it over quick, but the goal is to take him into custody, not to neutralize him (notice that here I am even thinking in cold, professional language). The plan is to slam into him from behind with full body weight and leg strength at a slightly upward angle, slamming him into a wall and as he bounces off, swing him away, sweep his legs so that he lands face down on the concrete. I'll do a double knee drop, kidney and neck if there's still a little fight ... that's the plan.

I get the hit and he bounces off the wall, but he spins off of it, using the momentum and tags me with a hard hook punch or elbow–can't tell, it's too close and too fast. I'm going to freeze for a microsecond, partially because my plan has been spiked but largely because this guy has just shown me that he knows what he is doing and the fight has shifted from custody of a dangerous threat to survival. I've dealt with that before and will unfreeze before he hits the ground, landing on his feet.

Part of my particular unfreeze is that I completely stop thinking. My body (hindbrain) has done this hundreds of times. I let my body do it. I'm also, by training and inclination, an infighter. I'll shoulder slam him into the wall, preferably keeping him off his feet. Infighters are rare and

I usually have the advantage. If he goes for a weapon, I'll slam him hard, using the wall as an impact weapon. I'll also snake a hand up to the leverage point under his nose and twist and extend his cervical spine, using that action to slam his head into the wall if I can.

If he doesn't go for a weapon, most people don't know how to generate power at super tight range. If he's skilled, he'll be trying to wrap around to hit my upper cervical vertebrae at an upward angle. I want him high, either taller than me or still off the ground, to make that hard.

If I can get his spine extended and it's a very bad situation, I have practiced short power and will fire a fast, hard strike into his lower ribs preferably with his spine extended away, so that the ribs break easier and preferably on his right side, over his liver. Liver shots suck. It's like getting punched in an eight-pound testicle. Spine extensions, using walls, furniture, corners and ground as impact weapons, close range power and multi-level/non-conscious thinking are part of my fighting personality.

However, when I get ambushed, hit from behind, slammed into a wall, especially if I take some damage, I have an entirely different personality. My eyes light up, I get this maniac grin. Sometimes I giggle. I usually spin with the force of the first impact and then I want to make a show. Let him know that I am faster, more skilled and more ruthless. I beat right past his pathetic little arms ...

Any way he stands and any way he moves all works for me. He's not only my toy, but he actively helps me with each pathetic attempt to attack. I just beat past his arms until I have his core and toss him in the air (not strength, there are a handful of judo throws that I love for this, but if you have ever used your hips to toss a hay bale, you know the action). When he lands (sometimes badly, but often I come back to my human mind when he is in the air and control his fall a little) I flip him over and cuff him. Casually. He's like a toy, a rag doll. Even when he is trying to fight.

Understand that I am not saying that this is the best way to think or feel. It is not something that I chose. These are states I discovered, who I am on the inside. The manic grin and giggling? Almost totally unlike my regular persona.

I know what these states feel like from inside and know the mechanics of what happened, largely due to reports and witness statements. I don't have reliable insight to what it feels like to be on the receiving ends, since bad guys don't write reports.

The point is that not only do I have two distinct personalities when things go bad, your characters won't look at, feel about or respond to the situations the same as I do, or anyone else for that matter. No two people fight the same or think about fighting in the same way.

✧✦✧✦✧

HOMEWORK:

This is for extra credit. Call your local police agency. Ask if they have a "Ride-Along Program." Many agencies have a program so that citizens can go on patrol with an officer as an observer. If they have a program, take advantage of it. You will see a new world.

TO RECAP:

- Professionals approach violence differently than OPIEC characters
- Professionals develop skills at reading terrain, dynamics and people
- Professionals try to avert uses of force and generally have the skill to do so
- Reformed bad guys reform for a reason and it is sometimes hard to stay reformed
- Be careful with your sources, including me
- The OPIEC character has a lot to overcome in order to win realistically
- People have distinctive fighting personalities

… 7 …

Gender Differences

Here's a big shock: men and women see violence differently.

It's bigger than that. We have both socially conditioned and biological reactions to danger and violence that differ. I haven't actually heard anyone say since the seventies that all gender differences are cultural (someone noticed the plumbing was different about then, I think) but there are a lot of very odd opinions out there.

Here goes. Boys and girls were raised differently. By the time a boy is ready to either start learning to fight or thinking about taking a job where fighting is likely, he has been wrestling and rough-housing for years. This means that most of the time he has been hit, he has it associated with fun, bonding and learning.

The 'don't hit a girl' ethic denies women this same chance. There are always exceptions, but for the most part if a woman or girl has ever been hit, she has been hit as a punishment. The hitting gets tied in her mind with shame. This even happens in abuse. A child who has done nothing wrong will still be told she is getting beaten 'for her own good' and that she caused it. That combination of beatings and shame make for an early and powerful association.

This is why women rarely train in martial arts and when they do they tend to pick classes with low contact. Tobi Beck (Duchess Elina of the SCA) wrote about it. I have used her information to plan tactical operations and to really help teach female officers.

http://forums.uechi-ryu.com/viewtopic.php?p=27215&sid=f4a748e1c9f45f08fe553d76dd725f61

The most important biological difference is in adrenaline reactions.

When something bad happens, men get a big spike of adrenaline and other stress hormones that quickly fades. Women have a much slower build up, the peak never gets quite as high and it tapers off slowly.

In personal relationships, where you see this most often is in arguments. I have an argument with my wife. I'm getting loud, she's clearly wrong but she's being infuriatingly reasonable and I finally get so angry, after just a minute or two, that I stomp out, slamming the door and go for a walk. A couple minutes later it's pretty clear that she was right. I decide I might as well go back and apologize now ... and I walk in just as she is getting to full fury.

To a man, since I got mad early and got over it quickly, she looks irrational. She wasn't mad when I thought it would be appropriate and was mad when I was over it. It actually has nothing to do with thought or rationality, that is just timing on adrenaline. (It's really a bunch of hormones and neurotransmitters, I use adrenaline for shorthand).

You see this in defensive shootings, where a man will usually fire about two shots as soon as he is aware of the intruder and a woman will retreat and retreat and retreat and then empty the weapon.

This is valuable and one of the reasons why I loved working with a female partner. Early in the encounter when a guy is going into his fight or flight mode, the woman can still think, plan and even do fine motor skill things like, oh, aiming. Her memory and senses in a quick encounter will be clearer.

What gets misinterpreted a lot is that after a very tense encounter (when the guy is going into his sleepy or sometimes horny mode) the woman has a tendency to burst into tears. It's just adrenaline burning off, but often neither the man nor the woman is aware of it and think it is an emotional issue. (Not sure how it will affect your readers and your writing, but be careful with yourself to distinguish between hormones and emotions.)

This does happen to males as well, but it is usually invisible. Because the male adrenaline reaction tends to happen during the action, small details like teary eyes are easy to miss. There is one place we see it. Buck fever.

When a novice hunter sees a mule deer or any big game animal, there is sometimes an interesting reaction. The body and hindbrain fully expect that in order to kill two hundred pounds of meat, you must run it down with a spear. The adrenal glands dump enough adrenaline into the system to do just that. Pulling a trigger simply doesn't burn that adrenaline.

Sometimes (as in my case) the first shot or series of shots is perfect, then the adrenaline hits. In others, the adrenaline has hit before the first shot. In a heartbeat I went from a text book stalker and marksman to a shaking mess. The rifle that I had learned to shoot on was suddenly a complex mechanism. I couldn't make the bolt work and when my shaking hands finally did, the bolt came completely out. Shaking, watering eyes … the whole bit. I would say that men get the adrenaline reaction worse than women but because the guy has his adrenaline timed to what is often the most violent part of the encounter, the things that might be misinterpreted as emotion are hidden by action. He'll probably get the shakes afterwards, they both will. But since hers will last longer no one seems to notice that they started later as well, and she was fine when he started shaking.

Evolutionarily, you can see why this works. Child-bearing women are the primary resource in a marginal hunter-gatherer society. If a handful of the younger men fight, even if the predator is too formidable to stop, it buys women and children time to get to safety. That time, if the predator breaks through, probably coincides with the female adrenaline peak.

One more evolutionary thing for the fantasy writers. The math doesn't work on female warrior societies, not unless they have a huge surplus of resources and people. Not because women can't fight. Trust me, in a lot of ways men are far less dangerous in a fight than women. It's because of children.

Let's say there are two tribes, all adults, each has ten men and ten women. Tribe A has its women do the fighting, tribe B has men fight. They get in a dispute. The battle ends in a draw and each loses four warriors. Both tribes now have 16 members, A has six women and ten men; B six men and ten women. The next year, assuming peace continues and war doesn't break out during pregnancies, all of the women can potentially have a baby. Tribe A now has 22 members, 9 of them female (potential warriors). Tribe B has 26 members, 11 of them potentially warriors. As this goes on, A will eventually whittle down and lose. Unless total destruction of the tribe was the alternative, women have been too valuable to risk in combat for most of human history.

This doesn't mean that such a society couldn't or hasn't existed, but there are reasons why it couldn't last without some extraordinary edge ... and it will take some real deep motivation for a group to risk it, knowing how dangerous it would be. (Another side note–in history and even in wilderness societies today people knew the world was dangerous on a gut level we have largely forgotten today. The people–tribal and colonial both–that I met in Ecuador were not "living at one with nature' they were frankly scared to death of the forest and the river.)

Sending young, fit males to fight also *doesn't* take them out of the gene pool and *does* serves a purpose. From my current Work in Progress:

Once upon a time, one of your ancestors was sitting on the savannah with about fifteen other men, women and children. He had a stick and was poking under a log hoping to find some ant eggs when Thog ran out of the brush, screaming. Thog was running as fast as he could for the biggest tree nearby.

Your ancestor ran too. Probably. There's a reason emotions are contagious.

Wugga, widely regarded as the snottiest of the tribe decided it wouldn't be 'cool' to run and looked to see what Thog was running from. So the lion killed him first.

MarMar and Roro, young males in the tribe, grabbed sticks and ran towards whatever Thog was running from. They were widely regarded as not very smart but sometimes useful members of the tribe. If they didn't die, they were definitely going to get laid out of it.

That's important, because without either stupid snotty people or stupid aggressive people, the math is bad. Men run and climb faster than women who run and climb faster than children. Without a few sacrificial males, the women and children die. So dies the tribe and eventually the species.

The stupid brave get breeding rights (hasn't changed much through rescuing princess and the modern action-adventure movie, has it?) because we will need more stupidly brave people later ....

Look at the small percentage of modern soldiers who actually die in combat. It's been over ten years since the first Special Ops groups went boots-on-ground in Afghanistan. In ten years combining Afghanistan and Iraq we have lost less people than we have in single days in WWI, WWII or the Civil War, despite huge advances in technology and fighting an urban insurgency, one of the potentially nastiest forms of warfare. In May, 1968 alone 2415 American servicemen were killed. Compare to 4488 in Iraq in the last *nine years*.

Even WWII, with 40-50 million killed, barely made a blip on the population growth charts. The 'baby boom' caught up nicely. Had a high percentage of those 40-50 million been women of the same age, it would have been a very different story as far as population growth.

These factors combine to make some cultural differences between men and women concerning violence. Because women weren't immersed in play violence as children and don't have the biologically driven 'monkey dance' programmed, they also don't have many of the subconscious rules that men have about fighting. When a woman goes physical, she is there to hurt you. In my experience, women go for eyes and try to cut (especially faces for some reason) far more than men do. They will often ignore the surrender signals that a man will respect.

Often, when a man goes physical, it is all about dominance and pride. When a women goes physical it is all about either stopping the threat or hurting him. There is a stage some women get to that can seem sadistic. Happens in men, too, but usually with less intensity and is somewhat less common. To put it another way, even an enraged man usually stops when the victim is dead. An enraged woman doesn't. (Careful... these are all generalities. Use them as they work for you.)

Hitting after death is not sadism, exactly, especially sadism in the modern recreational sense of the word. But it is horrifying, both to witness and to clean up after. It has more to do with the lack of social conditioning with and to violence. When guys are learning it can be fun to pummel each other, they also learn when it is appropriate to stop. Women tend not to learn this. Combined with the longer adrenaline curve, females can go into a longer, more brutal "dancing on the torn and twisted corpse" stage than males have the endurance for.

It's not making sure the bad guy won't come after her, it's not that conscious. Most of us have been conditioned from the time we were small not to hurt people. When hurting or killing someone is a necessity, that need often goes head-to-head with our conditioning. All too often, conditioning wins. It is really hard to kill in cold blood and that can be a really hard decision to live with afterwards, even in war.

For the record, I have fought men who outweighed me by more than a hundred pounds, experienced fighters, multiple opponents and men with weapons ... and none have come as close to killing me as the girl who tried to stick a knife in my back (current ability to breathe is due entirely to a reflection, luck and reflexes) and none felt as dangerous as a desperate brawl with a crack whore who wanted to gouge my eyes out. Women are dangerous, but they fight very differently than men.

To sum up, generally, women have three superpowers and two super weaknesses when it comes to fighting. If they can get over the weaknesses and use the powers, they can be incredibly formidable and skilled fighters.

Weakness number one: Many have no experience except on the receiving end and most of the physical violence they have experienced has been from an authority figure. And the authority figure shifted the blame to the girl. This creates a powerful and often freezing shame reaction when a woman gets hit, especially when she gets slapped.

Exceptions and fixes: The classic is the woman who grew up with four brothers who liked to fight and learned how to play dirty to win. Another exception is my wife. K grew up without brothers and in a peaceful household. But her father was a tough guy (former soviet bloc military with an interesting assignment) musician, painter, engineer and he got her into art and sports. When she decided to take martial arts, she had no preconceptions and no negative conditioning to overcome.

The most common fix is an act of will, the decision to learn how to fight, coupled with the right environment. It will require a supportive but not enabling instructor and training venue. People that can teach the woman that fighting is fun. Fighting isn't fun. It hurts and is scary. But fighting well is incredibly empowering and increasing ability is fun and satisfying at very deep levels. The training environment must accentuate that aspect.

Weakness number two: Most women have been taught to lose to men. Almost every good female martial artist I know is certain that there are men in her class she can beat, but she lets them win. She is certain that rather than lose to a woman they will escalate, break the rules and injure her. It is not worth it to her to injure them, and so she lets them win. This is deep conditioning and read the dynamic here: women have been conditioned that it is safer to lose than it is to win. Safer to lose.

There are two fixes I know of to this. One is dark but has motivated real people and characters for a long time. And that is losing. A person chooses not to fight as a victim and the predator plays and it is worse than anything that could have happened had she fought and she makes the decision never again to be a victim.

The other fix is less dark, but often motivated by the first: Find the right trainer or school. Where winning is rewarded. Where the focus is on making stronger students, not a stable hierarchy. Where the other students and teachers love the physicality of fighting but aren't doing it to bolster ego.

Superpower #1: That slow build up in adrenaline? That means that under an ambush a woman can fight skillfully. All of the deficits of the SSR (Chapter Four) do not necessarily apply. Not right away. A woman can fight skillfully in the first seconds of a fight where a guy cannot.

It's not easy. Most people need the adrenaline, need to read it as anger or fear, in order to let themselves fight. If one can get over that need and fight while still cold, a woman can fight like a machine. Like a sociopath.

Superpower #2: When the adrenaline hits you are stronger, a little faster and insensitive to pain. Unfortunately, in most cases, you're also kind of stupid. How cool would it be if you could plan in advance how to use your strength, speed and insensitivity? With the long, slow build up a properly-trained woman can do something a man cannot do–she can plan a rage. In order to make this work, your must be able to delay the sequence of events.

Superpower #3: No social rules. Ask any experienced cop or bouncer about their most dangerous fight and most will tell you a story about a woman. My most disgusting use of force was with a 300 pound methed-up naked woman. The two people that have come closest to successfully stabbing me were both women. Women are scary. They don't fight by 'the rules.'

It's a two-edged sword. Because most women were not socialized to rough house and play fight, they don't have a lot of experience at it and are often hesitant to engage. On the other hand, most women have never internalized the rules that men use when they fight. A woman's instinctive fighting is 'out of the box' and outside the experience of most men. Men rarely claw, bite or grab hair, and are usually surprised when someone else does. Most non-professional men and many professionals, will give clear signs that they are moving towards force. For some women, especially if they use the second Superpower, you never see it coming. And men have been taught when to stop, they tend to instinctively honor surrender signals. A woman fights until she either feels safe or she is out of adrenaline, and that last can be a very long time.

Women in the Violence Professions

It seems that lots of Americans feel that if we/they/me/Group X are only nice enough, everyone will like them/us. If we are accommodating, we will make people happy and comfortable and we will be liked. Women, in particular, are often taught that this is THE preferred strategy for fitting in and getting along.

There are a lot of cultures and subcultures that admire strength and courage, and that involves going head to head with problems and disagreements. Being too nice reads as obsequious and untrustworthy in those cultures.

In law enforcement, there is a dynamic with new female officers where they can feel harassed and marginalized. There are some instances where misogyny is in play, but that is relatively rare. It is actually a dynamic that guys who played competitive team sports have dealt with for much of their lives but women, even if they were top competitors, haven't experienced. Because they haven't experienced it, they have no idea how to act.

Cops believe (with a lot of justification) that a 'pleaser' personality stands a much higher chance of getting killed on the streets than anyone (and I mean anyone) else. When someone comes in with a pleaser personality, the veteran cops, especially the FTOs (Field Training Officers) push and they push. Not necessarily to get the person to quit (and this is the part that men learn in locker rooms and women don't) but to get them to fight. Not to get someone else to fight for them (filing formal complaints and lawsuits) but to stand up, get in their faces and set boundaries.

I was one of the 'pleasers'. Far too nice for the job. Everything changed the day after I got in a shouting match with my sergeant in the lieutenant's office, something to the effect of, "That's bullshit! I don't care if I'm on probation. I won't do something stupid just because you tell me to!" It was actually a lot more colorful than that. I thought, for a short time, that I had reached my limit and lashed out. I wasn't even in the vicinity of my limit and I did not at the time, like many people, know the difference between 'lashing out' and simply standing up. That's something you must learn in order to thrive in a dangerous profession.

If the rookie never once stands up and tells his training officers to pound sand, the rookie doesn't have the confidence to do the job well ... and can't even do it safely. It's a big responsibility to put someone out on the streets who you believe will die.

I've had success with explaining this dynamic to women rookies. I don't think it's a matter of gender as much as experience. Some rookies, male or female, literally can't grasp that what the FTO wants is an argument with some righteous indignation and anger. Once it's explained, they see it. Not all can do it, of course. Sometimes the conditioning is too deep.

Female officers need different and extra training and they will never get it officially. Because of current labor law and practice, everyone going through the academy must be treated the same. Our need to pretend that everyone is equal turns a blind eye to the fact that everyone is different.

There are a lot of the problems that you imagine—criminals, especially sexual predators, try to intimidate female officers. Many of the more violent subcultures in America have serious sexism issues as well and taking an order from a woman is almost always met with defiance ... and if the female officer shows cultural sensitivity and calls for a male officer to handle members of this subculture, other criminals see her as weak and she can't do her job. If she tries to handle it herself it will be dangerous, but if she doesn't the criminals won't respect her and will push her continuously.

Some officers (male and female, but any officer who isn't used to conflict and violence and those are more often female or upper-middle class male) are so afraid of losing control that they become little martinets, trying to badger and bully.

But probably the hardest thing and the one that women especially need special specific training for is how to function in a paramilitary, testosterone-drenched, extremely political and violence-driven field. (I don't consider any of those things negatives, by the way. Except maybe the politics, but even there I understand the need.)

> There are a number of attitudes that only work within narrow parameters in the real world. Break those parameters and you may get naïve readers to go along, but people with any experience will be lost and maybe angry.
>
> A common example is the maverick. The guy who doesn't follow the rules, who bucks the system. There are effective mavericks. But almost every maverick I see or read is an ego-driven idiot who will get his team killed or the case dismissed. The rookie who comes on the team and shows everyone up … exactly how does he get there? How does his special genius outweigh all of the cumulative years of trial and error paid in blood? The rules he is bucking are the rules that get convictions, the rules that keep people alive.
>
> The effective mavericks tend to be older, widely experienced, and willing to sacrifice their careers for their team and the mission.

When you are dealing with large numbers (my deputies were routinely working at ratios of 75 to 1, locked into the dorms in direct contact with the inmates) of violent people, the field *is* violence-driven and a big dose of testosterone and a good, clear organization contribute hugely to handling things safely. And all of this is new to most women.

They think people are being cold and unfriendly where a guy would know that they were waiting to see how he would handle stress. If someone is easily offended by words, it's not about being crude or sexist or Neanderthals—guys believe that people who freak out over words will panic over actions. "Sticks and stones may break my bones but words will never hurt me." People who believe that words really hurt haven't had bones broken yet.

A good female officer doesn't try to act like a male officer. There is a distinctive style to staying both feminine and in charge. The best are awesome at it. But because the academy classes are taught together, there won't be a class on "Feminine Authority and Power Dynamics in Law Enforcement" and there really should be.

One of the common mistakes women make is trying to act like one of the boys, trying to be cruder than the guys are. Being crude has its own unique set of rules. Cross one line and you have burned bridges that cannot be rebuilt. I'm aware I am being vague here, largely because these rules are instinctive to me. Too close and I can't see them, but I do know when they are violated. So do other people.

As a TL (Team Leader) I liked the energy that women brought to the team. The guys would be a little more polite and clear-headed.

We expected women to be morally superior in a way and we wanted them to want us to live up to being our best, chivalrous selves. When a woman tried to be cruder, she didn't do it well (just like in any society, cross gender there are lots of different subtle rules about what is appropriate and where and when) and it also tarnished that ideal.

Remember that most of the people that get involved in these career paths are something of idealists.

One of the expectations is that women will have to really work to go hands on and fight. When a woman is ruthless and determined and unafraid (or fakes it) it really impresses men ... and when they do fight women tend to be more clear-headed and controlled than men, and that's very impressive. Remember that the clear-headed calm is because adrenaline curves are different. That has two side effects in that a woman usually must force herself to fight as an act of will and she gets the adrenaline affects after it is all over which can include shakes, crying, horniness or all three. Guys often interpret especially the crying as a hormonal weakness, fear, or "inability to deal". That's not what's going on. Most women take great pains to hide this phase. So do men. Much of the time many feel the after-effects of adrenaline as shakes or nausea, but I have seen one man, a big, tough experienced cop after a very intense few seconds say to me, "Sarge, I feel like I want to puke and I'm going to cry. Is this normal?" Yeah. That's perfectly normal.

Another factor is that violent places can get really sexually charged. One of the common side-effects of violence and danger is an incredible urge for sex. Biologists have even joked about the "Four F's" of survival stress: Fight, Flight, Freeze and Fuck.

The best women operators are strictly off limits. Very few women can engage in sex without emotional issues (even as basic as 'will he talk?' and 'what will the others think?') and even those that can, the men don't believe that these issues aren't coming up. It gets into a nasty cesspit of rumors and innuendo. It can tear a team apart, especially a team that is doing well enough to incite jealousy with the rest of the organization.

Like the best male operators, the best female operators have good relationships outside the team. And that can bring in another dynamic because some guys cannot handle a woman with a more macho reputation or job description. Unless the guy is strong, he will have ego issues.

Staying feminine and in charge is difficult. Very, very few do it well. Far too often the idea of a powerful female is a bitch. The two most powerful (by acknowledged rank) women I know in my field worked hard to be not-feminine and have resulting health issues, largely related to weight.

The most respected are healthy, with the special beauty that comes with that, extraordinary athletes and absolutely (in front of everyone) fearless. They have proven their competency and maintain the feminine largely by the games they don't play. When the guys get obnoxious, they just raise an eyebrow and you feel like you told a dirty joke in front of your mom. It's a mix of a medieval lady archetype, a mom, and someone you really, really wouldn't want to mess with.

A lot of good women operators don't try for rank. They are both satisfied to be accepted at the operator level and disgusted with how other women have advanced their careers. That's not a woman thing. Many of the people who achieve high rank in dangerous jobs sucked at the job. They were bad at it, it scared them, and so they worked and connived to move up in rank because the higher you are the farther away from the danger.

A woman who has worked hard as an operator has a huge disadvantage in the political field (integrity is valued highly in the operator ranks because these are people you rely on to keep you alive; career expediency is valued, sometimes even over lives, in the administrative ranks.) She also, often, doesn't want to be associated with the women who have made rank, and she will automatically be lumped in with them ... and every last one of them will hate her and try to destroy her career.

Violence Professionals and Relationships

There is a stereotype that men are threatened by strong women. I can't speak for everyone, but in a strong relationship a strong woman is empowering, not emasculating. The emasculating paradigm only works if the guy has a need to dominate (which is common, maybe the baseline for most cultures).

"Can't you control your woman?"

"Partner, you couldn't even keep up with her."

When both members of a relationship are in high-risk jobs, the relationship can be very difficult. Lots end badly. Lots start badly for that matter. Some of the reasons:

Shift work: Your character may work or will have worked some of the lousiest hours there are. I was lucky in my agency—we had three shifts and bid annually by seniority (theoretically in my 22nd or 23rd year I might have a chance at day shift with weekends off). Some agencies rotate weekly between day, evening and graveyard shifts. One that I know of works twelve-hour day shifts for four days, takes three days off and then works three twelve-hour night shifts. It is damn near impossible to keep any relationship (social, going back to school, volunteer work) going on that shift. Or get a sleep cycle.

Nothing to talk about: I think this goes for most couples. If both are doing the same job and living together, they were there for most of the things they would normally talk about.

Nepotism, or accusations of: Unless both members of the couple have dead-ended or decided to dead-end in the job (lots of people choose to stay on patrol, I had no interest in becoming a lieutenant, since that was exclusively a desk job) one will promote faster than the other. That can hamper their careers and create a headache for scheduling, especially in a small agency since most have policies prohibiting family members supervising family members. If one of the members rises to sufficient power, the other one (no matter how good) will face whispers and gossip over ANY positive action—getting promoted or even getting a medal for valor.

Out of about five hundred officers in my agency, I only know of a handful of long-term relationships where both were on the job. One has a wide disparity of rank, but seem to be doing fine. Most of other couples were pretty troubled. There were other relationships and marriages that all ended badly and most quickly. A lot of it has to do with maturity. With mature expectations for a relationship and understanding of self, others and the job ... but I still have no idea if a good relationship fosters that maturity (I believe it did in my case) or the maturity enables a good relationship.

When only one of the couple is on the job, the stresses are different. And most are avoidable. It is very easy when you spend your workday dealing with the part of life that civilization seems designed to deny, to come to believe that no one understands you. That you alone see the real world. That everyone else is no better than blind sheep ... and in a few years you start saying, "You can't handle the truth."

It's bullshit. This is something we as professionals do to ourselves.

It's true that most people can't understand. When someone dies, you see something leave their eyes, and it is a different feeling when it is someone young who desperately wants to live. Children should outlive their parents, not be killed by them. Telling someone that a brother is dead is hard enough ... I never want to tell a child he or she is an orphan.

There are aspects of this that people who live safe lives will never understand. But they will listen. And they, largely, will accept that you deal with it.

This is something that ties in to the long-term solid relationships. We share. We talk. I used to have a fear that the more icky stuff I dealt with, that it would somehow rub off on me, infect me. It's not true. Maybe because I work to spend time with good people, and the good people are the reason for all of this.

Good people don't need to understand. We do this job largely to keep that world away, to keep the good people not only from ever being victimized, but from ever really having to look at it closely. But good people will accept, and that can save your protagonist's mind.

For the partner who is not in the profession, it can be hard. The unpredictability of it can be hard. Most of these jobs are relatively safe, most days. Most soldiers come home. Almost every cop comes home every shift ... but some don't, and that is always scary.

Some partners live in happy oblivion and just never think about it. Some obsess on it and that is very hard on the relationship, since the obsession won't go away unless the marriage breaks up or the other leaves the life. Some express faith, whether faith in a higher power or (sometimes ridiculous) levels of faith in the partner. Some partners require constant reassurance, and that is a horrible, wearying strain on the operator. Others are a constant source of reassurance.

I went home, every day, and saw why I do this. It is worth it.

Women in Criminal Subcultures and Organizations

I can't speak authoritatively about this. My experience is limited.

From the blog:

Love Letters From Prison 26July2007

... One of the early mild shocks in this job was reading mail that inmates would send to their loved ones. They would ask for help with spelling sometimes. I was amazed, because the letters had the depth and imagery and poetry of the love letters that I had sent to K from Basic Training and AIT. Not having read love letters from people other than myself and those sent to me, I'd thought mine were uniquely deep, soul touching and true.

Now I read almost the same words and surely the same sentiments scrawled in pencil and sent from jail.

Sentimental poetry from people who showed the physicality of their love with fists, boots, cigarette lighters and electric cord. Over the years I've read incestuous rapist wax rhapsodic to their victims; listened and read tales and dreams of love from people who have prostituted their own children for crack. Compared the written words to the threats over the phone ('You are my angel in a darkness, baby' versus "Bitch, you put money on my books tomorrow or I'll fucking cut your whore face off!").

The criminal subculture is a dangerous place where the strong take from (or use) the weak. In my experience both in levels of violent subcultures in the criminal world and traveling, the most violent groups also have the most defined and restrictive sex roles. Men do *this*. Women do *that* ... and anyone who dares to cross will be punished. Will meet violence.

If you have the access, you will hear pimps, dealers and gangbangers talk about their women the way they talk about their cars or their dogs. As pets and ornaments. As property. In certain OMCs (Outlaw Motorcycle Clubs) if a member really likes you (and you are male), he will order 'his woman' to "Show him your tits, baby."

This is the world of violence as it is, not as we romanticize it.

From the blog:

Bad Date 16October2006

I'm not going to try to defend or explain or justify prostitution. It's not a victimless crime–by living outside the law, prostitutes become victims, prey to the stronger and more vicious. It's also not victimless when you see the world their children are raised in. It's not like "Pretty Woman" and I have yet to meet the "whore with a heart of gold."

It's also not just a lifestyle choice that happens because of economic concerns or poverty or ... it is just a piece of a very self-destructive montage of abuse and addiction and many subtle or not so subtle attempts at various types of suicide, some physical, some emotional, some social.

It is a hard life. I have pictures of meth prostitutes (first big fact, my friend: there are meth whores and crack whores and heroin whores and even alcohol whores but you will search this great nation from coast to coast and never find a prostitute who doesn't use drugs. This has been a running challenge, an informal contest with cops from coast to coast for decades.) ... where was I? Yeah. Pictures. Meth prostitutes. Anyway, the same woman early in her career and five years later. She looks like her own grandmother- toothless, wrinkled, with shrunken, hollow eyes.

It's a dangerous life. Rapes, beatings, robbery. Some have nowhere to go for help or support, others turn to a pimp who must be worse than her other predators and she just has to hope he won't be worse to her.

Knowledge is power, and in certain sections of Portland (including the health clinic at the jail and some of the female cell blocks) you will find slips of paper, usually in colorful pastels, headed "Portland Bad Date Line!"

It is a warning newsletter from prostitutes, by prostitutes and for prostitutes. A list of events and horror stories:

"ON BICYCLE "GENE" - Downtown, W Male 29 or 30 y.o., bright blue eyes, goatee, tatoos on face, hands, and left leg, 5'6", scars from broken back, skinny. Knocked out, bit, restrained, cut, sedated, raped/sodomized, ejaculated on. Wrkr released 32 hours later"

"BURGUNDY VAN- NE MLK & Shaver. Male, African or Cuban with thick accent, 6'3", dark complexion, clean shaven. Offered $40 for BJ, pulled out big butcher knife and cut worker. She got away."

There are warnings about known predatory sex offenders in the area, requests for information in cases of severely beaten women, a request from a police officer who is working one of the cases–a "W Male big, thick glasses, beats w/ pipe, rapes" who has attacked five times.

This is a monthly newsletter put together by women who want to save themselves, want to have some power in their lives. In such a little space are hints of stories that would horrify Hollywood, acts of savage survival (heroism?) reduced to a few words: "kicked him in the face and got away".

If your character is a woman in these circumstances she will have been exposed to horrible things and, as a survivor she will have to be very tough and likely very dark. If you envision a female crime boss or major player, think this through. She will have had to survive an environment where her gender is seen as a commodity; where violence is just a tool and the males around her (who will be threatened by her competence) will use that violence both casually and brutally to either teach her her place or simply kill her.

There are matriarchs in modern, American criminal subculture. An astonishing number of criminals have been raised by their grandmothers. Father absent, dead, in prison or else just drifting between the women who make up his stable; Mom frequently addicted or in prison or jail ... grandma steps in. Not all, but many criminals have an unconscious and automatic respect for elderly women. You might be able to use that.

✧✦✧✦✧

HOMEWORK:

A Mary Sue is a female character so perfect as to be annoying. Smart, pretty, rich. Probably a size three. We'll call the male version a Gary Stu. Remembering that criminals don't like to get caught, don't like to get hurt and therefore tend not to choose large athletic men to victimize ... make lists of the crimes Mary Sue and Gary Stu are likely to be targeted for. Think hard about the differences on those lists and what kinds of violence your male and female characters are likely to experience.

TO RECAP:

- ✧ Men and women were raised to have different attitudes toward violence
- ✧ They have different biologies, especially regarding responses to fear
- ✧ These differences serve an evolutionary purpose
- ✧ The differences get misinterpreted, hormones seen as emotions
- ✧ Women in violence professions have to adapt to a new culture
- ✧ Relationships between two violence professionals have challenges
- ✧ Relationships between citizens and violence professionals have different challenges
- ✧ Women in a violent criminal subculture are at an extreme disadvantage

8

UNARMED

It's a little artificial to break this up by unarmed, impact weapons, edged weapons, firearms and less-lethal, but I'm going to do it anyway. The actual mechanics and use have a lot of things in common. For instance, in most cases, aggression beats skill. A skilled knife player (say *silat* or *arnis*) usually chokes when confronted by a prison-yard-style shanking. A good shot tends to be killed by someone who charges blasting away. And blackbelts getting crushed by untrained streetfighters are almost a cliché.

It works the other way, of course. Aggression coupled with good skills and tactics makes an incredible foe. Add the clear predator mindset and it is more a force of nature than a human being. Mix timidity with bad skills (or, especially, bad skills with false confidence) and the person is almost more a danger to himself or bystanders than he is to the bad guy.

First break down: How people learn to fight unarmed

1) Martial arts. What follows are generalizations and include a lot of my own prejudices. Just be aware that these are informed prejudices.

1A) Traditional martial arts: These are the things practiced by rote, usually in a uniform in a nice dojo (Japanese for "place of the way") or kwoon (Chinese training hall) or dojang (Korean, same name as Japanese). People from these traditions sometimes learn really good physical skills, but most have no idea of what they will be facing. They practice against techniques that bad guys don't use at ranges that bad guys avoid. The rules and rituals are as important as the technique.

That said, most of the traditional arts arose in very violent times. I find the body mechanics to be superb for a real assault. The weakness is that most instructors, having no knowledge of violence, tend to guess how things happen and how techniques should be used. They rarely guess accurately. Main point: unless your character has great instincts, some real world experience to put things in perspective or an extraordinary instructor, martial arts training tends to be a very visually interesting way to lose.

1B) Martial sports. This is stuff like boxing, judo, Brazilian Jiu jitsu (BJJ) full contact karate and Mixed Martial Arts (MMA). Again, the training usually misses the context of a real assault. These guys don't train against the ambush and they have to limit techniques for safety (there is NO SUCH THING as no holds barred *and* full contact sport in the civilized world). However, they tend to take solid hits in training, something many traditional martial artists miss. Since they have a very real possibility of being hurt, they tend to train much harder than other martial artists. Though there are skills they don't practice (blinding, strikes to the throat and cervical spine, for instance) the skills they do practice tend to work and are developed to a very practical level. With the possible exception of the closed fist punch to the head. More later.

1C) Reality-Based Self-Defense (RBSD) schools. These range from weekend workshops to entire systems. The idea is to either from the ground up or using a traditional martial arts base create something effective for real assaults. The results are mixed, largely because anyone can start such a system and the definition of 'reality' or 'research' varies hugely. Basically, some of the systems are completely made up. Even the good established systems, such as Krav Maga, Systema (a Russian art derived from folk wrestling and filtered through Russian Spetznaz– special operations) or the Fairbairn/Applegate WWII combatives have a wide variety of instructors. A good instructor in this system can give your character a great edge. A bad instructor can pass on his bullshit macho fantasies to your character.

1D) Miscellaneous. This stuff mixes, and some of those mixes make for very good training. I trained in an ancient system of jujutsu. We actually learned how to bow properly while wearing armor and practiced sword defenses while kneeling. That training was filtered through brutal reality in a jail ... so I've been the guy with training and experience teaching in a garage. One of my dearest friends and mentors is a former librarian, graduate of Maharishi University, Vietnam combat veteran, former cop and has almost as many blackbelts as fingers. That's some pretty unique training. And he teaches in his garage, too.

2) Military or Police training. People who haven't been involved with either tend to vastly over-rate the UAC (Unarmed Combat) or DT (Defensive Tactics) training that soldiers and officers get. UAC is not a primary tool for anyone in battle. The person who conserves ammo and has a bullet left will win a fistfight. It is still taught, but they get little time for it and the purpose of the training is more to get over the idea of closing and grabbing an enemy than to instill specific skills. Military skills are designed to do as much damage as quickly as possible. The target students are young men in peak condition. An aggressive young man in good condition can make a lot of things work that would fail if attempted by someone else.

Police DT training also has limited time but it is considered a more important skill. It generally emphasizes take-downs, locks and pressure points. It is taught in an intensely political environment. Public agencies are far more concerned about getting sued than losing officers. For that reason, the skills tend to be concentrated on less damaging techniques (regardless of whether they work) and taught by rote (to prevent cadets from claiming the training was in some way unfair.) 40 hours of training in DTs at the academy and eight hours a year of refresher training is about standard, but varies by state. It is not enough to get good and most of the best officers train on their own. Which is hard because of shift work.

3) Experience. Trial and error, by itself, rarely makes a good technical fighter (I define a good technical fighter as someone who can consistently defeat a bigger, stronger threat). That's a lot of error to overcome and error has a price. (I've been well trained and by most standards enormously successful, but I sometimes have trouble remembering names, my left eye is blurry and the cornea rips if I let it dry out, my fingers go numb every so often from all the shoulder dislocations, I have a slight limp if I get tired or the weather gets cold...) What experience can give you is resourcefulness, toughness and an understanding of other violent people.

4) Combination. Obviously, I find that training under a good instructor coupled with experience makes the best fighter. I will even go so far as to say that a mix of traditional skills (where they can learn very dangerous techniques) combined with hard-contact sport training (where the students get inured to impact and pain) grant a huge edge.

Second breakdown: What people can do to each other

This is another thing that can be broken down a lot of ways. One way to look at it is Movement-Pain-Damage-Shock.

Movement: In a fight, you can move the threat or part of the threat. You can shove him, throw him, make him lose his balance. You can plant him into a wall or slam him down the stairs or into traffic. You can also move part of him, shifting his arm so that his ribs are exposed or twisting his head up to expose his throat.

Pain: Causing pain is really variable. Most people are not beaten. They give up. If a threat really, really wanted to keep fighting you need to either shutdown the brainstem (people have kept fighting even with extensive damage to the neo-cortex) or break every long bone in the body (and even then, they can still pull a trigger). Pain is to make the threat give up. To decide he doesn't want to play anymore. Not everyone feels pain and not everyone reacts to it the same (some give up, some get enraged, some panic, some don't feel it at all). Pain can be caused by light strikes, gouging pressure points, pinching, pulling hair and joint locks ... that's just a few off the top of my head.

Damage is breaking something to the extent that the threat loses ability. Break a leg, the threat usually has trouble standing, running or kicking. Break the elbow, the threat can't punch. But you must understand it is not automatic. Break a rib and it hurts to breathe but, until you get to a flail chest or punctured lung, the threat can still fight. I've known threats to keep punching with a shattered (not merely broken) hand. In the end, most threats give up when taking damage not because they were unable to fight but because the stakes are now raised too high to make it worthwhile to stay in the game.

Shock: This is shutting down the system, essentially shutting off the brainstem or severing the upper spinal cord. A bullet to the back of the head, strangulation and smothering, even a rib punch that lacerates the liver and causes internal bleeding. Except for massive trauma to the brainstem or upper cervical spine, none of these are instantaneous.

There is an old gunfighter saying about the "Dead Man's ten" which are the ten seconds that someone can stay in the fight to kill you after being shot in the heart. A good blood strangle takes a minimum of seven seconds. An air choke takes a minute or more. Bleeding out takes as long as it takes.

Marcus Young's Story
http://www.lawofficer.com/article/training/officer-down-marcus-young-inci

**Third breakdown:
Combat training by technique**

Most systems will have a mix of what follows. Few have all of them, even fewer have only one. Almost all specialize in a few and this becomes the core of their strategy.

Hand strikes: almost every surface of your hand, wrist, and arm can be used to strike. Some styles emphasize closed-fist punches, others feel it will do more damage to your hand than to the threat. Some target critical areas like the throat and cervical vertebrae, others count on massive damage to the head.

Kicks: can be delivered with the foot, knee or shin. They have a lot of power but pin your mobility on one foot for long enough to be dangerous. Kicking in boots is entirely different than kicking barefoot.

Throws: range through flipping someone over your hip, sweeping out his legs, twisting his spine to break his connection with the ground to simply getting out of his way and letting his own momentum drive him into the floor. A good thrower can make them work against much bigger, stronger people and it is easier to do in a real fight than in a martial arts setting. Many throwing styles combine with locking. The modern reason is to try to limit damage and not injure the opponent but the historical reason is that locks and throws work on armored opponents.

Gouges: Some styles actively work causing pain (and occasionally tearing muscle) through gouges, pokes and pinches. Some systems have elaborate mythologies of why they work and what amazing things can be done with them—at least one system ties their pressure points to acupuncture and teaches that if you hit five points in the right sequence, it will kill. Might be good for a fantasy setting, but if the paradigm is correct it is impossible to survive a massage.

> I was designing close-range defensive tactics course for my agency. In the process I was going over all of the kicks I knew could be effective from clinch range–toe out kicks and grinds and heel stomps and … A friend, an Air Marshall said, "That's bullshit. The only kick you need at that range is a toe kick to the ankle. Think about it, dude. You're wearing boots. Every last one of those martial arts kicks is designed to protect your bare feet. They aren't designed to injure the bad guy."

Strangles: I differentiate strangles (cutting off blood to the brain) from chokes (cutting off air). Both have similar effects, but chokes take longer and are more likely to trigger a panic response. Sometimes a strangle will put the person unconscious and they won't even know it is happening. A strong neck helps fight them, but these are the only techniques that work on everyone despite insanity, drugs or rage. They can be done with bare hands, a tool (like a rope or garrote) or using the threat's own clothes.

Pins: Moving someone on the ground is an art form and grapplers play at it like chess masters. Pins are holding someone down. Generally in sport-style pins the opponent is face-up to make the contest more challenging. Cops, soldiers and bad guys prefer that pins are face down, to make restraining or executing easier. Going for a pin makes you vulnerable to a third party. The usual winner in a ground fight is NOT the best grappler but whoever has friends who show up first and start kicking.

Locks: Locks are attacking a joint in a way it was never intended to move, or too far in a way it was intended. They can be used standing or on the ground. Locks can be used to force movement, to immobilize, to cause pain or to dislocate the joint (damage). Some can be modified into takedowns and throws.

Head butts are AWESOME. They deliver tremendous power with a big bone at close range and usually too fast to evade, as well as being a surprise (except in the UK where they are very common and they used to be common in Korea, for some reason.) But they require technique. Your head has flat places and corners. You hit the threat's flat places with your corners. Far more concussion to him than to you. They go much better with some neck strength and when someone tries to thrust or spear with the head, (like driving your character's head into a bad guy's stomach) it tends to strain the neck severely. You can do it to the nose, which hurts a lot, makes the eyes water, and gets blood everywhere. I don't recommend the mouth or jaw. It does a lot of damage but teeth break and broken or not, teeth cut. The character who does it will get somebody else's blood and saliva in fresh cuts, and that makes for some nasty infections and disease possibilities.

Miscellaneous: Don't forget head butts; shoulder and hip slams (not much damage, but they also cause movement and tend to cause surprise) and using the environment. Those are the things that make a fight so dynamic.

Stacking: A skilled fighter will use many of these things in combination. Strikes and gouges can both set up a throw and do damage during the execution. You can lock a limb while sweeping a leg. You can use a lock to slam the threat into a corner or over a coffee table. It's all good.

Specific styles

I'm not going into this here because there are thousands of styles and systems and most are searchable on the internet. If you emphasize that your character studied a system, spend a little time with an instructor from that system and let them double-check your scenes. That's more important in the training scenes than the fight scenes. Fights are messy and should be messy and won't look like it is supposed to look.

That's cool.

Self-Defense Schools and Instruction

There are some pretty definite gender differences in fighting. That affects how self-defense is taught greatly. Rather, it should affect it. Far too often you have large, male martial artists who envision violence as the fights they had in grade school trying to teach women with far less size, strength and training.

First of all, a lot of SD instructors have little or no experience with violence. Those who have none tend to make stuff up, and it winds up being more about the instructor's fantasy life than anything else. Some have limited experience and too often try to cram all violence into their single focus. Others are teaching as part of their own therapy, trying to get control of their lives and identity.

From the blog:

Assumptions and Biases 24December2011

We all have biases and assumptions as instructors. So does your instructor. We can't help it. We see the world a certain way and certain things have worked for us. The things that worked (for us, in our environment) are where we concentrate our teaching.

An athletic martial artist who has worked as a bouncer will believe and teach that you see things coming and your physical attributes are key.

An instructor who has survived a rape attempt may well believe that the key is unbridled ferocity, slipping the leash. If they won despite disadvantages in strength, size and position they will believe and teach that strength, size and position are secondary to mindset. If they could not even think of a technique in the moment, they will likely teach that technique is irrelevant.

So here are my biases and assumptions, to the extent that I see them (the thing with blind spots is that you can't see them, so there are many I will miss.)

1) Unarmed arts only exist for emergencies you didn't see coming. If you can predict it and plan it and force is unavoidable, it is stupid to go in without a weapon. For that matter, without getting every advantage you can.

2) Which means that the basic environment of an unarmed encounter is the position of disadvantage. Bad structure, positioning, footing, injured, overwhelmed and behind the curve.

3) Almost always, the ones you see coming you can ward off by positioning or verbal de-escalation. As such I've often and (so far) successfully, put myself in positions that weren't tactically optimal in order to talk stuff down (strategically preferable).

4) I don't think conflict is a physical problem most of the time (see number 3) and even when it is a physical problem, there are minds and social rules and the world involved. The more of those elements you can manipulate skillfully,

the better off you are. Sometimes you play the cards, sometimes you play the person and sometimes you play the table.

5) I expect the threat to have the advantage in size and strength or to be crazy (mental instability or drugs). Because almost all of them were one or the other. Potentially sampling error ... but I think it makes sense, since you'd have to be crazy to routinely attack bigger and stronger people.

6) I believe in the primacy of infighting. This is the prejudice that is most likely to be incompatible with a student's nature. Classical JJ is an infighting system– weapons were assumed and there was no safe way to finish it at long range. Early I learned that people freak out more when someone tries to close, and that shaped my personality. Thus, by nature and training, I'm an infighter. I tend to reject techniques that keep distance and most of the techniques I prefer (and therefore teach) put you at clinch range. If that's not a good range for you, I'm unlikely to be a good teacher.

7) I tend not to injure people. That was the preferred outcome on my job– maximum control with minimum injury. That's shaped a lot in that I have very few strikes I consider reliable. Marc consistently gives me a bad time because I don't always treat potentially deadly threats as seriously as he thinks I should.

8) Weapons: I'm completely cool with improvised weapons and using obstacles, etc. But for the first ten years of my career, we were not allowed to carry anything. When OC was finally authorized, I just never thought about it. On the other hand, my weapon training was completely offensive, centered around hostage rescue tactics with a team. My mindset is completely different when I pack versus when I don't.

9) I have very weak social instincts. This means that I don't tend to get emotional or competitive when I fight ... and I don't really understand why other people do. It's good in that the lack of anger never makes me want to overstep bounds, but some of my basic things–the range, positioning, not bothering to make eye contact, smelling, face contact–are sometimes hard for others. Many people have to force themselves to grab a face, for instance, whereas grabbing a collar or neck is (emotionally) easier. Just rarely as effective.

There are more, I'm sure. Do this analysis for yourself, your style and your instructor. It all adds up to this: Each of us train for a generally narrow range of conflict. Including me. Be aware.

Remember that people with only a single experience of violence learn what is false and never learn what is true? Some dedicate themselves, subconsciously, to creating a story that satisfies their need to believe that they understand what happened well enough to be in control ... and the students are then pawns in the instructor's fantasy. This isn't true for all, but it is definitely something to be leery of. Part of the problem is that almost everyone is a "naive consumer" and doesn't have any way to tell a good instructor from a bad instructor.

Generally, self-defense instructors or schools have an orientation. I consider that there are three essential elements to self-defense: Awareness, Initiative and Permission.

Some schools focus intently on awareness–how to recognize and avoid bad people and how to stay alert. If the instructor knows what he or she is teaching, that's fine. Few really go much deeper than "Check the back seat and under your car before you get in" or similar trite (to me) advice.

Some focus on what I consider initiative or technique, trying to get the students to act. Hitting becomes more important than how you hit. If the techniques taught actually reflect real crime, they can be useful. Otherwise not so much. Some of these also completely gloss over the legal aspects.

Some classes, especially Women's Self-Defense (WSD) focus entirely on the Permission aspect. The big thing in model mugging and similar programs is to get the students to let go, unleash themselves and really whale on an armored "bad guy" role-player.

All three of these are necessary, but some completely miss parts or don't understand them. Many male instructors are particularly bad at realizing that permission to act and hurt someone is a very serious problem with many women.

There is another dynamic that you should be aware of–gender politics in self-defense. When I tell someone that 'the most important thing a young woman can do to avoid being raped is to avoid places with lots of young men. And if you absolutely have to go to such a place don't drink.' The dumb responses range from, "Girls have a right to have fun" to "You're just blaming the victim" all the way up to the ludicrous, "A woman should have the right to walk naked into a biker bar and not be bothered." These are political ideals. They might even be the way the world *should* work. They are not the way the world actually works.

The responsibility for self-protection has to rest with the potential victim because the potential rapist has no interest whatsoever in her safety or rights. The potential victim is the one who cares. Counting on the people who don't care to do the right thing makes no sense at all. I have seen some very, very bad advice given to support an ideal of the world, even if it endangered the student.

Women are often reluctant to ask men for advice and sometimes it is because they wisely understand that the men don't get it. Most have never dealt with the psychological blocks and conditioning. Too many SD instructors are fit young men and can make bad techniques work. I prefer female, small and even old or crippled instructors because if they can put me down it is skill. 300 pounds of steroidal muscle putting me down means nothing. There's also the factor that most instructors will try to teach what *they* would do, and there are often profound differences between how and why men and women fight. A successful woman has a huge advantage in mentoring another woman to be successful.

A lot of people (this is definitely not a male/female thing) want multiple things and sometimes multiple incompatible things. *I want to run, but I want to do it in shoes that were not designed for running. I want to battle at close quarters but look cool. I want to break bones and rupture livers without any twinge of conscience. In the end, I want to be able to go through the most intense, dangerous ten seconds of my life where everything I counted on about human interaction is revealed to be a lie and I want to do it without changing who I am. I want the experience without sacrificing any illusions ....*

✧✦✧✦✧

HOMEWORK:

Take a self-defense or introductory martial arts class. Ideally one with some impact, like a Model Mugging course, Impact or some Krav Maga schools. Judo or jujutsu if they let beginners take falls. I want you to feel some impact. Get hit.

TO RECAP:

- The classic 'fight' is a stupid game, played by amateurs
- People learn to fight by studying martial arts, getting police or military training, by experience, or by some combination
- Fight effects break down to movement, pain, damage and shock
- Fight techniques break down to strikes, takedowns, locks, gouges, pins and strangles
- Self-defense schools have different focuses
- The instructor will make or break the skills

... 9 ...

WHY PEOPLE CARRY WEAPONS

Knife and Gun 18December2007

My captain used to say, "For most people, carrying a gun is like a fifteen-year-old with a condom in his wallet. He's not going to get a chance to use it and if he did he wouldn't know what to do, but it's cool to show his friends."

In a similar way, a person with a knife out scares me more than a person with a gun out. Some of that is personal–in most of my knife experiences, the threat was trying to kill. In the very small number of gun encounters, I got the impression that the threat was sort of hiding behind the gun.

This goes to a lot of shooting. I know a handful of very serious gun guys (who consider me a knife guy) and a smaller number of very serious knife guys (who tend to consider me a gun guy). In my estimation, the knife guys are more serious than the gun guys.

This, of course, falls to my definition of serious.

The serious gun guys I know practice with a cold, surgical precision. "Slow is smooth, smooth is fast." Dry fire every day. Four count draw. Weapons transition, long gun or SMG to sidearm. Immediate action. They practice turning corners at retention in the house. Walking with a rocking motion of their feet. The best (and civilians rarely have an opportunity for this) practice with ConSims in uncontrolled environment with all of Force policy and statute in effect, working their judgment in tandem with their skills.

The serious knife guys are a different level. Stay close, here, because my definition of serious knife guy may not match anyone else's. Knife is not a precision skill, not at the serious level. It is a matter of intent and will. Knives are close range and messy and the serious knife guys I know focus less on motion than on the context. They prepare themselves for the smells; the transition when things go from technical to slippery; the feeling of parting tissues transmitted up the blade. The screaming and struggling. It's easy to play with a knife or a gun or any toy ... but actually using a knife hits almost every social button, every uggh and disgust and "Oh, Hell No!" a human being has.

Just for the record, slaughtering and butchering animals is valuable. I struggled with that word–it's not important in all ways, not critical. You won't learn a lot about knife work. Cutting through a skinned animal with a good set of boning and butcher knives isn't the same; gutting a bled-out deer is very different from the warm, slippery gush of a live disembowelment. What you do learn is about yourself and a tiny, itty bit of how much a death can affect you. You also learn how some things die very hard.

Much of the difference is in the mechanism. A gun is a joy of engineering. It is a nifty machine that throws a rock in a straight line. It is classically civilized.

A knife is anything portable and sufficiently thin to cut. I've found eyeglass earpieces that were sharpened to scalpels (more for torture than assassination or combat) and plastic toothbrushes sharpened to puncture. A knife is primitive. No matter the skill and technology that went into it, the knife is an exemplar of more primitive, less civilized times.

Part of the difference is in use. In combat neither a knife nor a gun is used for winning fights. Get over that. They are used for killing people. That is a profound difference. A handgun (as opposed to a rifle) is used defensively. As one of the rookies put it, "My Glock is just to buy time to get the shotgun." Simplistic, but the sentiment is there. A handgun is a compromise–portability and concealability for a profound drop in accuracy and power. The handgun is something you pull when bad shit happens to you or you expect it to.

The knife (dueling systems aside) is used offensively, usually in a close-range ambush. The threat appears to be walking past his target and suddenly grips the shoulder or arm with his off hand and pop-pop-pop-pop hammers staccato thrusts into the kidney or liver.

Neither of these examples are universal- handguns can be used offensively, but no professional does as a first choice. If you are going on the offense, you get a rifle, AR, SMG or shotgun. Knives can be used defensively, but usually increasing range is a better choice than working in the knife's required range- and when bad things happen in knife range, you can take a lot of damage while making the draw ....

Note well, this isn't about why people use weapons. Weapon use is easy to understand, as long as you haven't been brainwashed. Physical force is one of the most effective ways to get what you want. "Violence never solved anything" is not just a myth, but one of those statements of breath-taking absurdity. Violence has solved most of the problems that people have had until the modern era (it's pretty much the only thing you can do about eating and not being eaten). Weapons make violence easier and safer.

But the world, for the most part, is already safe and easy. So why carry?

1) Social
2) Superstitious
3) Preventative
4) Defensive
5) Offensive
6) Professional/Practical
7) Habit

Social carry. In some cultures and sub-cultures, carrying a weapon is just something you do. Sikh men are required by their religion to carry knives, a constant reminder that they are warriors. The *buke* of Japan (samurai were a subset of *buke*, the warrior caste) carried two swords, a long and short, even though the bow and the spear were both acknowledged as superior weapons on the battlefield.

I was raised as a ranch kid. Everyone in our little redneck corner of the world carried a pocketknife and having a rifle and shotgun in the parking lot of the high school was no big deal.

Read Sherlock Holmes. In the late 1800's a gentleman didn't leave his home without a revolver and a walking stick. Look at the social rules for carrying a rapier during the renaissance.

Swords, for that matter, have always been a symbol of wealth. It was something that, generally, the upper classes carried. Maces and axes were just as good and much cheaper to make. Both worked better against armor than swords. The spear, except indoors, was clearly superior to the sword. But axes, maces and spears were cheap. Peasant things.

Making a good sword required a lot of work and time from a highly skilled professional. Tempering was an art and very imprecise–it was incredibly difficult to get an evenly tempered long blade.

Like having a bodyguard in the modern western world, wearing a sword didn't mean that you needed one or even knew how to use it. It was often simply a statement that you could afford one.

Superstition. This is my phrase for it. And there is a little contempt in it. Carrying a weapon of any type is a huge responsibility. If you've ever lost your keys or cell phone, think how much greater the stakes are if you misplace a gun ....

Some people don't grasp that and they get a gun (or another weapon) and think that this will make them safe. Understand weapons *are* the big equalizer. Up until the introduction of very efficient weapons that did not rely on strength (think the revolver, first) might *did* make right. Not morally, but any moral argument put forward could be beaten to the ground.

Quick aside here on a gender issue. There are exceptions, but men are generally bigger and much, much stronger than women. Size, strength and reach really matter with any hand-held weapon ... and stronger people tend to be quicker as well. That is a huge genetic stack in men's favor. The default to make a woman character who can prevail is to decide that she had more training or better training or trained harder. But for all of history men have, on top of the genetic advantage, had more time and opportunity to train as well. AND more time just horsing around pounding on each other.

And all of that was neutralized by the introduction of the handgun.

Back to superstition. The weapon will not make you safe. It is a tool you can use. But people fall into magical thinking: "I have a gun (or a black belt) so I can go down into the dark basement with the weird noises after all of my friends have disappeared and it will be okay."

Preventative is the other side of the superstition coin. Maybe. The presence of a weapon can prevent violence, but only certain kinds. People do tend to be more polite around armed people. That's just common sense. The trouble is that in order for it to work, people need to be informed you have a weapon. That can destroy your tactical edge.

When we were going in to introduce ourselves to a newly appointed high-ranking Iraqi official, we went armed to the teeth, as did his bodyguards. It forced an extreme mutual respect. That was in a particular society. In a society such as ours where weapons are uncommon, it will likely make everyone so nervous that they won't be able to communicate at all. And if someone is planning a bad act, it gives them enough notice to decide exactly what to do about you and your weapon. In a dueling culture, carrying a well-worn, high quality weapon may prevent intelligent people from challenging … but it may influence stupid young bucks to challenge.

Defensive is the most common reason to carry a concealed weapon. It changes with culture, of course. In many eras of history violence was common and expected. Currently, violence is so rare that some people consider giving it any thought paranoid. Self-defense is nothing like fighting. If your character is a killer martial artist, it doesn't matter. If she sees it coming (kind of necessary to use her sparring-based skills) she can always avoid, de-escalate, or turn it into a kind of fight the bad guy is not expecting, e.g. get to a weapon.

Self-defense, ergo, only comes up when you are losing. When the situation is unbelievably bad. You've been grabbed from behind and your face has been smashed into the bar and you're dizzy and can't hear and the blood in your eyes makes it hard to see. Or you've been spun around suddenly and someone grabs your throat in a huge hand and literally lifts you off the floor to slam you into a wall.

Most unarmed stuff fails here. The threat isn't going to pick someone he has any doubt of beating, so he will be bigger and stronger. There may be many of them. He or they get the first move, from surprise and from a position of his choice. It sucks, basically. A weapon can turn this around.

But the primary skill, rarely practiced or taught, in defensive weapons is getting the weapon into play in the first place. Drawing under close assault.

Offensive is simple. You have a weapon because you intend to use the weapon. You use the weapon to make sure the target has no chance. Two levels of this. Simple assassination is really, really simple and very, very effective. It is rare for someone to survive and usually takes either luck or an insane level of awareness.

The other level is, in my opinion, a product of our legal system. Violence is investigated pretty thoroughly. An armed robber starts killing tourists, the police go into it hard. An armed robber intimidates the same tourists into handing over wallets and cameras, it's not investigated as thoroughly and the odds of a conviction are low. In this case, though still offensive, the robber uses the weapon so that the victim feels he or she has no chance and just goes along.

Professional/Practical. Sometimes it is your job to be armed. Sometimes you are going into a situation or place where it is stone stupid to be unarmed.

Habit. If you've spent a lot of time armed, you feel naked unarmed. For me, transitioning to civilian life it was a constant creepy feeling. I knew I had to get over it so I forced myself not to carry for a year, telling myself I was out of that life and didn't have a duty to act.

One of my friends, who is anti-gun, asked why I found it stressful. After some thought I was able to explain that not carrying a handgun diminished my sphere of influence. If I saw someone about to kill a person at, say, 25 yards, I couldn't do anything about it

So what weapon will your character choose? That depends on availability and to some extent on personality. But one thing is universal–when your life is on the line you will get the best weapon for your purposes that you can. As one of my friends puts it, "There is no such thing as a knife culture. Just people too poor to buy guns."

That doesn't always mean the most deadly or high tech. The beer bottle in your hand will often be better (faster) than the gun in your holster. Some people value reliability over anything else. As a friend said when looking over holographic and laser sights for weapons, "I don't want to rely on anything that relies on batteries." Individual choice.

Sometimes legal considerations enter into the equation. What is legal for your character to carry? A knife named "Ninja Commando" will get a lot more attention from a prosecutor than a similar knife named the "Hunter's Utility Blade."

Just some of the things your character may have to take into consideration:

- Concealability. Two ways. Handguns, for instance, are easier to hide on your person than rifles. But there is also concealability in use. A knife or a sap in a crowd will not draw attention like gunfire.

✧ Power. Big holes (guns), big gashes (blades), and big impact all tend to end things quicker. But sometimes the things that increase power decrease concealability or speed.

✧ Effect. Not quite the same as power. A weapon to kill has a different effect than a weapon to stun. Your mission, whether to kill, to capture or to escape will dictate the most effective weapon. That said, for defensive use, for surviving an ambush, multiple options slows your reaction time. The character with six options will not survive an ambush as well as the character with only one.

✧ Silence. Part of the concealability of use. Assassinations, you might want as little noise as possible. Other situations, you might want something loud enough to scare a horse. In my opinion, a longbow is a far superior weapon for killing people than the relatively slow and inaccurate musket. But the musket belches smoke and fire and lets off a thunderous noise and in a battle the side that breaks down from fear is the side that loses.

✧ Range. A knife is useless if you can't even get in the same room with your target. Conversely a sniper rifle on a crowded bus is an obvious and clumsy club.

✧ Specialty effects. A boar spear has a crossbar to keep the boar from running up the spear. A marked minefield denies access. Neutron bombs, theoretically, would kill the people but preserve the manufacturing resources. Grenades affect small areas rather than individuals. Improvised explosive devices (IEDs) like roadside bombs allow you to kill without being present.

✧ Specialty considerations. If you use a poisonous gas, how long will it be effective? If your fantasy character carries a sword that can cut anything, what do you make the scabbard from? Will a biological agent eventually doom your people as well?

✧ Legal considerations. These vary much by time and place. In some cultures only certain castes are permitted certain weapons. The castes forbidden swords, for instance, developed other weapons or fighting techniques for their work tools. In our world, different jurisdictions can have different rules on whether a pocket knife is a tool or a weapon.

✧ Ease and speed of use. Weapons that take time or teamwork to set up won't be a good choice for defensive carry, nor would a weapon you have to charge, whether a battery-operated beam gun that needs to charge up or a semi-automatic handgun without a bullet in the chamber.

✧ Availability. You can't carry something you can't get.

✧ Cultural considerations. Certain groups carry certain types of knives, for instance, because those are available there and everyone knows how to use them. Some are cultural identifiers. Some of those are driven by pop culture, e.g. switchblades are crappy weapons (a friend describes them as, "Basically a broken real knife held together by a pin.") But wannabe tough guys carried them after the gang movies and books of the late fifties to early seventies.

✧ Social reactions. Some weapons send messages. Had "Jack the Ripper" used a gun, it is unlikely we would remember him. Currently, several states are warning Syria of dire consequences if they use chemical weapons. Realistically, are chemical in some way more horrible than blowing people apart or blasting lead through their lungs and brains and organs? All societies find some weapons more acceptable than others. When your character wants to be accepted, he or she will be drawn to certain weapons. When the same character wants to show that she is an outsider, she might show up at the dueling grounds with an axe.

✧ Personal considerations. Lots of things can affect the decision. People who work in high-risk environments tend to be conservative. Not in the political sense, but in the sense that they are very, very slow to give up anything that has worked in the past. If you have survived your last four gunfights with a revolver, a list of reasons why semi-automatic handguns are 'superior' is unlikely to sway you. And some like being different and get a kick out of showing off exotic weapons.

A flippant note from my blog:

Wife and Gun Club 19July2009

This is probably going to be my weird thought for the week.

Long guns aside, I was raised on wheel guns and Colt semis. I learned handgun on a Smith and Wesson K22, moving up to a Colt Police Positive. Then the .45 Mark IV series 70. They pretty much defined what a handgun should be to me–solid, reliable, very fast from holster to hand and (with the exception of the K22, which was a kid's gun) they made big holes.

Over the years I played with other guns. I loved the sleek Browning Hi-Power. Giggled at the deadly accuracy of the Ruger Mark II. Had a passionate crush on the Sig Sauer, but she was out of my league, far more gun than I could afford as a starving student. During these swinging years of my life I often found myself falling back on revolvers, like a Smith 686 or Ruger GP100. Reliable, accurate, and they felt like a gun should feel.

Then the Glock. It was an arranged marriage. The team was going lethal. The Captain (was he still a lieutenant back then?) wanted everyone to have ammo and magazine compatibility. He wanted reliable and, with his bureaucrat hat on, he wanted cheap. We went with the Glock 23 in .40 caliber.

I hated it. It felt like a toy, too light to be a real gun. The grip was too big for my hand ... but it was a done deal. The way it was. And it was one of the things that I might never need, but if I ever did it would be the most important thing in my life. I didn't like it, but we were stuck with each other. So I practiced and came to learn that it was reliable. No matter how hard I shot or how much dirt I dragged it through, as long as my form was good, the Glock would fire every time. And she was accurate. If both bullets didn't go through the two-inch square, it was me. As long as I did my job, she would do hers. It was never really love, but after a few years we got along very, very well

My second arranged marriage was with the Beretta 92 (M9). The Beretta had a bad reputation around the barracks–unreliable and puny. Failed consistently to do her duty. Fit my hand better than the Glock, though, and that was something.

On the range, she lived down to her reputation–it was mostly bad magazines and I had to ruthlessly cut those out when found. She was picky and didn't care much for getting dirty and this can be a dirty place. Accurate, though. More so even than the Glock. The range master kept my qualification target around for months to scare the locals.

Picky and unreliable, but accurate and fit my hand. That was enough to work with, since we were stuck together anyway. I would just have to supply whatever she couldn't in the relationship.

Most people have comfort foods. I probably have comfort weapons. Blades aside, the revolvers are probably closest. Comfort isn't enough, though. You and your weapon are a pair. Without your weapon, you are unarmed and can only do what meat can do. Without you, your weapon is an inert lump of metal. Together is all that counts. Comfort isn't enough for that. It takes work and practice to make that pairing effective. Even more work to be phenomenal.

There are certainly passions as well. I love the way the Browning Hi-Power feels, the way it comes up on line effortlessly. But it still takes work to be good and no weapon is so thrilling or so reliable that you can ignore basic maintenance forever.

And there is commitment: "This is my rifle, there are many like it but this one is mine ...."

I was a little heavy handed above, but I noticed today that some people act towards the weapons that their lives depend on and the mates (that sometimes their soul depends on) in very similar ways.

Some won't commit until they find the one that is 'just right'. Some collect as many as they can but never really work on any one. Some get stuck with one they aren't interested in and instead of getting to know each other, leave it rusting in the holster until they retire. And some, whether it was a love match or an arranged marriage practice, work hard and never neglect maintenance.

I don't know if there is a correlation, if the officers with serial divorces are the same ones that go from weapon to weapon. If the same guys who notch bedposts are the ones with a room full of guns that they have almost never fired. If strong, stable marriages are the same households where the guns are quick and steady from long practice.

But it is an interesting thought for the day, and I never would have thunk it without an exposure to the local custom of arranged marriages.

✧✦✧✦✧

HOMEWORK:

All society has broken down. There are no police, no soldiers, no order. There is rampant looting, theft, murder and rape.

If you could have any weapon, would you carry one with you at all times? What weapon? Would you only carry it when you left your home/base? Would you have a different weapon in the home to defend? What would that be?

If you couldn't have any weapon, but only what you have on hand right this second, what would you use?

TO RECAP:

- ✧ Different weapons have different purposes
- ✧ Different weapons require different technical and emotional skills
- ✧ Weapon carry can be driven by social or practical concerns
- ✧ Weapon choice can be influenced by social concerns, practicality and access

… 10 …

WEAPON USE

Weapons are used for many different things. From quick and simple murder to communication. When a weapon is out and in play, there is a purpose, and that purpose drives how the weapon will be used. Weapons can be used offensively or defensively, to communicate to others or self; or to fight. And all of those categories are different.

Offensive. Fighting, even very aggressive fighting, is qualitatively different than offensive weapon use. The purpose of offensive weapon use is to give the other person or people no chance to turn things into a fight. Assassins shoot people in the head, they do not shout a warning to create a quick draw contest. Snipers kill from too far away to be seen. The lowly street criminal will bash in brains with a crowbar. If he has decided to use force, unless he is very young and inexperienced, he will never square off and create a fight.

Hunting, the way that tactical teams do entries (giving no chance to defend is what allows so many high-risk missions to be handled without loss of life on either side), military raids and the way that criminals target victims are all aspects of offensive weapon use. It has nothing to do with fighting. As a tactical team leader, if the bad guy got a chance to fight back it usually meant that I was doing my job wrong.

Sub-category: Offensive shooting should be very similar to range shooting. You get your pick of targets, time, and place. It's not quite like range shooting, because of chance and adrenaline. People do miss. Experienced pros not so much, but even highly trained professionals tend to screw up their first real missions. Which is why the general rule is to add inexperienced people one or two at a time to an experienced group. The rookies can model the attitudes and behaviors of the veterans.

Defensive. There are levels of defensive weapon use. At the lowest level is simply reputation. If it is known that your protagonist has successfully used weapons in the past, people will think twice about attacking her. But if they do attack, they will take her reputation into the equation.

Defensive display ranges from the highly visible archers or cannons on your curtain wall to the gun on your hip to drawing and brandishing your sword to show that you are ready to sell your life dearly. It is almost always a stupid choice and a sign of a pure amateur. If your archers are visible, then they can be counted, their fields of fire graphed and they can be neutralized. Your character brandishes his sword in a heroic gesture and he has just told all the real warriors that he is nervous and NOT ready to kill.

The handgun on an officer's hip is an exception. Because in the US all cops are known to be armed, there is no information, misinformation or doubt possible, and so the increased speed of the unconcealed draw has no downside.

And defensive weapon use. It is nothing like fighting defensively or concentrating on defense (blocking, avoiding, not getting hurt) in a fight. These are the skills that you need when you are caught out by someone employing offensive weapon use. These are the skills you need to turn certain death into something of a fight.

The premier skill for this, with any weapon, is a fast draw. Getting weapons into play. It will be hard. The nature of an ambush or assault is that the attacker has stacked everything in her favor. She has chosen time, place, distance and even victim. And this means that almost nothing a fighter knows will apply. The distance, footwork, power generation, structure and facing positions are all distinctively different from the duel. Defensive use is not about fighting. It is about not dying when you begin profoundly losing. Clawing your way back from the brink.

Sub-category: Defensive shooting is your response when you are under attack. Ideally it would be a cold-blooded combination of moving to cover and aimed fire. In reality it is usually "spray and pray," blindly firing shots in the general direction that you think the attacker is firing from. Often with panicked running. Sometimes with the off-hand held in front of the face as if that might stop a bullet.

Under close assault–the threat is strangling or stabbing or pummeling you–defensive shooting is a contact sport. You have to get your weapon out. You likely won't be able to see the weapon. You will have to touch the threat to be sure to hit him and some angles will endanger you (I always want the classic hostage movie situation–one arm around the victim's neck, gun pressed into the other side of his neck–to end with the threat firing and blowing his arm mostly off.) If you press the barrel of most semi-automatics too hard into the body the slide will shift taking the round "out of battery" and the weapon will not fire. That close it is almost certain that the slide won't be able to rack fully and your fancy 18-round handgun will turn into a single shot.

Neither of these are problems with modern double-action revolvers unless the hammer gets held down somehow. Or the cylinder is gripped too tightly to turn.

At longer range, you are taking fire. You may not know from where in the first instant. Hit or not, you have to move. You were ambushed in this precise spot because it is the best place to kill you. You MUST get out of that spot (or "Off the X" as we say.) Move. American military trained people will charge the ambush. That's the highest percentage option, especially if you have a group. Solo and with less or different training, people will want to suck cover or run to cover and then figure out what is going on. Then decide whether to engage or escape. Deciding takes time and time is exactly what the bad guy needs to aim.

Long range or even medium range shooting where the bad guy knows exactly where you are and you are unsure is very bad. Most of the ways to find your target leaves your head in one place more than long enough to get shot.

Communicating with yourself. Weapons are powerful ego support. That's not a bad thing necessarily. Checking weapons can be a calming ritual. Many people throughout history have had a weapon preparation ritual on the eve of a battle. Almost everyone I have met who has been in the situation reflexively checks weapons when they get tense. It's a tell, and a great way to pick out who is armed.

But there is also a big downside. Weapons do not change your nature, only your reach and power. And they can make weak people feel brave or timid people feel safe. And timid people will sometimes believe that the mere presence of a weapon will make them safe, and so they do not train or make plans. It often ends badly.

"You don't respect me? Well, now that I have a gun, you'd damn well better! Ha!" When someone fires a gun for ego support, it is part of a dominance display. It is an attempt to intimidate, not to harm. Shooting into the ceiling. "I'm gonna make you dance," in an old Western.

It comes from a person with insecurities. Violence and the risk of violence goes up when the people are insecure. The insecure person will not, generally, want to shoot anybody–he is afraid to. BUT, if he is challenged, what do you think an insecure monkey would do if challenged? Yep, lash out. And lashing out with a gun is bad. Remember always that weapons embolden the insecure.

Communicating with others. An incredible amount of fighting, violence and conflict are about communication. European duels were rarely about killing, but about upholding social norms and showing social status. Even pitched battles in the Napoleonic era were not won by the mathematics of lead and death, but by which side broke and ran first, and that placed the value on noise and drums, chanting and marching, bright colored uniforms and tall hats.

To display a weapon sends a message. In many places and times, the weapon you carried told who you were. There are differences between the kukris carried by the Gurkha and other nearby tribes. In most of the Edo period in Japan, wearing two swords was a caste privilege. It was a symbol of status. To the educated eye, weapon choice shows affiliation, status, economic level and sometimes even training, skill and experience.

To brandish a weapon sends a message as well. You are letting someone know that you could kill him in order to force a negotiation or a concession. Armed robbery is the same dynamic as any dictator with an army demanding concessions.

Brandishing, especially in interpersonal situations, brings up some questions. Assuming the character doing the brandishing is not unbelievably stupid, you must be sure that what they want couldn't be gotten easier from a corpse. Shooting near someone to send a message will likely be prosecuted as attempted murder, which is significant hard time. Avoiding the murder charge won't be a motivation. And it draws attention like very little else. With guns, if there are people in hearing distance and they are likely to call it in, and there is a police force, the shot may have just started a clock.

The person being threatened, assuming a pro who can keep cool (as opposed to someone who just pisses his pants in panic) will get a lot of information from a shot that misses. Is the shooter unable to kill, like many people? Is there some reason it is necessary to take me alive? Or is he just a really shitty shot? In the case of a brandished sword, all except the last apply.

All of these possibilities, this information, give the target power. You shouldn't use a weapon to empower your enemy.

Seriously, if you need information, leg shots and tourniquets give you a range of options that simple fear does not.

This is a dominance display. It is raising the stakes expecting that the person threatening you will back down. Sometimes it works. Modern police officers almost always display pepperspray before they use it, giving the threat one last chance to surrender without force. The laser sight on the Taser (or on some firearms) puts a red (usually) or green dot where the dart or bullet will land. One company that manufactures laser sights refers to this as "Helping criminals make informed decisions."

Fighting. Realistically, fighting is a subset of communication. It is one of the least intelligent of human behaviors. With two exceptions, everything that fighting can actually accomplish can be achieved easier, better and more safely by ambush or assassination.

Those two exceptions? If you want to communicate, either to the person or the crowd that you are willing to fight and how and over what.

That's important because it shows who you are under stress. The second reason is if you need to prove the same things to yourself. Fighting is almost always ego driven.

People with extensive exposure to violence rarely fight. We play at fighting. We spar, box, grapple, fence, play paintball... it is fun and a way to stay sharp. But if someone were foolish enough to say, "Let's do this for real. What do you say?" A pro smiles and leaves. Or guns him down while he is waiting for an answer.

The essence of a fight is a contest. It shows physical skill, nerve and even tactical intelligence. Universally, it is fought for social reasons and follows social rules. Whether the protocols of 18th century European dueling, with seconds arranging time, place and weapons or even a schoolyard fight ("Meet me behind the gym after school unless you're a chicken!") or a martial arts tournament there are protocols. They change by culture, but they are always there.

The predictability is why they are stupid, to a professional's eyes. Predictability gets you killed, if killing is the goal. If killing (or handcuffing or escaping or...) is NOT the goal, why even play? Why give someone a chance to learn how you think and move under stress?

So, a fight–both sides know it is coming. Spoken or unspoken, there are rules. The driving factors are either social expectations and/or ego.

Sub-category: Gunfights are very rare outside of a military context. Even there, one side uses all of its resources to create an ambush hoping to annihilate the enemy without ever giving them a chance. People are hard to kill, though, and often some survive the initial assault and, if they are well trained and preferably well-led, turn it into a fight.

The western movie gunfight, facing down on a street at noon may have happened, but there are some issues with it. First and foremost, bullets are like dueling blades. There is almost no place you can hit a human that physiologically stops them from shooting back. Shot through the heart? You've got roughly ten seconds to shoot back. Nothing below the first or second thoracic vertebra prevents you from pulling a trigger. Headshots are not even reliable. A local man when I was a rookie took a .45 caliber slug between the eyes from three feet away and it bounced off his skull. In the 1977 murder of Baton Rouge officer Linda Lawrence, the threat took ten shots from a large caliber revolver including a contact shot "to the solarplex area," a contact shot through the rib cage from side to side (The threat grunted and said, "You got me a good one that time" and threw Steve Chaney, Officer Lawrence's partner, across the room) and a contact shot through the top of the head.

Even after the headshot the threat got up one more time to fight.

From the blog, the first time I was invited to give this class:

Gory Details 30August2005 For the writers of fiction:
In November, my lovely wife has arranged for me to talk to a large group of writers, readers and people who want to write. "What do I say?" I asked.

"Talk to them about the things that they write about but they don't know. What criminals are really like, how and why they fight, what it feels and sounds and smells like when you're fighting for your life. They same things you try to tell martial artists."

Oh. That stuff.

We had to put down Gazelle, a paralyzed goat. Put down means "kill". Maybe it means, 'kill for its own good, for the cessation of pain.' I went out early in the morning and dug the grave. It is a sin in my family to waste meat, but since the paralysis was probably due to loss of circulation the meat may not have been safe. I dug the grave close because I know that limp bodies are much harder to move than stiff ones. I took aim from about a foot and a half away with a .40 caliber semi-automatic handgun and pulled the trigger.

First note: "Putting to sleep" i.e. euthanization from drugs is the procedure used in a veterinarian's office. It looks very peaceful and is much easier on the grieving owners ... but one of our family friends, a veterinarian in Eastern Oregon did her doctoral thesis on euthanasia. She said it looks peaceful because of the effects of the muscle relaxants but that the EEG showed unmistakable signs of panic as the animal slowly died ... whereas a shot to the head went from normal to flatline instantly. She said that some people can't take the responsibility of killing their own animal, but if they can, a gunshot is more humane, though it can be messier.

The shot was very loud in the morning quiet. I'd aimed for the sniper spot, the brainstem. We are taught that in a hostage situation a direct hit on the brainstem will make the threat go limp, so they will not reflexively clench their hands and pull a trigger. I missed. I'm a very, very good shot with a handgun. That means that on my best days I'm about half as good as a TV hero. The miss (live targets move or I may have rushed the shot out of fear that Gazelle would move) was about an inch from my aim point, missing the brainstem but entering the brain cavity. It was a special expanding bullet and didn't exit the skull. Gazelle started shuddering and twitching.

She was dead–CSF (cerebral spinal fluid) and blood had erupted from both ears and her nose at the shot. Her eyes were fixed. I touched her eyeball and there was no blink reflex. She was dead, dead, dead. But the brainstem is old and animal and it kept her legs jerking and her heart beating and her breath going in little raspy gasps. For about a minute. I think I watched that long because I was convincing myself that she was dead and I didn't screw up. But K was there (my excuse?) and it was hard on her to watch (oh, no, couldn't be hard on me ... I've been butchering animals since I was a kid! Bullshit. It's still hard. I just do it more efficiently and with more respect and with clearer reasons now). So I fired again, this time hitting the sniper spot, and Gazelle went limp instantly.

People don't die much different.

Is this what the writers will want?

✧✦✧✦✧

HOMEWORK:

For a fantasy world, design three weapons. The first has no other purpose than to intimidate peasants. The second is simply for killing trained and armored warriors. The third is something effective and cheap—you must outfit an army of conscripts quickly and you will have little time to train them.

Describe the weapon, how it is made, who uses it and write one scene of the weapon in use.

TO RECAP:

- Weapons are used for reasons ranging from communication to murder
- The purpose drives the way the weapon is used
- There are levels of defensive weapon use
- There are many levels of communication with self and others
- 'Fighting' is social communication and follows protocols

... 11 ...

Impact Weapons

The chapters on weapons and unarmed fighting will never be detailed enough. There are thousands of things that can be used as weapons. A friend said, "anything longer than it is wide, which includes people" but billiard balls work fine and they are exactly round. And there are lots of ways to use them.

There is a description, I believe in Robert Ardrey's "African Genesis" of a pre-human fossil with a depressed skull fracture. The depression exactly fits the humerus of an antelope. This means that people were killing people for millions of years before there were people.

Impact weapons are cheap, easy to find. They can easily be lethal, especially if they can concentrate a lot of mass in a small area, like a hammer. Or they can do serious injury, by breaking bones (axe handle) or rupturing organs (especially when thrusting a staff).

Impact weapons are the notorious 'blunt objects': the candlestick in the library; the ASP expandable baton; the *bo* staff; the quarter staff ... on and on. Even the lowly brick can be a fight-changer.

I tried to find a link to a crime that happened near where I grew up in the early nineties. I found the memorial, but not a good article. The officer was called to a domestic. He had history with the threat and evidently decided he could handle him with OC (pepper spray). The threat yanked the waist of the officer's zippered jacket up over his head, blinding him and pinning his arms (a very common move in a fight in that region) and then beat the officer to death with a piece of firewood. It took a while.

Why use a blunt object? There are a bunch of potential reasons.

You can find a serviceable one almost anywhere. A piece of kindling. A rock. A vase. Blunt weapons, even good ones, are significantly cheaper and easier to make than edged weapons. There may be concerns about killing or doing too much damage. Or your protagonist may live in a society where weapons are restricted to certain castes.

How are impact weapons used? You smack people with them. You can spend years learning nuances of *jo* staff or *bo* fighting or try to recreate quarterstaff technique from old manuals, but the basics aren't that hard. You hit people.

Now the details. Blunt weapons can be swung, thrust or flailed.

When you swing a club, the faster the impact end goes, the harder it hits. The heavier the impact end is, the harder it hits. Unfortunately, those same two factors slow you down when you need to recover after a swing, whether you hit or missed.

The best targets for a swing with a club, unlike a blade, are bones. You can bruise muscle with a club or staff and even get a 'charley horse' but for the most part an adrenalized threat won't feel the pain, won't notice immediately and it won't swell up until long after the fight is over. Smash his finger bones, however and he loses the ability to hold his sword immediately.

The other primary targets are the head (going for a concussion) and the muscles at the base/sides of the neck (especially with a sap--this is what police DT trainers call a "brachial stun").

Most blunt weapons (but not flexible weapons, like saps or flails) can also be used to thrust. This is the one really dangerous application of most staff work. Except for the brainstem/neck/head hits, which are relatively tough to get, most of the swing targets don't do lethal damage. The thrust can, and it tends to be slow and sneaky damage.

A thrust, particularly over the liver (your own right side, extending to below the lowest ribs) can cause internal bleeding. Kidneys, spleen ... lots of ugly ways to bleed. The hollow organs (bladder with some frequency, I haven't heard of a stomach rupture) can be popped, flooding the peritoneal sac with fluids and gunk that were never designed to be in there–a very, very painful death from infection. Even a strike that penetrates the abdominal muscles without damaging the organ can result in a hernia.

Flailing applies to weapons that are swung, like a medieval flail, *nunchaku* (two sticks connected by a short chain), or the *manriki-gusari* (two weights connected by a longer chain.) A simple length of chain works here as well.

They develop a hideous amount of power, have a tendency to go around shields and blocks (and that wrap-around speeds their rotation and increases damage). They are relatively cheap and easy to make, but do tend to break. All that torque works on the weapon as well.

Some specialty flail weapons with a longer chain, like the *manriki-gusari* (a weight on each end of a three-foot chain) or the *kusarigama* (up to a thirty foot chain with a weight on one end and a stabbing sickle on the other) are used to entangle the opponent as well as to bludgeon.

You can often disrupt a flexible weapon by attacking (preferably with a thrown object) the controlling hand or the chain.

Note: when you think of martial artists getting all crazy with *nunchaku,* ignore it. Those drills are for practice and coordination. When a weapon is used to fight, it is snapped out to do damage and snapped back in to guard. Swinging things around in complex patterns not only invites the person to disrupt the pattern but frequently results in hitting yourself. Controlling a flexible weapon, like a flail, takes a lot more skill than just swinging it.

It's hard to ascribe a specific mindset to blunt instruments. Chimps will throw things and almost anyone in a panic will pick up anything and swing it in a hard, repetitive, over-arm style. At the same time, a cold enforcer who wants to send a message but not leave a corpse (since it's harder to get money out of a corpse) may prefer one of the classics, like a baseball bat.

Cops use the expandable baton (ASP™) or the PR24 (side-handle baton, almost identical to the Okinawan weapon *tonfa*) for an option that can put someone down but isn't likely to be lethal. Old school cops used to carry a sap (as did gangsters who wanted to take people alive) a flat, hand-sized leather sack filled with lead shot. Fairly reliable concussion (done at the base of the skull, a quick loss of consciousness) and left less obvious marks than a baton. You can get similar effects with a plastic water bottle.

(In case it's not clear, don't try any of this stuff at home. There is nothing that can knock you out that doesn't also have the possibility of serious brain trauma.)

So there isn't a club personality. Untrained people will tend to swing it from over the shoulder down. Very predictable. Skilled people will tend to use less heavy sticks, striking at bones (particularly the hand, wrist, elbow and forearm) and thrusting at the abdomen and throat. A thrust to the liver not only hurts like hell, but can break the lower right floating ribs and the bone fragments might lacerate the organ, causing shock and death.

Skilled stick fighters will use heavier weapons on the skull or the neck, if it is safe to get that close. Part of the advantage of using a weapon is keeping the victim at a distance. Striking the head, especially from the front, often puts you in range for retaliation.

Cops, on the other hand, (though most know that clubs work best on bone and joints) are taught to strike the big muscle groups of the legs. It is the place where batons are least likely to work and that contributes to many baton incidents where the officers used a lot of blows.

Last note: sticks, including batons, canes (canes are a great potential weapon for your character and can even be taken on airplanes) and staffs can be used for locking and sweeping. So can chain weapons. It's a rare skill but can be impressive.

Knockouts

There are three basic kinds of shock. Shock is "inadequate perfusion of tissues with blood and oxygen" and it is what causes organs and people to shut down, to die. A paramedic will argue that shock is the only thing that can kill you—everything else are the mechanisms to get to that state. Hypovolemic shock means inadequate fluids in the blood stream for whatever reason (dehydration or hemorrhage). Cardiogenic shock means the heart isn't pumping hard enough; Anoxic shock means the blood is getting there, but it is out of oxygen. Neurogenic shock means the brain has done something, usually dilating the blood vessels faster than the heart can compensate (this is basically what happens when you stand up and get a 'head rush'). One of the subcategories of neurogenic shock is psychogenic–nothing went wrong in the brain but following a psychological or emotional trigger, the person faints.

If someone passed out without neurological trauma, they didn't get knocked out. They fainted.

It probably won't make much difference in writing, but people get immediately knocked out one of two ways–either the weapon overcomes the structure of bone so that it either compresses the skull or damages the skull and part of the bone and/or weapon intrudes on the brain, or the weapon (falls can do this as well, of course) moves the skull so fast that the brain slams into the inside of the skull and bounces, called a contra coup injury.

Those are the only MOI (Mechanisms of Injury) I know of that can cause enough brain trauma to turn someone off ... and most don't. Most pass out later as part of the brain swells like any other bruise and pieces get squeezed. Any injury that can cause even a temporary loss of consciousness will involve this swelling, hence the standard protocol to hold for 24 hours for observation. If the swelling is not too severe it will go down on its own. If it is, the pressure will have to be released.

(Side note: some weapons, like saps, are favored less because of the injury than because they leave so few marks–redness and swelling that entirely disappears in a few hours coupled with sometimes severe contra-coup brain injuries.)

Taking head blows even without ever getting knocked out, "microconcussions" have some very bad long term effects. I think everyone should try boxing, at least until they get over the fear of being hit, but I don't recommend anyone stay with boxing.

There are some possibilities for non-concussive unconsciousness or unconsciousness without significant brain trauma. With strangles (sleeper holds, vascular restraints ... there are a lot of euphemisms) the person goes out for twenty seconds plus, and unless there is a pre-existing condition (heart problem, arterial plaque or blood vessels weakened by excessive drug use) there are no ill-effects.

Theoretically, a strike to the side of the neck a little towards the front will induce syncope (fainting) by triggering the baroreceptors, the points where your brain reads blood pressure. I haven't seen that work, but I also haven't talked twenty people into letting me try to punch them close to the throat.

A light slap to the point acupuncturists call Gall Bladder 20 gets an immediate stun reaction. Put your hand on the back of your neck, cradling your lower skull. Now slide it to the side so that the bottom of your palm touches your ear and you are cradling one of the rear corners of your skull. Slap, lightly, in and up to that juncture of skull and neck. It's a fairly reliable shock stun (short term, no loss of consciousness but the threat freezes). The acupuncturist told me it worked because it dilated the blood vessels. If true, it would be a faint and a no-side-effects knockout. I'm skeptical because hitting directly over the brainstem and at that angle doesn't take a lot of power to do severe trauma to the very upper spine and the parts of the brain that controls stuff like breathing. Potentially lethal.

To be clear—head trauma can definitely put someone down, but rarely, if ever, without some pretty severe other effects, like nausea, dizziness, seizures, impaired vision, impaired coordination ....

Hammer wounds:
http://emedicine.medscape.com/article/1680207-overview#showall

✧✦✧✦✧

HOMEWORK:

This will jar your shoulder so please be careful: Take a baseball bat and go hit a tree. Feel it. Go into the woods or a park (I live in the Northwest, so this is easy) and pick up random sticks and hit trees. Feel how light sticks hit light; how not all are fitted to grip, how bent ones torque in your grip.

Now, take a long sock, preferably a nylon and wad up a sock in the toe. Tight enough so that it swings like a medieval flail. Now flail it around. Hit things. Try to keep it moving and still hit on command. Try not to get hit too much when it bounces back on you. Play.

TO RECAP:

- ✧ Blunt weapons are common, cheap and easily improvised
- ✧ They can be simple to learn
- ✧ Blunt weapons can be used to swing, thrust or flail. Some can be used to entangle, joint lock or takedown.
- ✧ Head trauma and knockouts have specific effects and mechanisms of injury (MOI)

... 12 ...

EDGED WEAPONS

A note from the late Carl Cestari (used with permission):

KNIFE DEFENSE MYTH

Instead of talking about a lot of B.S. concerning so-called unarmed "knife" defenses, let's reverse roles for a moment.

Let us assume the "role" of the attacker, instead of the "defender".

First, let's consider the "choice" of weapon.

A knife or any edged weapon is an "up close and personal" tool of ferocious and brutal mayhem. You have to close with your mark and physically, violently and with extreme prejudice stab, slash, and hack him to bits. It's not like a gun, which could have an element of detachment. No, a knife is about as personal, brutal and ruthless as it gets.

So what kind of "mind-set" does this entail? You are going close with your target hard and fast, using deception, surprise or simply a committed and brutal pouncing. You aro going to be determined, ruthless, brutal, ferocious, vicious, and most probably filled with hate and rage.

You are going to seize the target with abject brutality and stab, slash, hack and eviscerate with totally committed rage, ferocity and hate. OVER and OVER and OVER.

NOTHING is going to stand in your way. NOTHING! You are going to DESTROY whatever DOES attempt to thwart your murderous assault. You will attack repeatedly with ALL the strength, speed, and brutality you are capable of. And THAT will be heightened even MORE by rage and adrenalin.

You KNOW that you MUST get this over with QUICKLY. Your attack will be a frenzy of hate, rage and murderous INTENT.

You WON'T "feint" with your blade, you WON'T "spar" with your blade, you WON'T "half-step" with your blade.

You WILL attack with brutal and ruthless rage. You WILL punch, kick, bite, gouge, butt, and do ANY and EVERYTHING that will accomplish you GOAL in as ferocious a manner as inhumanly possible.

Unless YOU are killed outright, NO injury will dissuade you from KILLING your mark. In FACT, anything LESS than your death, will ONLY add MORE FUEL to YOUR FIRE. NOTHING, short of your immediate demise CAN stop you. Rage, hate, murderous intent and adrenalin are fueling you to an almost superhuman state of FRENZY and FEROCITY!

Even when your man goes down, and DOWN you are determined to put him, YOU still continue the assault. You stab and stab and stab. You kick and stomp OVER and OVER and OVER again.

You DON'T even begin to "disengage" until your "blood" lust has been quenched, and your mark taken off the count.

THAT is what REALLY happens when one human being uses a knife on another.

Face that FACT squarely. Too many are "playing" knife gymnastics without EVER even realizing what the street has in store for them. It isn't going to be pretty!

Are you REALLY preparing to DEAL with THAT? Or are you kidding yourself and others? REALITY sucks, as they say. But it is what it is!

Sobering? Carl had a way with words.

When Carl was writing, he was trying to wake up martial artists on the subject of defense. The difference between practicing against a training partner and someone trying to kill you is huge.

The knife-wielder isn't always emotional. Knives work just as well with a detached mindset. There is still (except in sentry-removal style assassinations) this kind of fast, hard, implacable onslaught ... but it can be cold.

This is one thing to be careful of: people who write fight scenes sometimes make the character sound like a chess master, with moves and countermoves.

A killer kills. He allows no countermoves. That mindset can be cold or hot, but it is there.

Here's the deal about knives: using a knife is more of an emotional skill than a physical one. If you ever use a blade you will feel the different layers of tissue. You might feel the signs of life, the heartbeat, the muscles contracting in pain, transmitted right up your blade. You will feel stuff gush over you and you will smell it, the coppery blood and sharp, stomach-acid polluted shit smell of open guts. You will be close enough to look in the eyes and see the intelligence and life fading from them. If you ever see that fade, you will probably come to believe in a soul.

And some will revel in it. Killing with a knife is profound. Profoundly sobering and sometimes, for some people, profoundly empowering and liberating. You have to decide for yourself if that emotional response is automatically evil.

If I could assign homework for you I would ask every one of you to find a local farmer and help out at slaughtering time. To wield the knife yourself. To take the life of a big, human-sized animal and watch and feel it die. To know that things rarely die easily.

There is a lot of technical stuff with blades. I'm going to start with knives. Here's the big shocker. Knives are not used to win fights. Knives are used to kill people. You get as close as you can and you stab (usually) or cut. A lot. Often holding an arm or the head so that the victim can't move.

Do knife duels happen? Maybe. But one of the more qualified people I know once said, "I'd rather be unarmed against a knife, because knife on knife I know there are two crazy stupid people in the room." Or, in the immortal words of anonymous: "There is one thing worse than coming in second in a knife fight. Tying for first." People smart and vicious enough to use a knife tend to be too smart to use them stupidly, and that includes dueling. The knife-on-knife training is just bullshit macho fantasizing (my opinion, of course. Feel free to disregard.)

With a knife, you can thrust or slash. The thrust is to get to organs. Heart, liver, kidneys, bowels, bladder, stomach. There are some specialized thrusts–behind the collarbone to get to the ascending aorta is a classic assassination. Thrust behind the trachea and then pushed out through the front of the neck used to be taught. Into the femoral artery/nerve. Through the pelvic gap (Directly at the bottom of the crotch you can stab upward through the soft spot. Hits the bowel and large intestines. Ugly way to die. Not quick.)

Slashes are aimed at muscle. If you can sever a muscle completely, that limb is half useless. People in medieval times regularly survived slashes, which led to the belief that thrusts were more dangerous. It was definitely true before antibiotics. I'm not sure today. Most of the survivors I know were slashed and most of those that died had thrust wounds, but a lot had both.

In either case, slash or thrust, bone near the surface is a bad target.

A lot of people don't notice any pain from a knife assault. Several have said after being stabbed repeatedly that they thought they were being punched. A friend didn't know he was stabbed until he noticed one of his sneakers was full of fluid. He thought he stepped in a puddle, but it was his own blood filling his shoe. Seeing your own blood and realizing it is yours tends to make most people panic. The fear turning into a righteous rage "I will make this bastard pay!" seems to be the survival mindset with the best track record (See Sanford Strong's "Strong on Defense").

Swords. I have a fair amount of training in swords but have only ever used them to kill goats. I've been trying in these chapters to stick with stuff that I know and avoid speculation. You can get speculation for free in other places. So some observations:

✧ Fencing has vastly changed how we think about swordfighting. With the advent of guns, the advances in metallurgy and the decline in armor, the small swords and rapiers changed the fighting world. For the first time the same tool could be used for offense and defense without being irreparably damaged.

✧ Specifically, up until the advent of fencing, you tried to avoid blocking with your sword. It was better than dying, but if a heavy sword hit another heavy sword, both would be too damaged to be reliable.

✧ Older European weapons were balanced to cut, not to defend. They feel completely different than a modern replica.

✧ In Europe especially, defense was based on the shield and armor.

✧ In older Japanese systems, the same was true, but never having developed the shield, defense relied on continuous movement and quick killing.

✧ Older Japanese systems look and feel very different from systems that were influenced by kendo.

✧ Dueling systems (post-kendo and post-fencing) emphasize a balanced offense and defense and layered strategy.

✧ Pre-kendo/fencing systems were simpler, more brutal and emphasized closing and cutting

✧ These older styles were also much more comfortable with using body crashing, sweeps, strikes and environmental opportunities than later styles.

✧ The few times I have played with armor it has been hard to slash through and disturbingly easy to thrust through (but I've never tried it with metal plate)

✧ A good sword is a three-foot razor blade. It doesn't take any power. While butchering the goats without adding any strength, just letting the blade's weight fall from my shoulder it went through eighteen inches of spine–eighteen inches of bone–and I never felt any resistance.

✧ Stiff or set targets are easier to cut than limp targets.

✧ Swords are not just for cutting. They are often heavy enough to break bones and some can shear through bones.

✧ I've played with some old Filipino weapons. I believe that the reason they emphasize flowing draw cuts so much is because the handles were attached so poorly that a heavy stroke would have snapped the hilt off.

✧ Which means that technology drives technique: the reason Japanese blades are curved is because of the folding process. Japanese swords were straight before that was introduced. The Vikings were able to figure out how to do something similar with a straight weapon, but never (as far as I know) discovered differential tempering.

- Toughness refers to durability, the ability to take a beating. Hardness refers to how hard something is to scratch. High hardness holds a better edge, but tends to be brittle (shatters or chips) while tough swords don't break (but some bend) tough swords tend to dull quickly.
- Hardening, annealing and tempering are the combined art form of trying to find the right balance of toughness and hardness.
- The longer a sword, the harder it is to get these good qualities evenly along the whole length without weak spots. That is why they were so expensive and a good, tested sword was so prized.
- If used against flesh, you can sacrifice a lot of toughness. Less so against armor.

Infighting With a Sword. A lot of weapons, particularly swords, can be used infighting. Very few train it, but it is devastating. Infighting with a sword is easier to show than to write about. Let's give it a shot.

Hacking is swinging a blade to hit the target at 90 degrees. Slashing swings the weapon in a similar way, but with the weapon angled back from the swing so that slightly more of the blade gets drawn through the wound channel. A draw cut uses either of these mechanics and then, on impact, you draw your hands closer to your own center to pull the blade through the wound. A press cut does the slash or hack dynamic and on impact the hands push out, pushing the blade through the wound channel. You could play with these geometries on a piece of Hunter's Sausage or dry pepperoni to see the effects.

Infighting with a sword depends a lot on an ability to close and to cut angles and is done almost all with the legs and waist. Imagine a katana coming straight down at your head. A modern, dueling system fencer would dodge back, dodge to the side or parry the weapon to one side and counter-attack. The infighting solution, which is common to battlefield styles (and very different from dueling) is to charge, angled slightly off from his center. Where a dueling system tends to lead with the point, an in fighting system tends to lead with the hilt.

For the downward slash, if my timing (as an infighter) is poor, his slash will connect with my sword, which is angled back and down, hands/hilt in front, above and to one side, tip trailing over my shoulder. My weapon glides his weapon. If he can't control his slash and recover, I'll be behind him.

If my timing as an infighter is decent, a similar motion will happen but it will be his arms, not his blade that impact and slide on my weapon. I'll be behind an armless man.

If my timing is good, I'll be so far inside the range of his slash that my edge will go into his torso or armpit (if I know I'm faster, I may have dropped my blade lower to belly level). I lever the blade against his body and step away with a twist, which gives draw cut mechanics plus the effect of pressing directly on the back of the blade. You know when you cut frozen meat how you push on the back of the blade with your hands? Infighters wind up doing that a lot but often with their own hips or shoulders.

It has a lot of the mechanics of rugby, because there is a lot of rush and body impact. Some elements of wrestling, because you find that there are ways to control the threat's elbows with your shoulders. It integrates with some sweeps, throws and locks (battlefield era systems weren't big on punching and kicking, since they were ineffective against armor. Throws and locks work just fine on armor, though).

The battlefield/infighting was based on the idea that one of you was going to be dead in the next instant. Using dueling techniques on a battlefield could easily end with someone else sticking a spear in your side or back. That made continuous movement critically important. Staying really close to the enemy helped shield you from his friends. It's another example of the huge difference even in a fight between fighting and killing.

Spears, axes and other cool things. The spear, not the sword, was the primary weapon on the battlefield before firearms. It had superior reach; thrusts were generally more effective against armor than slashes; and spears were far cheaper to make than swords. Use in battle required team planning. Used solo for dueling, the spear could become quite acrobatic and there would be opportunities to use the butt and shaft. If you see a staff form (kata) with a lot of thrusts, it often descended from a spear form.

Spears varied in length, from pikes that could be over twelve feet to the short stabbing spears of the Zulu, the assegai. The longer weapons were used in formation, turning the whole unit into a lethal porcupine. The shorter ones were individual weapons—even in well-coordinated mass battle, a Zulu warrior wanted to make a name.

There have been a lot of spear-based and combination weapons, usually trying to add slashing versatility (an edge, either like an axe or a short sword) armor piercing (putting a spike at 90 degrees to the haft) or disarming/dismounting abilities (hooks).

Common to swords, axes and spears—big swings make you vulnerable to closing attacks. A good fighter would attempt to rush inside the arc of the swing. That gave some short weapons an advantage and made even swinging weapons, like an axe, something that you held in a thrust position to defend (unless you were using it with a shield.)

Axes have a lot of the advantages of an impact weapon, like a mace. They put a fearsome amount of force on a small surface area. I have not used an axe against armor myself, but have read that it crushes through. They are also extremely useful tools, cheap to make and maintain (notice that expense comes up a lot in weapon descriptions- that's important) and versatile. Even big axes can be thrown and they can be used to hook over shields and yank them out of the way (an arm strapped to the shield will result in the whole body spinning, probably exposing the back) and can sweep legs. Some of the head configurations increase the versatility with a thrusting spike on top and an armor-piercing spike on the back.

A bayonet allows a musket or rifle to be converted to a spear. Remember that the spear was the superior weapon on battlefields. The bayonet/musket combination played a large part in making pikemen obsolete.

Improvised weapons. Almost anything can be used as a weapon BUT not all of these weapons are actually an improvement on no weapons at all, unless they give confidence. And confidence based on inferior stuff is really close to superstition. For a little more on found weapons, see Chapter 15 on concealed weapons.

WARNING: The following links can be graphic.

These are the pictures I use to show non-serious knife wounds:

http://www.dlsports.com/knife_dangers.html

A cut throat (at autopsy, cleaned up):

http://www.pathguy.com/~tdemark/0050.htm

Defensive wounds:

http://library.med.utah.edu/WebPath/FORHTML/FOR026.html

More graphic stuff. Machete wounds.

http://www.documentingreality.com/forum/f149/machete-wound-42126/

This website is sick enough I don't want to endorse it in any way... but it does have some graphic pictures of Brazilian machete victims.

http://www.bestgore.com/murder/brutal-machete-attack-brazil/attachment/man-brutally-hacked-machete-brazil-02/

Quick note about the graphics. My goal is not to make you sick. If your character uses a sword, if she has ever had to take a life with a blade or chooses to go into that profession, this is something she had to get over. She may have been raised with it, just as adults in Rwanda now were raised with rafts of chopped up humans drifting down the river.

In fiction and movies we pretty it up, but there is nothing pretty about this. It is fear and horror, and it is also infinitely empowering and it can be addictive. If your heroine can walk in this world she can handle things with a self-possessed precision that others can't really understand. And for all the horror of battle, there can be a weird and powerful joy in it, too. Nothing else takes everything you have–your body, mind and soul–and puts it all out there in one big gamble for everything.

Free solo climbing touches that, and so does heavy weather solo sailing. Many things that require your complete mind and body where you face death completely alone. But only battle pits you against another person doing the same thing. You go to a place inside yourself where you are a perfect animal. And, with experience, you become a perfect *human* animal. None of the social hang-ups that an alligator or a raptor can't afford and, simultaneously, the judgment and intelligence of a human.

An article I wrote for a friend's blog:

http://thestrikingpost.blogspot.com/2009/12/enter-dragon.html

Enter the Dragon 23December2009

You have three minds. Depending on how you look at it, you may have more and in the end you only have one brain ... but for our purposes you have three.

Your human mind is thoughtful and aware, reasonable if not always purely logical. You are not in this mode nearly as often as you think you are. When you are, you weigh the costs and do the right thing regardless. You live up to your highest ideals.

Your animal mind, your lizard brain, is older. It is concerned with you as a physical animal – it deals with danger and hunger and movement. When you are in your animal mind, you move like an animal, like an athlete. It is pure. It can be vicious and it is ruthless. It is older than human concerns like justice or mercy ...

In the middle is your monkey mind. We evolved from social primates – animals that lived in tight groups completely dependent on the group for survival. Our interdependence drove an evolution toward social skills and social strategies to deal with conflict. Your monkey mind is concerned, always and obsessively, with what other people will think about you.

You are rarely in just your lizard mind. When absolute terror kicks in and you break out of fight-flight-freeze and just act, it is an animal thing. Sometimes a few feel it when they have trained for a long time and hit the zone, a mushin where they can act with absolute grace and without conscious thought. Many, today, only hit this zone playing video games, where they have trained to reflex on the controls and can play without registering what exactly they are pretending to do or caring who might see.

It is just as rare to be in your human mind. When you have done the right thing even though people you care about will be angry; when you have stood by the facts even though everyone said it was wrong .... When Galileo recanted the truth out of fear of the church, he gave up his human mind and did what a monkey would do.

As much as we are ever just in one of these minds, it is the monkey. Obsessed with the tribe, with others: Angsting over how other people really feel, worrying whether someone really likes you, following celebrity gossip (on what world is it important who Angelina and Brad even are?) concerns about whether you blend in enough or stand out too much... This is monkey stuff. The insecurity of an animal who needs a community because it knows it is too weak to survive in the wild on its own.

The monkey mind interacts with the other two obsessively. When a gunshot goes off and people start looking around to see what other people are doing, that's the monkey mind. When you don't duck or hit the dirt because you are afraid of what people will think, that's the monkey mind. And when your first instinct is to slam the door in a stranger's face and you don't because 'that would be rude' that is the monkey mind. In all of those cases, people have died or been raped because they were worried about what others would think.

It interferes with the human mind as well. Writers struggle constantly with the 'inner critic' – the voice constantly whispering to them to give up, that they aren't good enough, don't know enough. The monkey mind is just as concerned with being too special, too successful, as it is with being rude or looking silly. Being too good can also push you out of the tribe. Monkeys die if they are alone.

Same with every incident of hiding the truth or ass-covering or sucking up: the monkey wants to belong, and that need to belong is more important than the truth or, often, even survival.

And that is huge, because the monkey mind doesn't distinguish between physical death and humiliation or isolation. Any profound change in you, even learning a new skill, might terrify the monkey. It sees change as what some call "ego death". Your monkey mind constantly fights to keep you in your comfort zone, where nothing changes. No matter how much that comfort zone sucks to your human mind (when you don't live up to your potential; when you feel the shame of taking the easy way instead of the right way) or your lizard mind (and so people die rather than take the chance that fighting might be rude or running might seem cowardly). Your own monkey brain will fight you if what you need to do to survive might impact social standing.

This impacts martial artists profoundly. When training becomes a hierarchical series of ritual it recreates the monkey tribe. Socially secure, everyone knows their places and what to do ... but that's not really what martial arts is about. Is it?

When students are afraid to ask why or how something works, or when students continue to practice flawed technique because even though they can't make it work it looks right, then the monkey has won.

Martial arts should be about the human mind and the lizard mind. Developing an ethical understanding of force and violence and educating and training an animal body to new levels of efficiency. Martial arts should be, fundamentally, about empowering students.

When the training caters to the monkey mind, it robs the students of power. It cripples students who may, some day, need to do the right thing (human brain) with absolute efficiency (lizard brain) to survive. The monkey has no place here.

When you silence the chattering monkey (meditation works for some, simply recognizing it works for others) and get the human mind and lizard brain to work together, you have something new. Something that uses the human abilities and virtues– thoughtfulness, righteousness, planning, goal setting and decision making– with the deep abilities of the ancient lizard– efficiency, ruthlessness and absolute focus.

Enter the Dragon.

✧✦✧✦✧

HOMEWORK:

I love this one. I've done it in the past to get a surprise reaction out of my students. You won't get the surprise, but it can be illuminating. You'll need a knife. A heavy, sharp kitchen knife will work (a light steak knife probably won't, but that might be good to try, too). A can of warm, shaken up soda. Not diet. You want maximum stickiness and mess. A big steak. Some old clothes. Be sure to wear old clothes.

Take the can and roll it up in the steak. Then take the can and steak and roll it up in a t-shirt. Tie it with a string. Give it one more shake. Hang it up outside by a string. Wear old clothes. Slash and stab it. Feel the gush.

TO RECAP:

- Knife is more of an emotional skill than a physical one
- Knives are not used to win fights. They are used to kill people.
- Thrust, hack, slash, draw cut, press cut, trapping with quillons, pummeling
- Pre-fencing sword work was very different than later styles
- Swords, and many other weapons can be used infighting
- Spears were the primary weapon on early battlefields
- Axes are versatile and cheap
- Blade wounds can be horrific

... 13 ...

FIREARMS

There is so much going on with firearms and so many details that I am going to skip and gloss over a huge amount. Here's the deal: if your character is going to use a specific weapon, go to a range, rent one and shoot it. Make notes so that you don't make really stupid mistakes, like putting a safety or a silencer on a revolver (or having a detective pick up brass from a revolver).

If your character is a professional, she will know her weapons. They keep her alive. She doesn't need to know about all weapons, but she will certainly know about hers.

To demystify things a lot: a gun is a nifty machine that throws a rock in a straight line. Sure, the rock is usually made of lead and comes in a number of configurations and goes really fast ... but the idea is dead simple.

An excellent source for little details, like whether you can shoot a lock off, is the Box O' Truth. http://www.theboxotruth.com/

First breakdown:

Handguns are small, portable and concealable. They don't have a huge amount of power, range or accuracy. That's a balancing act–if you ever need a gun, you want a rifle or shotgun, but handguns are quicker to get into play and you can take them almost anywhere.

A revolver has a cylinder. When you pull the hammer back (required on a single-action pistol) it rotates the cylinder so a fresh bullet is under the hammer. You pull the trigger and the hammer falls. A double-action revolver, like most modern ones, the trigger pulls the hammer back, rotates the cylinder and lets the hammer fall. With a DA, you *can* cock the hammer separately and it makes for a shorter, smoother trigger pull (and hence more accuracy) when you fire, but just squeezing the trigger is faster. Common calibers are .357, .38, .45 long colt, .44 magnum.

A semi-auto has a magazine, usually jammed into the butt of the gun. Each time a bullet is fired the expanding gasses push the slide back, kick out the old casing and slam the next round in the magazine into the chamber. A semi can shoot as fast as you can pull the trigger. A single action semi, like a colt 45 requires the hammer to be pulled back on the first shot (pulling the slide back and releasing to load one in the chamber also cocks the hammer.) After the first shot, the action cocks the hammer. In a double-action semi, the trigger can cock the first round. Common calibers are .45 APC; 9mm; .40; 10mm. There are also .357 and .44mag semi rounds but they are not compatible with revolvers of the same caliber. There are both revolvers and semis chambered for the small .22 round.

Rifles are shoulder-fired weapons. They have threading in the barrel to spin the bullet and make it more accurate. They are more accurate than handguns, and hit harder.

There are a variety of *actions*. Actions are how the bullets get into the chamber. Examples are semi-automatic, automatic (as long as the trigger is held down the weapon keeps chambering and firing) bolt action, lever action and pump (rarely pumps–they are believed by some people to be unsafe in center-fire rifles.)

There are many types of *sights*. Scopes; variable power scopes; night-vision scopes; thermal scopes; open sights (a vee notch in the back and a post up front) sometimes called iron sights; peep sights (a circle in the back like a peep hole and a post in front, common in military weapons) laser sights (an after-market addition that shoots a laser along the barrel. The bullet will hit about where you see the dot. Available for handguns as well). AimPoints and Eotech sights look like a short scope but show a red dot on the target point. One of the main advantages is that you don't have to be exactly aligned with the weapon to shoot accurately.

There are a huge variety of calibers. Rifles range from .22 used mostly for training, plinking at bottles and cans or shooting squirrels and rabbits all the way up to elephant guns and .50 sniper rifles. Modern sniper rifles in Afghanistan have hit targets at over 1.5 miles.

Shotguns are big-bore weapons with smooth bores (which differentiates them from rifles). With the exception of the .410, shotguns are sized by gauge. 12ga is the biggest common shotgun today, but in the past 10, 8 and 4ga were built and used. The 4ga must have been like a cannon. Gauge is a weird number. It is defined as the number of spherical shot you could make of the same size as the barrel from a pound of lead ... so a 4ga ball would weigh four ounces.

Shotguns don't shoot single balls today. The most common rounds are shotshells and slugs. A shotshell has a specific number of pellets inside. In buckshot, the pellets are about the same diameter as a .30 caliber bullet. In dove shot, about the size of a BB. The larger pellets travel farther and hit harder than the smaller pellets.

A slug is a single big round coming out of a shotgun. It will blow a big hole, roughly the diameter of the barrel of the weapon. Most slugs are 'rifled' meaning that there are grooves in the side that compensate for the lack of grooves in a shotgun's barrel. Rifling causes the slug to spin and increases accuracy.

One of the cool things about shotguns is that they are extremely versatile. Rounds have been made for them to pierce armor; to cause fires; to deliver chemical munitions, like pepper-spray; to not harm (rubber bullets and baton rounds); to shatter locks and, recently, as grenades.

Machine guns are rifles that fire continuously as long as the as the trigger is held down. Some are reliable, some are not. Most have problems under continuous fire in that the barrels get too hot to touch and may even bend. Most heavy machine guns today are belt-fed, meaning that rounds are linked by little bits of metal and feed through the action with the cases and the links being ejected.

Assault rifles (like the M-4, M-16 and AK-47) are designed to be light weapons that are easy to carry. They tend to use smaller caliber ammunition than hunting rifles or what used to be called "Main Battle

Rifles" because ammo weighs a lot. Most are select fire, which means that they can either be fired semi-auto or, with the flip of a switch, set to full auto (the M-4 and some of the later M-16 A-2's have a 'burst' setting that fires three rounds instead of a full auto).

Some are accurate (like the M-4), some are durable (like the AK).

Submachine guns (SMGs) are basically pistol-caliber weapons with slightly longer barrels, more accuracy; much greater magazine capacity and usually the option to select fire between single shot and full auto. They are the preferred weapons of many entry teams and groups that specialize in close quarters hostage rescue.

Caliber is done in millimeter diameter of the bullet, e.g. 9mm; percentage of an inch, designated by "cal" e.g. .45 cal is 45/100 of an inch across. Sort of. .357 and .38 caliber are actually both .38, but a .357 has more powder. So you can fire .38 rounds from a .357 weapon, but if you try to do it the other way around, the weapon may be damaged or even explode.

Wounds. Don't go overboard with handgun wounds. Physically, a .45 bullet does about as much damage as a half-inch stick being pushed through you. It's not always that simple, of course. The bullet is going through pretty fast. The bullet hits a bone and fragments of bone can go slicing away in different directions. Bullets often follow the path of least resistance and sometimes go between tissues instead of penetrating.

Some bullets are designed or modified in an attempt to do more damage. The "Glaser safety slug" is described as 'frangible' and the bullet breaks into small pieces on impact. A 'dum dum' is the idea that if you cut a cross in the top of the bullet it will expand and make a bigger wound channel. A hollow point has a scoop in the tip of the bullet designed to help the bullet deform. A wadcutter is flat across the top and originally designed for target shooting—the clean holes it punches in paper are easy to see. Wadcutters in flesh create wound channels that don't close by themselves and bleed profusely. The flat tip means that they do not feed well at all in semi-automatic or automatic weapons. Some new rounds are designed to 'star' when they hit flesh and the soft lead core will force a split outer jacket into a jagged star that lacerates tissue in a bigger wound channel. Armor piercing rounds, the so-called 'cop killers,' are designed to punch through armor. They also have a tendency to punch through the body without deforming or deflecting, and so do slightly less damage than a regular bullet. Jacketed bullets have a layer of harder metal, like copper, around the lead bullet. It makes for a cleaner hole and also feeds better.

Note I said *designed* in an *attempt* to do more damage. Actual results from the field are less positive. When I have called the manufacturer to ask why an expanding 'star' bullet didn't expand they said it probably got clothing stuck in the nose and didn't expand. Well, duh. People wear clothes.

The other factor in bullet damage is speed. Gun nuts argue about this ad nauseam: for some reason a bullet going over about 2300 feet per second does a lot more damage than one going slower. No normal handgun, by the way, gets to anywhere near that speed.

People don't fall over or get knocked back or knocked through the air by the impact of a bullet. Many don't notice it and quite a few that feel the impact never even consider that they were shot.

Sometimes those that know they were shot curl up and die from wounds that aren't physically lethal. A lot of gunfighting, any fighting really, is psychological.

Shots to the pelvis and stomach can be excruciatingly painful. The chest is rarely that painful. Bones can be broken. People bleed.

Except for a shot to the head, specifically the brainstem, people don't die quickly.

Gunfights are fast, dynamic affairs. They go bad quickly.

This is an analysis of a local shooting, all identifying details removed.

A teenage girl had called in to 911 reporting that there was a man in her house, that she had locked herself in the upstairs bedroom and she believed he might have already killed her grandmother.

Three officers from two agencies were the first on the scene. The grandmother was lying in a pool of blood outside the house, dead. The officers entered to clear the house and rescue the girl.

They entered, weapons out, and started to clear the building. In the first room, they saw the threat, on his knees, in the kitchen to their flank with a knife. They ordered him to drop the knife. He screamed, leapt up and charged.

Analysis of an Officer-Involved Shooting

3 Officers

1 Threat with knife, charging

Distance: 10' closing to 5' from the nearest officer (C); maximum of 15' from farthest officer (A) at start of incident, but A did not fire until threat was closer

Officer A armed with a 9mm estimated firing 1-2 shots.

Officer B armed with a 9mm estimated firing 5-6 shots.

Officer C armed with a .45 estimated firing 3-4 shots

Criminalists (what these agencies call their Crime Scene Investigators, CSI) found eight (8) 9mm shell casings and four (4) .45 caliber shell casings. This adds to twelve, but in the criminalist report they say that thirteen cases total were found.

The officers entered the building with weapons drawn. The suspect was sitting on the floor through a doorway on their right. He was ordered to show his hands and drop the knife. He charged, screaming, weapon extended.

Officer C, the closest, opened fire while attempting to step back and create distance.

Officer B fired his first shot through the wall. He says he did not see the knife at first and fired because hearing another officer fire was sufficient indicator that it was a deadly force situation. As he explained his reasoning, it appears to be a clear example of time dilation- he remembers more conscious thought than there was time for.

Officer A distinctly remembers his point of aim as center mass between the hip and the armpit. This is the bullet that probably struck the threat in the side of the head, the only shot that clearly came from the side, which is where A was positioned.

Of the twelve or thirteen rounds fired, there were seven hits, two of which were deemed fatal by the medical examiner. In two of these the bullet was recovered.

One bullet entered the side of the head (9mm)

One bullet hit the center of the neck and did some damage to the spine

One bullet entered the right side of the chest and would have proved fatal (9mm)

One bullet hit the right upper arm/shoulder

One bullet grazed the left hip/thigh

One bullet hit the left groin/lower abdomen

One bullet hit just above the left knee

All officers have been trained to fire center mass. Weapons were out and in hand. Ranges were approximately ten feet or less.

These were guys who were good shots at the range. They were responding to a call, a teenager who thought that someone was in her house. Her grandmother had already been stabbed to death outside.

It is not like shooting at the range.

Geeks. Everything has geeks. There are computer geeks and martial arts geeks and tactical geeks and definitely gun geeks. Getting really upset or picky about word choice to me is a sign of a geek, and geeks are rarely operators. So some people will get excited that a revolver isn't a pistol (but semis and flintlocks are)... it's a geek game. A pistol in standard usage is any firearm designed to be held and fired by one hand (despite the fact that most times you shoot two-handed.) In geek terms, a pistol only applies if the breech (where the bullet goes in) and the barrel are contiguous. Whatever. The same kind of issue comes up in 'magazine' and 'clip'. The only people likely to care are geeks (but stick with magazine).

Don't use this as an excuse for error of fact. 'Revolver' for instance is specific because it is a description of the action. If you make the mistake of calling a .45 semi-automatic a revolver, it's roughly equivalent to someone talking about typing a manuscript on a 'manual' laptop.

The 'hydrostatic shock' thing. I already mentioned that for some reason, bullets above about 2100-2300 fps (feet per second) do a lot more damage than slower rounds even when they don't break up. 'Cavitation' is one of the theories- that is the idea that a wave of air, like a sonic boom follows the bullet and causes the tissues to explode away from the wound channel. Hydrostatic shock is another theory, that basically kinetic energy travels through the liquids in the body and can cause damage distant from the wound channel. So it's not a myth, per se (though hand gun calibers don't get to the speed where it happens) but it is one of the theories to explain an interesting fact about terminal wound ballistics.

One more note on wound ballistics. Outside of war, rifle (high velocity) wounds are extremely rare. Most of what ER docs and coroners deal with are handgun wounds. When it is a rifle, often it was used at very close range (ala suicide) and the muzzle flash can do more damage than the bullet. Makes it hard to figure out cavitation vs. hydrostatic. It also allows for a lot of 'twilight zone' effects with rifles.

A very experienced coroner said that he had no problem with the so called 'magic bullet' in the JFK assassination because the people questioning it were comparing the behavior to low velocity (handgun) ballistics and, simply, outside of war, not enough people are shot in the head with rifles to have any feel for what can happen ... and in a war, medical personnel are too busy for that kind of forensic research.

Soft Body Armor (SBA). Soft body armor are the "bullet resistant vests" currently issued to most officers.

Details: My first couple of sets had white inserts, the later had blue. The inserts are the Kevlar part, the armor. They blue ones feel like slick plastic, the white ones felt like stiff cloth--you could see the weave. They have Velcro circles at the very top where they go up the shoulders.

The inserts are slipped inside a carrier that was black. The top of the carrier had matching Velcro circles on the inside to keep the actual Kevlar from slipping. The carrier was in two pieces, adjusted with Velcro straps at the top for length/height and Velcro on elastic at the side for width. A well-fitted vest went down to just above your belt buckle, had a slight v-neck and the layers would over-lap slightly on your lower ribs.

The armpits have no protection at all and that is one of the primary reasons that very few police agencies teach the Weaver stance anymore. The carrier has an extra pocket for the 'trauma plate,' which is just another very thin piece of Kevlar that fits in the pocket over your heart. Many officers keep a laminated card in the trauma plate pocket with blood type, allergies and next-of-kin information. There are cloth panels hanging from the front and back so that you can tuck them into your pants and keep the vest from shifting.

Can't speak for everybody, but mine smells like cat piss when I've been sweating in it for eight or twelve hours. It's not super heavy or that hot, but you definitely notice it and it doesn't breathe. You can wash the carrier like any other Velcro and elastic clothing. It washes fine but it's a mess when it comes out of the dryer. The panels can be sprayed with Windex and wiped off (or water, I guess). A lot of guys kept Febreeze in their lockers.

The stuff degrades over time and has an official shelf life of five years.

The article "The Selection and Testing of Soft Body Armor" by David S. Katz has more detail than most street cops know about ballistic vest failures and ratings. It is available with a quick on-line search.

Theoretically, the vests are rated to stop:

I	.22, .25, and .32 caliber handguns, .38 Special lead round-nose
II-A	.38 Special high-velocity, .45s, low-velocity .357 Magnum & 9-mm, .22 rifles
II	Higher velocity .357 Magnum and 9-mm
III-A ...	.44 Magnum and submachine gun 9-mm
III	High-power rifle: 5.56mm, 7.62 mm FMJ, .30 carbine, .30-06 pointed soft point, 12-gauge rifled slug
IV	Armor-piercing rifle bullet, .30 caliber (1 shot only).

I was issued a III-A, most times.

If the vest doesn't fit quite right you can almost strangle sitting in a car. It really slows down any cross-body reach, like undoing your seat belt. And thought it gives a little protection from punches it really hampers your own grappling skills.

The current military armor is either horrible or really good. It will stop even rifle bullets if they hit the plates straight on (which could then ricochet of course, maybe up under your helmet. That's life in the big city). But those plates are inch-thick ceramic. It's roughly the equivalent of wearing a brick shirt. It is heavy, over thirty pounds. And hot. Bulky, it is hard to run in and you have to be very careful in placing your pouches on it. My left shoulder has problems and I had to get creative placing my magazine holders so that I could get them out.

The stories are kind of dry, lacking in the detail that would be most useful to an author, but the Kevlar survivor's club might have some hooks you can use.

http://iacp.dupont.com/SurvivorClub/Search?

I have seen bad tactics taught based on the idea the vest would save you. That's gambling. Pros use their armor, they don't rely on their armor. Yet there is also an element of talisman to a lot of people and officers, both regarding equipment and training. People think that the vest will protect them and then don't think about what it might save them from. People believe that they have earned a black belt and can now survive a fight, without ever once looking at what a real fight is like and whether it matches their skills. People seem to believe that merely owning a gun will somehow, magically, keep them safe.

I'd say most people carry guns and even use them like amulets-- "As long as I have a gun, I'll be okay, I can handle it." Many cannot pull the trigger. That said, a few hours of training with a rifle allows a peasant to defeat a warrior who has trained all his life with a sword. That advance in technology made the concept of equal rights possible.

✧✦✧✦✧

HOMEWORK

Go to a range, ideally with a friend who knows what to do. If not, definitely take a handgun safety course first. But go to a range and fire a weapon. Extra credit if you take a good handgun course.

TO RECAP:

- ✧ Guns are nifty machines that throw a rock in a straight line
- ✧ Handguns, rifles, shotguns, assault rifles, machine guns, submachine guns
- ✧ Actions, sights, calibers and gauges, bullet configurations
- ✧ Gunfighting is different than range training
- ✧ Geeks exist. They get upset about terminology. Don't sweat it.
- ✧ SBA (Soft Body Armor) is the modern standard for protection

... 14 ...

LESS LETHAL WEAPONS

Less-lethal weapons are a designation that has come to the fore in the last decade or so. In a lot of ways, the holy grail of law enforcement is a tool that would put a violent person down at least as reliably as a handgun, but without permanent injury.

Chemicals: two versions of mace (tear gas) are CN and CS. Users translate that as "Cry Now" and "Cry Sooner". They are mucous membrane irritants, eye irritants and cause your skin to burn, especially if you are sweaty. It seems to react with water (sweat) and so affects people who fear it more than people who don't. It is relatively safe, though some people do have breathing problems.

More importantly, most people can fight through it, especially if they have been exposed before. Exposure to tear gas is a staple of army basic training. I assume the other branches do it as well.

CS and CN have a sharp smell and make your eyes really burn. It makes your nose run, too, and soldiers leaving the gas house with huge trails of snot hanging down their chest, hunched over and wheezing is a common sight.

The CS and CN are really crystals and if gear worn when exposed isn't properly washed, it will gas off later when it does get wet. Makes putting on a used gas mask (called a 'pro-mask' for protective mask) and then sweating really interesting.

OC, which stands for Oleoresin Capsicum, is what cops call pepperspray. OC is believed to be safer than the military tear gasses. It is a food by-product. It feels about like you would expect crushed hot peppers rubbed in your eyes would feel like. Which means it hurts and your nose runs and the skin it touches feels like a sunburn. It doesn't affect breathing, but many people feel like they can't breathe (if someone is screaming that they are suffocating, their air flow is fine.)

Pepper spray comes in different concentrations and what they call Scoville Heat Units or SHU. It is supposed to be a measure of how painful a particular batch is. It's actually kind of arbitrary. Same with concentration. Usually a 10% spray feels hotter than a 5%, but not always.

What does matter is the delivery system. OC comes in pressurized canisters of different sizes. Most cops carry a 4 oz bottle, but they came in larger "party canisters'.

Some canisters are 'stream' which squirts liquid OC. Easy to aim, penetrates the eyes quickly.

Aerosols penetrate the fastest and get into the mouth and nose. In my opinion, aerosol OC sucks the worst BUT it is also the one most likely to get blown off course by the wind and always affects everyone in the area, including the person using it.

Foam is an attempt to keep it from gassing off and affecting the officer using it. It hits and looks like creamed carrots. It does gas off and will affect the user as well, but not for a while. Unfortunately, it also tends to take a bit to affect the person it is used on.

Some OC details:

OC is an oil and if you use too much it will make everything slippery. Trying to handcuff a guy dosed in OC can be like a greased-pig contest where the grease burns your skin.

Air and water wash it off. It usually takes about a half hour for the burn to get down to a decent level. If you drive with your car windows rolled up, though, the concentration will increase in your car.

It doesn't affect everybody. I've watched inmates wipe the foam from their faces and eat it or try to throw it back at us. Some didn't even shut their eyes.

Hot water opens your pores and reactivates the residue. In other words, a hot shower after an OC incident, especially when the water flows over your sensitive parts, can be an interesting experience.

The Taser®. First of all, the Taser has nothing in common with the hand-held shockers usually called tasers on TV shows. The real taser is a device shaped roughly like a pistol that uses compressed air to shoot two barbs up to thirty-five feet (the civilian version has a range of fifteen feet). The two barbs leave the weapon, one in a straight line and the other at a slight downward angle. Each barb is attached to a thin, plastic-coated wire.

When the barbs hit, an electric shock goes down the wires. The shock runs for five seconds in the police model and 30 seconds for the civilian (to give a good head start running away). The shock has a maximum of 50,000 volts, which sounds like a lot, but it is only 2.1 milliamps. That's about 1/7600 of the amps produced by a wall socket.

Those are just numbers.

Tasers hurt like hell. When I took my hit it completely blanked out my brain. There was nothing but pain. I'd had frostbite before and run on a broken fibula and thought I was pretty good with pain. This was a whole new level. A few seconds into the 'ride' I was able to think a little. I was able to lie down by myself and not scream, and that was something to be proud of.

They also tend to freeze the muscles between the two probes. That means that even people who don't respond to pain are usually frozen while the Taser is cycling.

Cool thing–the only injury in a Taser use are from the two barbs, or possibly from falling.

That brings up an important detail—injury and pain are completely separate issues. You can be grievously injured with almost no pain and in great pain without injury. Officers and people who deal with force on a legal basis are required to distinguish. Pain is preferable to injury, injury is preferable to killing. The huge pain of a taser is preferable to the potential injury of a wristlock or takedown.

Other cool toys:

There are a number of delivery systems that can be pretty versatile. A number of LL (less lethal) rounds have been made for the shotgun, including a self-contained Taser unit. There are rubber bullets designed to hurt a lot and bounce off and "ferret rounds" designed to penetrate a car window or drywall and spray OC on the other side. There are also bean bag rounds--small cloth bags filled with lead shot, intended to act as a long-distance sap.

There are 40mm and 37mm launchers. These are essentially grenade launchers. 40mm is the same caliber used by the military and so it takes a special license. The 37 cannot use military explosive grenades and do not require the same licensing. The 37 and 40mm versions are usually single-shots but there are six shot versions, like big revolvers.

There is the M203 40mm military grenade launcher, a single-shot device that can be put under the M4 or M16 barrel.

Munitions for them include:

Direct impact rounds, designed to be fired directly at people. Some have a single impact ball that looks like a racquet ball; others are like big shotgun shells, filled with a bunch of .60 cal hard rubber balls (I've taken a hit from the .60s. It stung and left a welt but definitely didn't take me out of the fight.) "Bean bags" are cloth bags filled with small lead shot.

Indirect impact rounds: heavier and larger, they fire thick rubber discs. The discs can do considerable damage if fired directly into a body. They are designed to be fired into the ground and ricochet into the threat's legs.

Chemical munitions: gas grenades are the classic munition that you see on TV. OC is used more often now than CS or CN. Some are designed to penetrate walls first and then splatter OC. Some on impact 'pop' and scatter three smaller canisters that burn and produce CS gas.

The PepperBall and FN303 are weapons designed to fire OC pellets. The FN303 is very accurate and relatively long-ranged. There has been one reported death of a young woman in a crowd struck in the eye.

The PepperBall is a paintball gun, but the balls have been filled with OC powder or water. The water stings a lot, as a kind of impact round.

Distraction Devices are the technical term for 'flash-bang' grenades. They make a very loud noise and a very bright light. A flash-bang is a hand grenade with no fragmentation and limited high explosive (HE). It is basically a blasting cap in a container. Loud and bright, but no shrapnel and much less of a pressure wave. The stingball and stingball/OC versions look like a black rubber softball. A regular flash-bang looks like a cylinder, black, about 1.5 inches in diameter and maybe four inches long. They have a 'spoon' and pin like a military grenade but without the extra safety clip.

Technical detail: they make a slight pop first, something to do with the detonation, which draws the eyes for the bang.

Teams use them to make people freeze and, hopefully, prevent more dangerous force.

I've been within a meter of a flash-bang (and a stingball, see later) with no ill effect. You could feel the pressure wave and it was loud, but even at near contact, no damage. Throwing one in an enclosed space and trying to close the door, I've been knocked back about six inches from the pressure wave. A door has a lot of surface area.

A stingball is a flash-bang with rubber pellets in it. Theoretically it adds pain to the noise and blinding light. I've never noticed the pellets hitting, but part of that may be due to adrenaline.

Flash-bangs can also have OC in the mix.

There are lots of other weapons. Always remember to do your due diligence when finding experts on weapons. Some may have a lot of technical knowledge but never used the weapon in combat. Manufacturers make claims based on what their weapons can do in controlled conditions (and what they can get away with.) Weapons don't always work the way they're supposed to, and they can break. It makes them difficult, sometimes frustrating, and fun to use (and write about.)

Tasers and Death, Less-Lethal Technology and the Media:

Tasers almost never cause death. The charge is low amperage and doesn't penetrate deeply enough to disrupt, say, the sinoatrial node. If the pain can trigger a cardiac condition, death is possible.

Deaths following use of a taser do happen. They are rare. In this instance following doesn't imply causality. Tasers tend to be used on people in extremely emotionally disturbed states, and a certain percentage of these die anyway. The medical examiner's term is excited delirium. Some–usually activists and attorneys–dispute that excited delirium exists. ER docs are given lessons on how to deal with it, as are some cops. It is an officially recognized cause of death. In some instances, liver temperature at autopsy has been over 108 degrees. That's not survivable, nor is the temperature related to or caused by any force used. I've written an analysis of one of the scary studies before.

The taser is more incapacitating than wall outlets because the points of contact are spread much farther.

So is the outcry against Tasers (and, about ten years ago, Pepperspray) all television sensationalism? Not all, but that seems to be the driving factor from where I sit. The partial information, misinformation and, in some cases (one that I have a personal stake in–a major news outlet was reporting American deaths in Baghdad 100m from where I slept that never happened) deliberate lies that make it into the news can really shake up your confidence.

That said, there are bad officers. They are rare because it is not a profession that tolerates stupidity. If you think citizens don't like bad officers, just know that other officers hate bad officers–and there are young, inexperienced, stupid and aggressive officers (who make for a lot of bad press). There are also timid, gullible and overly-sensitive officers who never generate bad press but frequently get themselves and other officers hurt or allow citizens to be unnecessarily hurt by failing to act.

There are also situations with no good answers: You get a 911 call, a family, terrified, saying their son is out of control and he has a knife. You show up and the kid is whacked out on the driveway, stripping off his clothes, howling and screaming threats, waving his knife around.

You try pepperspray (at great risk to yourself, getting that close to a man with a knife) beanbag rounds and the taser. He shrugs them all off. Then he turns and sprints back for the house where his family is hiding. In one second you need to make a decision: do you shoot a disturbed young man in the back and live with those consequences? Or do you let him run into a place where he has access to victims and you can no longer see or do anything about it? Kill him? Or take a chance that he will kill his entire family? The consequences of either decision will be on you. You have, maybe, one second to decide.

How often police do things that citizens think they shouldn't? Almost every day. Not because there is anything wrong, but because people have lived so far away from dangerous people that they forget the danger exists. Any use of force seems shocking to the inexperienced. I'll frequently watch a video and wonder why the officer didn't use decisive force earlier, whereas someone else will wonder why he used force at all.

Many of the Taser incidents that have been filmed and are available on the internet show a level of pain that is shocking to many people, but a professional looking at the same incident sees every other option as having a higher risk of injury.

There are also some gut level things. Ours is supposed to be an egalitarian society. What is wrong for one should be wrong for all. But when an officer puts cuffs on you and throws you in a car it is an arrest, and legal. If a stranger does it, that's kidnapping. This stems largely from having a society that seems to feel that all violence is wrong, and yet knows that only force can stop violent people. So there is a need for people to be assigned a role to use force in the name of and for the benefit of society. Our culture's answer was to make it a profession open to all. Other cultures made it a caste.

In early Christianity, there was no pretense that God was good. He was the boss. God was not an example to live up to but a voice to be obeyed. The infinitely good concept was tacked on much later ... and God didn't fare too well. Bad things happen to good people. Exploitive people have happy lives and the exploited die young and hungry. Clearly, nothing in nature is based on human concepts of justice or goodness. God failed at being infinitely good and wise, just and kind, always knowing and punishing the wicked, always protecting the righteous. God failed at that, and yet that is the standard that people try to hold officers to. No mistakes. No accidents. Compassionate and forgiving to groups that I like; harsh and inflexible with groups that I don't like (and, of course, to respect that like/dislike line for everybody at all times equally). It makes me want to laugh or cry, sometimes.

There is no violent solution that will make everyone happy. Not all people respond to words. Not all people respond to beatings or pain or the sound of their own bones breaking. Some people must be stopped.

When an officer swings a baton, he has judged that he needs to stop the threat and either a lower level of force will not work in time or has already failed.

If the baton fails, what then? Switch to the higher level of force, which is the handgun and take the threat's life? Or keep swinging the baton again ... and again ... and again ....

The Taser seems so ideal—no injury, as safe as it gets but a level of pain that makes the most hardened street-fighter rethink his options. Effective on all but a handful of people. And safe. Those are the exact same factors that could let a sadist vent, the same factors that could turn one of the greatest advances for humane law enforcement in the last fifty years into a device for torture.

In the end, everything always has and always will come down to the judgment and integrity of the people in the crisis. The protagonists. Making, and living with decisions like this is the heart of 'protagging.'

Speculation. There are some cool possibilities for futuristic weapons out there.

One company is experimenting with a cordless Taser, basically using lasers to ionize two streams of air and running the current down the ionization paths. It would be like a Star Trek phaser, but without the kill or stun setting, just a mind-numbing pain setting.

Lights that work in patterns and cause seizures in most people.

Nets and glue bombs for the 40mm launcher

The Area Denial System (ADS) uses microwaves for crowd control—it feels like you are on fire. ADS triggers that burning sensation with no injury (theoretically). It also, currently, requires a huge amount of power and is mounted on a big truck. Not something bad guys will use when simple molotovs are cheaper and easier. It's the kind of thing that only an organization with incredible resources and an equally incredible reluctance to injure would have commissioned.

✧✦✧✦✧

HOMEWORK:

Describe the attributes of three weapons. The weapons are designed to quell mass riots. The cause of the riots is irrelevant–if you want variety or need a motivation, mix-and-match: in all cases protesters are destroying public property and injuring people. In one world, a loose group of shadowy, unidentified people have convinced large groups of students that protest will actually work against a government with thirty years of history of torture, rape and exploitation. In another world, workers are protesting because the government's planned economy has led to 5% annual starvation. In the third world, protesters are upset because after an economic crisis, the government's promise of three months vacation a year and retirement at 50 will have to be cut to two months and fifty-five.

Design a weapon for crowd control for each of three governments:
#1 The government has no civil rights, does not care about media and wants to send a message that this behavior will not be tolerated.
#2 The government has no history of civil rights but will be embarrassed and possibly lose trade if foreign governments are offended by the process of riot control.
#3 The government can be removed from power if its own citizens, many of whom are related to the protesters, are offended by the methods used.
In all cases, for purposes of this assignment, the protesters must be stopped, this is non-negotiable. Have fun. Be both evil and goody-two-shoes.

TO RECAP:

- ✧ Less-lethal technologies are an attempt to invent a tool that will take a bad guy down as effectively as a handgun but without injury
- ✧ Modern LL chemical weapons are CS, CN and OC
- ✧ The Taser is a directed energy weapon that hurts. A lot.
- ✧ Impact, chemicals and other specialty munitions can be fired from a 12 gauge, 40mm or 37mm platform
- ✧ Distraction devices are "flashbang grenades" and some configurations have impact pellets and chemical sprays added
- ✧ Paintballs have been modified to fire OC powder
- ✧ Media and civilians freak out over LL technology regardless of lives saved

... 15 ...

CONCEALED CARRY

There are weapons for battle and weapons for emergencies. For emergencies, you want something light enough to carry at all times, easy to conceal (and that is cultural–people in our culture panic when they see weapons, in another place and time NOT carrying a weapon openly might mark you as a peasant) and quick to get into play. That makes most of the weapons you can carry concealed inferior to the ones you would take into battle. A stiletto up your sleeve is inferior to a broadsword. A handgun is an inaccurate, anemic compromise compared to an assault rifle.

Concealed weapons usually fall into the 'emergency category'.

There are three approaches your characters may consider- concealing a weapon; training and practicing with something not considered a weapon; or fashioning something that doesn't look like a weapon.

I'm going to start with the last two because they will be way shorter.

Practicing with a non-weapon. We've already mentioned canes. Something that can be carried everywhere, doesn't ping the radar as a weapon and can be very versatile. There are stainless steel pens (I believe Cross is the brand name) that can thrust through a sheet of plywood.

Old school Marines used to practice with their belts and heavy buckles. I'm not big on the keys through your fingers idea, it rarely hits squarely and will tear the shit out of the flesh between your fingers, but it is the idea that is important.

What do you carry with you that can be a weapon? There's a lot, it just takes some creativity.

You also have to think through which are really only useful for assassination. A pen, for instance, is not intimidating. No one will decide not to fight you just because they see that you are holding a pen. It is useless for defense, in that it will not stop another weapon. It is not particularly effective. You can kill someone with a pen but it will take either extreme precision, an unmoving target and/or some fairly extensive time. You have to have it clear in your mind (and so must your experienced protagonists) that some weapons may be used to make it slightly easier to kill someone else but are not good tools for self-defense.

Non-obvious weapons. You can change things, a lot or a little, and turn them into weapons or shields. You can now buy kevlar sheets for your briefcase that make it bullet resistant. I think a holy book with a stainless steel cover (possibly kept in a sturdy purse with a long strap) would make a great weapon. I've seen chain mail pouches for sale at RenFaires. Even a good leather pouch on a short rope filled with half a pound of coins would make a hell of a weapon. Two hefty bunches of keys on the end of a three-foot length of chain would be, essentially, a *kusari-gama*. I've been looking for stainless steel solid beads for some time. Many religions have some sort of prayer bead and it would be cool to say, "I didn't hit him, I just blessed him vigorously." When chopsticks for hairpins were stylish, I had a pair made for my wife with long steel needles concealed inside.

This overlaps with the found weapons somewhat. Be creative.

Concealing a regular weapon. Most people are incredibly unobservant, so it is not nearly as hard to carry concealed as you might think. There are some pointers, though: shiny weapons don't hide as well as those with flat finishes. Small weapons conceal better than large weapons, but tend to either have less ammo, less power, or both.

Make sure you have retention (like a thumb strap), or the weapon may fall out and people *will* notice (like, my personal shame, if you are dancing with the bride at a wedding and your .45 pops out of your inside-the-pants holster onto the dance floor.) Make sure you can get to it. I'm not big on pouches and purses because most people keep them closed and they are complicated to access quickly ... and if you need a handgun, you need it quickly. If you had time, you'd be going for a rifle or shotgun.

Make sure you can get to it and practice drawing in different places–in the car with your seatbelt on (an officer in my state was killed when she couldn't undo her retention straps while seated in her car. Investigators estimate that she had over three seconds. It wasn't enough time. Practice.) On the toilet. Bundled up in winter clothes. Your most vulnerable times are the times a bad guy will pick.

When you start carrying all the time you may develop severe lower back problems. The key is to balance the weight on the other side. A spare magazine, multi tool and tactical flashlight do it for me. It does make me look fatter, though.

If your weapon has an external safety make damn sure the safety won't pop off by rubbing against you as you move. If you ever kill somebody, you want it to be on purpose. And you never want to shoot yourself in the leg. Most of my holsters keep the weapon pointed away from me. Just in case.

Be careful with placement. The waistline is convenient and I prefer it (your hands are in that vicinity most of the time, so it's fast), but if you get knocked down, it will hurt. The small of the back is an excellent place for concealment, but if you fall on that it can do serious spine injury. You (or your character) will have to make some choices. Shoulder holster is decent concealment, especially on big-chested people, but it is slightly slower and you have to reach across your body, which means in close you can be easily slammed and have that armed trapped with no weapon. Also in a shoulder draw, when you pull the weapon, the barrel will briefly be pointed at your own left arm and will pan across 90 degrees on the way to lining up with your target. Every shooter is taught from the first day, never to point a weapon at anything she does not wish to destroy. 'Muzzle control' the constant awareness of where the barrel of a gun is pointing and the ability to never accidentally point it at others is considered a basic skill. Anyone who fails to control the muzzle is despised by serious shooters.

The shoulder holster automatically sets you up for this problem. A shoulder holster, however, is the absolute easiest way to carry concealed and draw while sitting.

Unconcealed, given my choice, I prefer a drop holster.

Basically, the weapon should be near wherever you habitually hold your hands. If you put your thumbs on your belt, a weapon may go there (appendix carry, front quarter between your hip bone and your navel). If you wear a shoulder rig, uncrossed arms (arms like a crossed arm position, but the weapon hand on or near the weapon, the other arm over it, nothing crossed) puts thing in reach.

We've found that wasp-waisted and/or wide hipped women have trouble drawing from a waist holster, especially a high-rise. There are holsters that fit on the belt but lower the weapon a few inches that make drawing easier.

Another point–your skilled characters should practice drawing with the off hand. Just in case.

The weapon and placement is only part of concealment. What you wear comes into play. Shorts and a t-shirt make it hard (but I have a small Makarov, roughly equivalent to a Walther PPK .380, that is invisible at the small of my back under a t-shirt, as long as the shirt is untucked and I have good posture.) Your character will have a need for jackets or big loose shirts, which won't be appropriate everywhere.

You have to check your state ordinances for unlawful carry. The USSC (United States Supreme Court) just handed down some rulings that are really rocking the gun control world. Your bad guy characters won't care about the law. They are worried about dying. Jail (as a concern) ranges from an inconvenience to a vacation, unless they have made a lot of enemies inside. (Understand the difference between Jail and Prison.)

Your good guy characters will be more complicated. They can get permits, but that varies by state and in some it is almost automatic provided there are no histories of felonies or Domestic Violence and no mental health issues. In other states, it is almost impossible unless you are hooked into the political machine. A CCP (Concealed Carry Permit) is for the state that issued it, though some states have reciprocity agreements. For a reciprocity map:
http://www.usacarry.com/concealed_carry_permit_reciprocity_maps.html

If the good guy can't get a permit and chooses to carry, there is some risk. For most people, no big deal. They will never be in a position to use it, the handful of people who might notice are friends, blah, blah, blah.

But that's not what makes characters. The big risk with the character (or real people) is that if they use a concealed weapon that they carry illegally, they will be prosecuted and the state will make a convincing case that carrying the weapon is proof of premeditation. Especially in states that have made a strong political stand on banning guns, they will really pull out all the stops to get a conviction and maximum sentence.

Cops are a special case. Since the passage of HR 218, officers and retired officers may carry concealed in any state. If stopped, they will show their ID, the officer that stopped them will call in to have it confirmed and, provided they haven't done anything illegal or stupid (such as drinking) they will be on their merry way. Be aware that the on-duty officer making contact will not know or necessarily believe that the armed stranger is another cop and he will make himself safe. That may include doing a full felony stop. "Turn around, get on your knees, lace your fingers behind your head" and calling for back-up. Unless the off-duty guy is really stupid, really arrogant, or drunk, he will cooperate. It's stupid not to. Never make a nervous guy with a gun and a badge make a fast decision.

If a citizen wants to bring a firearm on a flight, he has to have it in a locked box in checked luggage with the ammunition in another box. The weapon must be declared and will be labeled. I hear anecdotally, that labeled weapons are frequently stolen. The TSA regs are here:
http://www.tsa.gov/traveler-information/firearms-and-ammunition

The TSA regs on officers carrying on a plane are here:
http://www.tsa.gov/about-tsa/law-enforcement-officers-flying-armed

So, the opening scene in Die Hard couldn't have happened.

One other stupid little detail. When I was very young and thought I would be a bad guy, I carried a flat throwing/fighting knife under my shirt down my spine. So if anyone ever said, "Put your hands behind your head and lace your fingers" my hands would be right on it ....

✧✦✧✦✧

HOMEWORK:

For one day, carry something odd, like a small stuffed animal. You have to be able to get to it quickly at all times. For one day, go about your normal business and make sure no one sees what you are carrying, and don't ever leave it anywhere that someone else can get to it.

TO RECAP:

- ✧ Concealed weapons are usually for emergencies and less powerful than would be ideal
- ✧ You can train in a non-weapon, create a non-obvious weapon, or conceal a weapon
- ✧ Safety, accessibility, concealment
- ✧ Clothing choice is part of the equation
- ✧ Laws exist pertaining to citizens on a state-by-state basis

... 16 ...

MASS COMBAT

I think I was shot at. We were tearing through Kirkuk on our way from our camp in Sulaymaniyah to FOB Warrior for our weekly mail and grocery run.

Tony came over the radio, "Did you guys hear that? I think somebody was shooting at us." By that time we were probably a half a kilometer away from the ambush site.

Maybe I should amend the first sentence to: I think I may have been shot in the general direction of.

I have been in a war zone. That doesn't even imply that I have been in a war. I've never been blown up by IEDs or caught in a successful ambush or engaged in a firefight. My time in Iraq was spent as a teacher. So there are better sources for some of the nitty-gritty details. Keep that in mind.

Wars are based on politics, getting *something*—either a tangible thing or a concession. Their purposes can be very cold-blooded because the people making the decision are far enough removed from the fighting that they can see the 'big picture' or what Liddell-Hart called 'Grand

Strategy'. That's important. It rankles most of us, but war is one of those things that should be entered logically and coldly, never emotionally.

However, to get people to fight and support a war (in a liberal republic) you have to build up support. That's where the othering comes in, the ability to dehumanize the enemy. Propaganda. Ethnic slurs. In the actual combat, you've bonded enough with your teammates that it becomes very tribal: "These are my people and those bastards are trying to kill my people." The part of your brain that would reason that, in fact, you are in *their* country, doesn't register. That bonding is emotional, limbic-system stuff.

The further we are away from a tribal core (always with definite us and them), the more we are taught that people are people (and this is a huge shift in thought, something that would have appeared literally insane at most points in human history) the harder it is to kill. Even in modern warfare with all of our technology, the current wars have an unbelievably low incidence of collateral damage. Soldiers, not just by policy but by character are risking their lives and taking extra chances to avoid killing potential non-combatants. An unintended side-effect of this is that what our culture sees as strength, morality and restraint, specific cultures we are fighting see as fear and timidity and frequently use it against us.

"I don't understand Americans," Haider said, "From the time I was a little boy I always saw men walking the streets with rifles. Until the Americans, I never saw anyone trying NOT to shoot." –Baghdad, 2009

Those who were raised with a tribal identity 'other' very quickly and easily. Not only can they resort to violence quicker and easier and more extremely, there appears to be absolutely no PTSD or mental anguish associated with it. In one of the last chapters of "Machete Season" the author talks about a prison holding seven thousand perpetrators of the Rwandan holocaust. Less than a dozen have mental illnesses. Or nightmares about the killing or any of the effects that we would expect.

Different cultures see war differently.

Until the modern era almost everyone everywhere held that winning in war *involved* looting, raping and enslaving. When one culture steps beyond that and chooses to take a more moral way, the other cultures they are fighting might not recognize that they are losing.

Another example: Some Native American nations preferred'counting coup' to fighting. You proved your bravery by closing with and touching an enemy. Everyone knew who was brave and skilled and it kept the body count low. When nations that expected their very civilized and moral concept of counting coup to be the norm ran into peoples (such as the Europeans) who just simply killed, the skilled and noble warriors were slaughtered. Not because of technology–until the mid 1800s a bow was a far superior weapon to a musket (except for the intimidation of noise, smoke and flame, which was important). Nor because of skill. A few of the colonists were soldiers or former soldiers, but every Native American man was a trained raider and hunter. Cultural attitudes and beliefs about winning left them vulnerable.

That wasn't, believe it or not, a political diatribe. Especially if you are writing in speculative genres (this is one of my pet peeves) the late 20th/early 21st century middle class white American ideals of right, wrong, noble, ignoble are not the way the world works. Not most of the world, almost never in all of history anywhere in the world. Quite frankly, we've never before had enough excess food to be able to afford to look beyond tribal and family lines and recognize other's humanity.

So a *buke* (the warrior caste of Japan, that included the samurai) would cut down a peasant (*heimin*, farmer, one of the other castes) without hesitation for a perceived rudeness (rudeness, as is common in hierarchical societies usually translating to a lack of sufficient deference). A modern *Federale* will slap a child to the ground who dares to look in his eyes. A friend, raised in a California barrio, believes it is an insult not to use a weapon on a man. "Bare hands are for women and children," he says.

Back to war and soldiers. Politicians make a cold-blooded decision. It would be ideal if they could then turn to a group of predators to carry out that decision, but predators are notoriously difficult to control. Small numbers of predators would be effective but the politicians wind up using large numbers of regular people.

Regular people can't kill cold. Many can't kill at all. So they have to get excited, "motivated" in military terms. They turn their squad into a tribe. It is like trying to do a predator's job with a troop of monkeys (which, given that we're primates, it is). It will be inefficient and political, feelings will get hurt and there will be stress and drama. And the most egregious of the atrocities are not committed by the cold-blooded professionals or sociopaths in the ranks but by the scared and insecure primates.

There will also be a core of professionals. Some will be natural predators, people who have found that they 'other' people easily, enjoy the job or at least excel at it and have found a home in one of the few places that what they enjoy is legal. Some will be true believers who don't need to be 'motivated' and have decided on their own terms and for their own reasons that it is okay to pull the trigger. This small core of professionals can get a lot done and often wind up mentoring the rookies, trying to teach their worldview because it is both efficient and pretty robust against PTSD.

In the big picture, war can be looked at as a war of attrition or a war of maneuver. In a war of attrition, both sides beat themselves bloody, sending men and material en masse head to head to wear out the other side. Perhaps to kill all the soldiers, perhaps to use up all the weapons and ammunition and food and supplies. The war of attrition is a giant meat grinder, a test to see who gets exhausted first.

Conquest is easier after a war of attrition since the means to fight, including many of the able-bodied warriors and leaders have been eliminated. Taking the land presents little problem.

A war of maneuver relies on breaking the adversary's psychological will. By rapid action, great flexibility and an ability to put arms and men where the enemy has no hope of prevailing, you overcome the enemy's ability to cope. Shock and awe. Guerrilla hit and run tactics. Early horse archers.

It leaves the enemy with many resources intact, and the peace that follows is often only as good as the paper the treaty is inscribed on. It tends to cause a political change in regime, which may or may not benefit the winning side.

As John Keegan described eloquently, the goal of war is not to destroy the enemy but to break the enemy's will. In a war, to truly 'beat' a nation, you would have to kill every last person capable of throwing a rock. Wars are over when one side becomes afraid or too tired to throw rocks.

Or when factions within a side start forbidding retaliation in order to forge peace.

(This is true also in single combat. Unless every long bone is broken or the brainstem is shut down, a sufficiently motivated person could keep fighting. Exhaustion or fear of injury or fear of humiliation or some other psychological element is what stops most people.)

This is one of the big disconnects between soldiers and civilians in our population. In a liberal republic or democracy, war is not only a logical, cold decision. It is also a symbol that factions can use to manipulate popular opinion. The party in the minority can almost always use the fact of war and sometimes the fact of a refusal to engage in war, to try to remove another party from power.

In the civilian world this is rarely thought of and, when it is, seems fair, if political.

On the frontlines it is perceived not only as betrayal (remember that on a gut level, soldiers understand that winning is a matter of will and they can lose based on the lack of will of people who are not there) but as if the people back home are being deliberately manipulated for political reasons in ways that serve the enemy.

American soldiers (the type I have been and know best) pride themselves on their history. The have lost very few battles. Between technological superiority, training and tenacity, they tend to inflict extremely lop-sided casualties. They do not feel they have ever lost a war and rarely lost a battle. But they have been pulled out of wars by those with weaker will or for political expediency ... and running away, even under orders, feels infinitely worse than being beaten.

There is yet another factor that affects how soldiers and civilians see war. Especially in modern times, information is closely guarded. Those who actually know what is going on not only stay silent out of prudence or to maintain a tactical advantage. Almost everyone is under direct orders or contract to say nothing.

By definition, almost anything civilians hear on the news came from a source without direct information. Even when the information is incorrect or seems a blatant lie the people on the job are prohibited from denying information or pointing out inaccuracies.

When soldiers have been caught in this trap, notably Vietnam veterans, they see the civilian world as easily manipulated, misinformed sheep.

This means that modern war must be fought on several levels. It is not merely a mass of men and weapons vying for supremacy. Gathering intelligence, and conducting tactical and strategic operations against the enemy have always been a part of warfare. But managing public sentiment back home and abroad and trying to mitigate media damage–or play the media, which the military seems to be very bad at–is a critical aspect of war that only in the last fifty years has become a decisive factor.

An important aspect of this, which also marks a huge change in philosophy, is that there is no longer any such thing as "acceptable losses." Deaths, whether of soldiers or collateral damage, play poorly in the media. They are wasteful as well, and every commander I know considers every friendly death a mistake. My first commander long ago, Lt. Whalen, said, "There are only two things. Accomplish the mission and survive on the modern battlefield. Everything we do must serve those goals."

This is a philosophy, however, and soldiers have to deal with the practicality. How do you deal with an enemy who hides in the civilian population or uses children as shields? You can't avoid all casualties and zero friendly deaths is a dream. And there is a very real possibility and it is a common fear among warfighters, that taking this philosophy as truth will leave us helpless against an enemy that had the means and desire to wage a war of attrition.

Terrorists. When Americans try to write terrorists they want to give them some big tragedy in their past–family killed by an Israeli bomb or something like that. That's not the profile. There are voluntary and involuntary terrorists.

Voluntary terrorists are almost all from wealthy, western-educated secular families. (Hmmm, exact same profile for cult recruits, huh?) They have usually lived for some or all of their lives in the West. As such, they have always felt like outsiders, never fully part of their ancestral world or the world they are living in. Always outsiders, hungering to belong ... and someone offers them a guaranteed entry not just to one of those worlds but to the elite of one of those worlds. It's not about the virgins in paradise. It is about a human's sometimes pathological need to belong at any cost. It might take some work, but it's important to understand this from their point of view. Some volunteer for the army or join gangs because it is far more important to belong than to not be shot at. People volunteer for suicide bombings because death is abstract and belonging is real.

Involuntary terrorists

L, one of our translators told us the first day in-country:

We will be good friends. We will work together and you will like me and trust me. Never like me so much that you can't shoot me in the head. Listen to what I am telling you, this is how they are doing it now. I may come home and find the {Name of specific militia redacted} with my family tied up. They will point guns at them. They will point guns at me. They will give me a vest bomb. If I say no, they will shoot my youngest daughter. If I still say no, they will shoot my other daughter. Then my wife, then my youngest son. They will keep going until I say yes or they shoot me. If I take the vest, they will let my family go and give them ten thousand US dollars and protect them. I love you all like brothers, but I will wear the vest even to save my youngest daughter.

Most of this chapter has been background and based on modern war and modern perceptions of war, the idea of the 'big picture' as seen from the ground. What follows is more personal. It is a list of things that have often bothered me in fiction. They are details, things to think about. Use as you will:

- War is mostly boring. There is a lot of waiting, often in places that have terrible climates. Battle is anything but boring.
- You can't tell what is going on. Whether close range riot control or a pitched battle, your adrenaline is spiked, which almost automatically guarantees that you will have tunnel vision and auditory exclusion. Even without the biology, it's usually dark or too bright. The enemy doesn't want to be seen, and neither do your own guys. In a matter of seconds, especially if the team isn't tight or the leadership is weak or commo goes bad or it is at night, you lose track

of where everybody is. It is a mess of noise and light and deafness and darkness.

✧ Repeating in a way, but in much of history you could not see, through musket smoke, cannon fire or dust of marching infantry and charging cavalry, much of anything. You couldn't tell if you were winning or losing unless you saw that the guys running back were from your side. On horseback was best–it gave you some elevation–but it still sucked.

✧ Nobody really knows the big picture. There are political considerations, strategic considerations and tactical considerations. If you have good leaders they will share what they know. This is one of the reasons that obedience is important: the people making decisions have more information than you. Trust is huge in this, but obedience is critical. There is a reason why the bigger, stronger Germanic and Celtic people with home-court advantage were easily defeated by the Romans. Individuals on a battlefield are meat. Organized units with good leadership are power multipliers.

✧ Communication is always bad. I've worked with some relatively high-end radio systems designed for tactical operations. They all had dead zones in certain buildings. Microphones work loose and quit transmitting. Batteries die that should be fresh. In older systems they tried trumpets and drums and flags, most of which were hampered by the din of battle or the dust and smoke. Those with good commo have a huge edge, but it always seems to suck when it counts.

✧ Supplies are critical. Armies, even roving bands of bandits, need a lot of food and ammo. Hunting takes time. Pillaging takes a lot less time. The idea of supply lines really made a difference not just in how wars are fought but in who won AND how the populace felt about invading armies (when invaders treat you nicer than your own nobles ....)

✧ Battling is anaerobic, usually, and very much a matter of nerve. Soldiering is aerobic and very much a matter of endurance. Fighters win your battles. Soldiers win your wars. Fighters bring down hell on the enemy. Soldiers are the ones who get to the right place at the right time.

✧ Warfighting is not the place for heroism. Individualism may be valued in fiction and in our society, but in mass battle you must be able to suppress your ego and accept your place as part of a larger machine. An individual on a battlefield is just meat. At best, he will get killed, at worst he will get everyone else killed as well. What civilians see as rugged individuality we see as suicidal ego. Or, as the saying goes, "Hero is a four-letter word for someone who gets all his friends killed and manages to look good in the AAR (After-Action Report.)"

✧ Close range hand-to-hand combat, whether in a medieval battle (Not personally experienced) or a riot or mass brawl (have experienced) is a tangle of arms and legs. There is no room for big technique and people are almost as likely to hurt a friend as an enemy (one of the cool things about uniforms–if I'm twisting a blue polyester leg, I'm probably leg-locking a cop.)

✧ The randomness of it is overwhelming. This is something that not just civilians but that even people in danger have trouble wrapping their minds around. Not many people actually die in modern war. Ancient combat often had incredible death rates … but even then battles or wars where an entire side was wiped out were rare. Going to war is not the inevitable doom many seem to believe. *(According to Plutarch in the Battle of Granicus River, Alexander the Great lost only 34 men routing an army of forty thousand. The Persians lost considerably more.)* Even in really horrific legendary battles, few, relatively speaking, die … but those that do die … it seems random. Bullets and arrows fly. Sometimes they hit the best soldiers. There is no skill for avoiding what you don't see and what you don't see is what kills you. It makes every time you step into battle a strange and desperate act of faith. It breeds a form of fatalism that is the opposite of fatalism, because those who are in train harder hoping it won't be luck that kills them. This is hard to put into words, but it is part of a warrior's psyche: *nothing will keep me safe. Death takes who she wishes. Maybe not me, maybe not today.*

✧ Conversely, embracing that *(It is a good day to die)* allows you to do some truly amazing things. When you quit flinching and ducking you can aim, you can cut, you can become a cold predator and a force of nature. Those that embrace death care for their weapons. Everyone else does a kind of fidgety, ritualistic, preparation. They care for weapons but also pay obsessive attention to details of uniform and gear before a battle. Maybe it is a ritual, maybe it is just a way to not think.

I have been in riots and even when you are there to quell them the emotional force of a bunch of people losing control or even on the edge of losing control is intoxicating. For those in the riot, it is a feeling of enormous, anonymous raw animal power. *We can break things. We can destroy. We can leave our mark. We will never be known or punished.* It is the pure rage of a toddler's tantrum and just as free.

Teams are the essence of skilled group combat. It takes time and skill to make a team. Just throwing really skilled people together doesn't even approach what an experienced, well-led team can do. The ability to work together is a force multiplier like no other.

Teams must train together and they must fight together. Training will bring them to a level of skill, but actual operations will solidify the trust, and there are things that come up in real life that rarely come up in training: bad intel; bad commo; environmental hazards so extreme that your equipment fails; the sheer speed with which things can go bad. Until your first operation, you don't know who can really fight. You don't know who can control the fear. You don't know who is steady and who is excitable.

In a good team with experienced members, the ability to remain steady will grow over time as new members model veterans. The veterans know what to pay attention to, what doesn't matter. Details get you killed. *Which* details will get you killed is something you learn from experience or from experienced people.

Every time a new member comes on a team, especially an experienced team, there is a rough period. Sometimes for two reasons. The person being replaced will usually be missed. If the lost member retired or moved on (fighting is a young man's game) there may be little problem. If the person being replaced was killed or crippled, there will be some unprocessed grieving and a lot of resentment. If the person being replaced was removed because he was a danger, then there may actually be some guarded hope.

The second source of tension is that any new person is a risk. No matter the person's skill or history, she may not fit and that potentially endangers everyone. There are, sometimes, membership rituals (usually low-key, nothing like a fraternity hazing, you don't pull that shit on dangerous people) to try to ease the tension ... but the real membership initiation is the first operation.

A well-run team:

- ✧ Agrees on the goals and the methods.
- ✧ Communicates
- ✧ Are ordered to have balanced lives (seriously, some times you have to tell these guys to spend time with family) ... and we always watch for that, because someone who wraps his or her whole life around the team is a short step away from burn-out. We don't just do this, whatever 'this' is, for the team or an ideal. We are very aware that we deal with ugly things so that those we find precious never have to see or feel that kind of ugly.
- ✧ Trust each other. If I tell you to hold a door, I will not look to see if you do it ... and if I hear gunshots coming from you sector I will not look or come to your aid unless you ask. I trust you to handle it. Wrap your head around that–I trust you so much that I leave my exposed back to your protection and I don't even look. There is an old SWAT saying: "If you catch yourself looking over your shoulder to see if a specific teammate is doing his job, one of you shouldn't be on the team."
- ✧ Trains hard and fights hard. The harder you train, the easier you fight. They continually push each other to be better, faster, stronger and more creative.

There is a dynamic that comes up in the best teams (and marriages for that matter) where insecurity makes things constantly improve. The rookie comes onto a legendary team and thinks, "I don't know how I made it. I'm not good enough to hang with these guys" and spends the rest of his career continually getting better trying to be worthy of the badge/pennant/order/name/whatever. And this is one of the reasons why self-aggrandizing egotists are so despised in the Special Operations community. Some are gifted, but they simply don't work as hard as the good operators. There are a few who have made names in the public sector who are despised by their old squad mates. And this is also one of the fiction tropes that infuriates me–the hot shot rookie comes on the team and is simply better than everyone else and has to fight to prove that he is better so he disobeys rules and does things his way. In real life, this is an arrogant prick with a giant gap between what he knows and what he thinks he knows that will get people killed.

On the rare, rare occasions when one of these passes the test to get into a special unit, they usually find out very quickly that they are NOT special. Those that don't get it, have it proven to them. In criminal organizations the 'hotshot' is simply killed.

Leadership is not bossy. There is an absolute respect between a good leader and a good team. Your guys follow you because they trust you. If you have to order them, have to 'get their attention' it is almost always a lack of trust. You follow, because you trust the leader: He knows the plan. He has the team's interest at heart. He will not get you killed for his own career.

There is often a separation between the team and the people giving the orders. This may be a modern phenomenon, and it has good and bad points. You don't want people who are good at solving problems with violence deciding which problems need to be solved. That aspect of warrior/servant is pretty critical to modern ideas of civilization. That said, there is an often palpable fear and/or disdain from those who give the orders. They are aware that they could never do the job the team does, and to save ego, it is often easy to decide that the team is composed of savages or something not quite, and much less than a 'normal' or 'real' human.

Bad teams happen:

- When the goals or methods are not agreed on. Enemies make poor teammates. Pacifists don't blend well with meat-eaters. If the plan is to finesse/con the mission and one insists on going in with force and intimidation, the whole structure becomes weak, unstable and untrustworthy.
- When the leadership is weak. Operators do not rank weak and strong leadership by timid and courageous or quiet or loud or asking versus ordering, a weak leader is one who is not respected for ANY reason. Unskilled, stupid, timid, aggressive, or even morally questionable leaders lose respect quickly and lose control. Many try to take back respect by increasing aggression or loudness. It never works.

✧ When the members don't want to be there. Most elite teams in the US are voluntary and often the selection process is rough. The people who make these teams want to be there. In other places and times a bureaucrat decides who has the skills. These teams are often trained hard, even brutally, but they tend to be far less successful in combat.

There are a few administration issues that can damage or destroy a team. A connected resume packer may get a place on a team for the sole purpose of being able to brag about it later. The entire team feels cheapened, like their sweat and blood will be discounted to the value of his talk. Another is when the administration chooses to make a political statement by assigning members for reason other than fitness for duty. For instance (something actually somewhat common and a potential source of dramatic tension) assigning someone to an elite team in order to make it look more 'representational' (ethnicity, gender or religion) who failed the required tests to join.

✧✦✧✦✧

HOMEWORK:

Really want a taste of this? Just a taste, play American football or rugby. Or participate in a 'war' in the Society for Creative Anachronisms. http://www.sca.org/

TO RECAP:

- ✧ Wars happen for a specific purpose
- ✧ Different cultures see war differently
- ✧ Mass combat is chaotic and hard for an individual to see or understand
- ✧ Terrorists may be voluntary or involuntary and voluntary terrorists have a profile
- ✧ Teams, good or bad, are the essence of skilled mass combat

... 17 ...

VIOLENCE IN OTHER PLACES AND TIMES

This is a really hard subject to talk about without people's political sensibilities getting in the way. Universally, how you were raised is 'normal' and your ideas of right and wrong seem sensible and obvious. We live in what is possibly the most affluent time and place in all of history. There are many things that we accept as obvious truths that would be considered unnatural in almost any other century.

There are few things I find more annoying than a work of fiction set in a medieval or quasi-medieval setting where the characters have 21st century American values.

Some of the factors that lead to this disconnect:

1) Level of violence/personal proximity to death in the world. People who routinely kill their own food and expect that half their children will die before adulthood will have very different attitudes towards life and death than those who don't.

My mom had 13 pregnancies, six live births and three of us survived to be adults. That's really unusual today. For much of history, that was the norm.

By the time you were twenty you would have cleaned the bodies and buried relatives–babies and parents and siblings. A larger percentage of the deaths than we can grasp now would have been due to violence or brutal accidents. And the ones that weren't, the disease ....

You wouldn't have known what disease WAS. Without an idea of microbes and contagion, you would only see that death follows death, that maybe the dead want to recruit more dead ... and you would try to understand with ritual or superstition or religion or vampires.

2) Level of (for want of a better word) lawlessness. Before about 1780, there was no such thing as a police force. A king *could* send in the military if it suited his purposes.

Sometimes the village men would form a watch, but the primary purpose was fire prevention and stopping victimization was optional. There was no organization to investigate and punish crimes. If someone killed a family member you had a choice between revenge and sucking it up. You could go to the magistrate or equivalent and ask him to do something about it, but it would be his choice. This is compounded if there were active bands of outlaws or if the people lived on or near a war zone.

Unless a local lord or king (someone whose primary duty was to enforce social norms and protect the group by application of skilled violence) got involved, the only thing resembling justice was vengeance. If you refused to participate in vengeance, you were marked as easy prey and would continue to be victimized. The only safety lay in a willingness (and preferably ability) to meet force with force.

3) Difficulty of killing: killing well and efficiently hand-to-hand takes some skill and fitness. Peasants rarely had the time to practice. Medieval agriculture or fishing was a daily grind of backbreaking, exhausting toil with no guarantee of enough food. Repetitive hard work forged bodies into inflexibility. Farmers could be tough and strong, but they made shitty fighters.

The good fighters were the nobles, not because of the leisure time, but because fighting was their birthright and full time profession. Then start tacking on things like a weapon that no peasant could ever dream of affording, armor and a horse that would beggar and starve families just in upkeep, and you wind up with very segregated fighters and non-fighters ... and villagers were utterly helpless when the nobles wanted something.

Until the advent of the gun, especially the revolver. Something that could make a consumptive skinny guy (Doc Holliday) into a force to be reckoned with. Something that made nobility based on skill at arms obsolete. Something that, for the first time in all of recorded history, gave simple villagers and farmers the ability to stand up to people who ruled by force of arms.

4) **That means that a skilled fighter could take anything he wanted with almost complete impunity.** A Japanese noble could cut down a farmer, tradesman or merchant for not bowing quickly enough. A man with a sword could take any shepherdess he wanted and no one could do anything.

And, born and bred in a world where that was normal, no one saw anything wrong with it. They didn't *like* it. There was resentment and hatred and fantasies of revenge. But the idea that there was something inherently wrong, that there is an abstract and universal concept of good or evil or even justice, is a very modern idea.

When you hear the phrase "Divine right of kings" or even "insha'allah" it was a literal belief at the time. As I was told in Iraq, everyone hated Saddam Hussein because everyone had suffered. But Allah put him in that position AND Allah *made him who he was*. Everyone hated Saddam, hated the regime, but to say that what he did was inherently wrong would be to say that Allah is capable of being wrong. You just pray that God will give the next ruler a more merciful heart and move on with your life.

5) **Violence was, for centuries, the most efficient tool to get what you wanted, and everyone knew it.** The rape that naturally followed conquest for most of history was a far easier way to spread genes than

raising children. You could pillage food in a day that would take you six months of labor to grow.

It was not until the combination of free markets and a press that trade became easier and more profitable than conquest. The rise of mercantilism, slowly, made cultivating trading partners a better strategy than conquering, raiding, or enslaving.

6) **The world has rarely been secure.** We assume a level of stability that rarely existed in the past. In much of the under-developed world today, saving money and planning for a future doesn't make sense because it doesn't work.

Before banks, money saved could be stolen. When taxes were based on the whim of a noble or the tax collector, a rumor of money meant you would have it taxed, or simply taken away from you. It was a better strategy to spend it on others who may someday fall into money when you needed it.

If you are ever in a position to advise people in developing countries how to save and plan for the future, they will be resistant. For many, their future and institutions have never been stable enough to make that a good idea.

After the advent of banks, it wasn't immediately different. What was to keep the person running the bank from simply keeping the money? Even if it was guaranteed by the government, what did that mean when the government might be overthrown at any time? Or the banks? In the middle ages, the Knights Templar, though each had taken a vow of individual poverty, became a financial powerhouse, loaning money and transporting funds based on notes. In 1307, King Philip IV of France, already heavily indebted to the Templars, was refused a further loan. He ordered the arrest of all Knights Templar in France. What do you think happened to the funds the Templars were holding for other people?

7) **The idea that all people are equal, or even that all people have some value, is a very modern concept.** Not just what we today call racism, but the idea that anyone outside your tribe or not related by blood was fair game, non-human, was common in much of history. This belief still drives and promotes much of the violence in modern tribal societies.

Those are some factors. The one opinion that I will share is that the more peaceful a society gets (lenient punishments and ineffective/unarmed enforcement) the better being violent works, the more it pays and the easier it is to get away with.

Effective violence profoundly affects the survival of your children. Think that through. In Chapter 9, I mentioned that one of my friends says, with deep justification, "There is no such thing as a knife culture. Just people too poor to buy guns." Fighting with weapons is fighting for your life and it is serious stuff. As romantic as it sounds, as important as weapons are to cultural identity NO SOCIETY that has stayed with primitive weapons once better weapons are available has survived.

Japan's "Giving Up The Gun" was a totalitarian state realizing that arming the peasants would bring the total destruction of their caste system. The better weapons weren't given up, not entirely. An allotted number was kept under lock and key in case the rulers needed them.

Anthropologists have done extensive articles on how the introduction of a single metal axe has caused profound change in a lithic society. They lament the 'destruction' of the society, but that one metal axe made it possible to heat and feed more of your children with less work. Fewer people starve. All humans would rather lament the passing of an age than the unnecessary passing of a child. Going with the good weapons and the good tools is a no-brainer.

So, as much as it might be romantic to have swords on your spaceships, people who are worried about dying or their children dying don't give a flaming damn about romance.

In one of the colonial reconstructions (in Virginia?) they showed the jail cell. It was about ten feet by ten feet. It was the only jail cell for the entire colony. One of the tourists commented that there couldn't have been much crime back then. The tour guide said, no, it's just that people weren't held for punishment. The penalty for every felony was death by hanging. The cell was just a place to hold people while the gallows was set up.

✧✦✧✦✧

HOMEWORK:

This exercise comes from "Drills: Training For Sudden Violence." It is long and involved, but I believe worth your time. I usually run it as a moderated group exercise.

In Exercise #2 from Chapter Five, you got a little bit into the head of an addict by thinking of your starving children. Revisit that now, but as a literal problem. Not addicts, but real people starving. Understand that this was the baseline for much of human history. All organisms breed to their carrying capacities. All of our ancestors at some point hunted out territory or over-farmed the soil and had to move to other territory, territory that was already occupied. All of our ancestors did this, because any group that failed to make these decisions left no offspring.

The World-Building exercise starts with choosing one of the basic survival modes of early humanity. The participants can work from the viewpoint of a hunter-gatherer society or an early farming society. The people can discuss what those choices mean about the skills to get food and how children are raised and what things are considered virtues and how deviance is handled... all from the baseline reminder that this is a world where people starve.

This has been the base line for most people for most of human history.

Design your society. How do you get food? How are children raised? What weapons or tools are common?

Your natural resources have dwindled. Your children will starve this winter unless you get more food. Neighboring tribes are in a similar state and have none to share. You must take their stores or their land in order to survive.

First question–given a choice between peaceful farmers to your South, hunter/gatherer horsemen to your North and East and fierce cannibals to your west ... whom do you invade?

Do you steal the stores and hope that they starve before they can counter-attack for survival and revenge? Or do you take their land?

If you are willing to murder for food or money, what story do you tell yourself? We are humans and no matter what we do, we will convince ourselves that we are the good guys. What mechanism do you use to justify pre-meditated and socially sanctioned murder?

Note well: I'm fairly cool with "Because I don't want my children to die." But very few people are cool with simple justifications on big issues. They want something greater.

What story do you tell your children?

How do you teach them to kill, both the mechanics of it and the justifications. Seriously, how do you explain to a six-year-old why it is okay to kill a Taboolian but not okay to hit his sister?

Could you exploit without killing?

Can you demand tribute instead of killing and taking?

Would you take slaves? Is that better or worse than killing? If so, who would you take as slaves? Everybody? The young?

Social controls. Raiders require teamwork, discipline and clear lines of authority to survive. What do you do with tribesmen who aren't trustworthy?

Lesser levels of social control: How are disputes handled within a tribe that is very good at killing? Remember that killing tribe members weakens you in future battles with others. (And right here, in the social control, designed for non-lethal, in-house stuff do we get the first suggestions of what we would recognize as a modern martial art. Dueling, armed to first blood or non-lethal unarmed combat. Dominance games.)

Assume hunger was a factor for generations, and the stories that have been told to justify the violence have been told for generations. You have warriors now, maybe Holy Warriors. A religion that justifies raiding. What happens when the tribe is no longer hungry?

If you do go to war and one member of the tribe is very, very good at killing people and seems to enjoy it, what do you do with him during peacetime? He is a hero in wartime, someone that people fear at least a bit in peacetime. Do you need extra controls on the proven warriors? If so, what?

On one level or another, all of these problems still exist.

FOR ANALYSIS:

Do you see parallels between the types and strategies of modern criminals? Do many violent criminals have a personal mythology?

Do we, as humans assume that the mythology came first and the behavior followed? When we do make that assumption, we kind of forget that there was a need underlying it all.

This will likely offend some people, but try to give it some honest thought: how many religions suddenly make more sense when you start looking at them as justifying lies for children? How many of the purposes behind the myths simply no longer apply? Right and wrong may or may not change over time, but resources to fulfill needs do, and that drives a lot of the rules.

TO RECAP:

- When you write a twelfth century rogue, the character will slit throats without thinking or hesitation. He will care more about not getting messy than having nightmares. He won't try to hide evidence because no one will look.
- When you write the twelfth century damsel, bodice ripping isn't romantic–it is the prelude to a rape, something that she has probably experienced from those more powerful with no consequences since she was a child.
- When you are thinking about a violent person living in a violent time, they would do things that are unthinkable from the comfort of our places and times, do them with ruthless efficiency and be completely okay with it.
- Effective violence in most times and places was necessary for the survival of your children.

... 18 ...

BEING HURT

Being hurt is almost purely psychological, and pros distinguish carefully between pain and injury. If you can walk pain off, it's not an injury. When a Ranger or Ranger wannabe says, "Pain is weakness leaving your body" they aren't talking about injury.

And maybe the line is fuzzy, in some ways. If something has pierced your skin to the point that you bleed, you have been injured ... but unless it in some way hampers your ability to move (physically, not psychologically) we don't consider it injury. Put on your big girl panties and get back to work. Or 'cowboy up' depending on your team.

So you ignore cuts and scrapes and most bruises. Unless the blood dripping down the back of your throat interferes with your breathing, a broken nose is just a reason to fight harder ... and if it is interfering with your breathing you probably need to fight harder quicker and get it over with anyway.

Pain and pain threshold is, in my opinion, a function of experience and socialization.

It starts the first time a baby falls down. If you have kids, you have seen this. The baby falls. It is a big, new sensation. And the baby starts looking around for someone to explain what it means. If mom or dad rush over and acts scared, the baby learns that this new sensation is a *bad thing* and starts to cry, and will continue to cry whenever they fall.

If the same parents give a non-committal "Are you okay?" the child sees the attention, doesn't understand the words and may giggle, and learn to like minor bumps.

Pain and discomfort. What hurts? I was raised in ranch country. Like every other kid I knew, when rain threatened we had to get the hay in–no stopping, no resting. We milked by hand, and we didn't get to stop just because we were tired or our hands cramped and wouldn't grip. Every last drop or the cow would get mastitis. When I went to college and saw city kid athletes train, it puzzled me, because they quit when they got tired or went to muscle failure. It had never occurred to me that just stopping was an option. I didn't come from that world.

The first time you get hit in the face it is an immense new sensation. If you process it as pain it is shocking and often debilitating. The tenth or twentieth or hundredth, it is just a data point. But when you get slapped for the first time, that is new.

Your body changes, too. Beginners in judo go home every night with their hands red and swollen from slapping the mat while learning to fall. But over time that changes, and hitting the mat or taking a high fall doesn't register as pain and isn't scary–and your hands quit swelling as well.

If your character has the right background, he or she will be able to shrug off an immense amount of pain. Without that background, it doesn't make sense.

Look at people who walk into coffee tables or jam fingers or hit themselves with cabinet doors or walk too close to a piece of sharp metal. Some break down right there, howling. Not just children, either. Some talk about it as if it was a major life event. Some decide that they can't do anything. And others literally don't notice. Currently I have a scab on my left arm. I think it was going too close to an air conditioner while running through an alley ... but I can only guess that because my lovely and talented wife pointed out I was bleeding when I got home. Otherwise I wouldn't have even a vague idea of when it happened (which can be said for several scars.)

The reactions are purely psychological. And, interestingly, they often change when the circumstances change. Generally, animals don't show pain to strangers. Some humans hide their pain as well and in humans it is probably less instinct than conditioning. If you live in an environment that is caring and nurturing, where people take care of you when you are sick or injured, there is no punishment for showing weakness and possibly even reward. So people in the civilized world show pain. Some even exploit the dynamic (hypochondria.)

In an environment where if you are weak I beat you up and take your stuff (like most drug cultures) there is an incredible incentive to hide weakness (hide anything, really.) But many people who never show pain while on the street, game the system hard on the inside for the free medical care that the jail offers. They complain about insignificant aches and pains as if each was life-threatening.

There are some intense pains that I'm not sure about. They work on enough people that I want to say that they are beyond psychological, but I've seen them fail, too, so I'm not sure.

Groin shots. I've taken a perfectly targeted rear heel kick that lifted me over a foot in the air and not felt any pain for over a minute.

I just kept sparring. In about a minute I felt some pain and a lot of nausea, but it wasn't that bad.

Conversely, I've taken a light flick to a testicle that curled me up in a little ball of pain. That said, despite dozens of solid groin shots, only twice has it ever made me stop fighting.

The liver shot. Under the lowest ribs on your own right side is your liver. It is the reason that god invented the left hook punch. I already mentioned in Chapter 6 that a liver shot feels like a groin shot to an eight-pound testicle. I've put people down with it pretty consistently and been put down with it ... but it is not even close to 100% reliable, and there is a risk of serious injury associated with it. But it really hurts.

The most reliable pains strike I know is the slap to the ears. It's not just a pain strike. I ruptured a man's eardrum through a helmet with one and concussions are common (although, come to think of it, since dizziness and nausea are symptoms of both concussion and the balance disruption of an ear injury, can I be sure?)

But it hurts. It hurts like I imagine having a red-hot ice pick shoved in your ear would hurt. Used on me, I went down to my knees in pain and so far, I've seen that reaction every time. So far. But the sample is less than a dozen, so don't count on it.

Pressure points. There are a number of places on the human body that hurt worse than other places. We call them pressure points. They can be poked or ground or gouged. Some people really like to use them.

My thoughts: Pain is idiosyncratic, personal and unreliable. Sometimes pressure points work, sometimes they don't. Some people are virtually immune to them and most people are insensitive to some of them. The reliability decreases even more when the person is drunk, drugged, enraged or mentally ill ... which accounts for an enormous percentage of the people you may have to fight.

When they are used, there are three good reasons. Bargaining is implicit in a lot of pressure points: "You quit what you are doing and I will stop causing you pain." The second reason is that some have a reliable flinch response. If I gouge a thumb into the soft spot under your jaw (where you glands swell when you are sick) it will tend to make you go up on your toes and twist away from the pain, making it very easy to sweep your feet out. The third reason is that sometimes a sharp, unexpected pain can make the threat freeze or stop thinking for a second and buy you time to do something else.

Sampling error. I was having a discussion with a very good self-defense and rape prevention instructor based in Northern California. She has a dozen students that have successfully defended themselves with either nose strikes or groin strikes. Those two techniques have been 100% successful for her students.

In my experience, perfectly executed groin strikes have only worked 20% of the time. Nose strikes have stopped sparring sessions but they have never, ever stopped a fight. 0%.

The difference? I think it is the difference between a potential rapist who has chosen what looks like an easy victim, and someone who has worked himself up to attacking an officer. The level of commitment and the expectations of the threat likely have a huge psychological impact (pardon the pun) on what will work.

✧✦✧✦✧

HOMEWORK:

This goes for this lesson and the next as well: Take a good first aid course.

TO RECAP:

- ‘Hurt’ is psychological
- Response to pain vary by experience and socialization
- Showing pain also varies by situation
- Pain is unreliable and idiosyncratic
- Pain is used for bargaining, to draw a specific motion or to momentarily stop thought

... 19 ...

BEING WOUNDED

Most authors have been hurt but not wounded, and this is one of the places where I find action novels to fall apart. Being wounded is not the same as being hurt. When your ankle is hurt, you don't want to run. But with enough will or adrenaline you can run. You will run. When your ankle is truly injured, it will collapse out from under you despite will or adrenaline.

Exceptional people, like many of your characters, have continued to fight with horrific injuries. But they did not move the same. There were things they could not do. Glance over some books on anatomy and physiology. When your character gets injured look at what *that* trauma would do to *those* structures, and have your character debilitated accordingly.

If your character gets shot or stabbed or clubbed, there is a lot going on.

Shot: In Chapter 13 I briefly discussed wounds from firearms. Bear with me while I refresh your memory before I go into more detail: A handgun bullet does roughly as much damage as a stick of the same diameter shoved into your body. Roughly. It is going fast enough that if it hits bone, the bone can be shattered and fragments of the bone can cut more tissue. It can also deform or tumble, making the wound channel significantly wider than the bullet diameter.

Sometimes. There have been a lot of documented cases of a bullet following the path of least resistance and going around bones and organs, basically slipping under the skin and staying at that depth, circling the body. You can get some pretty weird wound channels and unlikely-seeming entrance and exit wounds that way.

Rifle bullets are a whole different animal. There appears to be some magic velocity (about 2100-2300 feet per second) where the bullet does much more damage than its size would indicate. There are a lot of theories about the mechanism. Suffice it to say that a rifle wound is far more serious than a handgun, many will blow through things that will stop handgun rounds. They are more likely to shatter bone and far more likely to cause internal damage that you can't see.

According to my handgun instructor (former USMC FAST team member and US Marshals Service SOG), only 4% of the people die from a single handgun wound. He claims that the number squares with each additional round, 16% with two, 64% with three. (People have survived way more than four rounds, though, so this is a rule of thumb, not a truth.) That's not immediate deaths or incapacitations, by the way. You can be killed by a gun without being stopped. And some people definitely stop (or run away) without being killed.

Blood, muscle, organ, bone and joint.

The round creates a wound channel that severs blood vessels. If it hits an artery (and actually, sometimes arteries are elastic enough to move aside and not be severed, especially with jacketed or round-nosed bullets) blood will start spurting with each heartbeat. That's bad. If it hits a major vein, there will be a steady flow. That's bad too, but the pressure is less so it is easier to stop or slow the bleeding with direct pressure.

If you lose enough blood, you pass out. Lose more and you die. That simple. Possibly in extremely fatty tissue you might get the proverbial flesh wound and not be in danger of bleeding out. Small caliber bullets, like .22 may close up and limit bleeding. Wadcutters (flat topped bullets, they feed poorly in automatics and semi automatics) create a wound channel that doesn't close up and thus bleeds profusely. Some of the expanding bullets, like the Ranger™, are designed to do this as well.

First aid slows or stops the bleeding, but be aware that if the wound channel goes into one of the body cavities, the external bandage is doing nothing for the internal bleeding.

A character bleeding out, internally or externally, will get agitated (I notice stupid and stubborn more in real life) sweaty and cold, then sleepy and die. This is not a choice. Willpower will not overcome this. This is shock.

Muscle: If the bullet tears up a muscle, the muscle won't be able to do what it usually does. That sounds obvious, but how many times have you seen it violated in fiction and movies?

And if it hits tendon or ligament, the injury (without modern technology) will be permanent. Range of motion and strength lost, forever.

One study (on mice, they frown on doing reproducible slashing on people) showed that a lacerated muscle given optimal treatment would be back to 81% after a month with the best treatment available, but only 35% of original function without treatment.

In people, if there is no tendon involvement (tendons heal very slowly, if at all) and modified by the amount of the damage, a lacerated muscle can take 12 weeks to heal (grow together) and another year to get close to normal (scar tissue normalizing).

Organ. Strangely enough, it seems that chest wounds (provided you don't die) are the one gunshot injury least likely to result in permanent disability. Yay.

Vascular organs, like the liver, gall bladder, kidneys and brain, put you at great risk for bleeding out when injured. A lot of blood gets cycled through those organs. Minor injuries can be a relatively slow (minutes to hours) shocky death. Heart, of course, though a muscle, is the ultimate vascular organ. Though people have survived getting shot in the heart:

http://www.lapdonline.org/inside_the_lapd/content_basic_view/27327#Stacy%20Lim

Don't count on even a heart shot being quick. It takes about ten seconds to bleed out to unconsciousness from a good heart shot.

Damage to the brain can be extremely idiosyncratic. The brain is a delicate organ that controls almost everything and influences what it doesn't control directly. Enough trauma or trauma to the right place and death can be quick. Trauma to the motor nerves might leave a thinking, aware person who cannot move, or cannot move a part of the body. Trauma to the occipital cortex can cause blindness.

Brain damage also gives some bizarre effects. According to my Neuroanatomy professor long ago, specific damage to the visual processing centers can create a state of conscious blindness. The subject would have normal visual reflexes– would stop something coming at his face, would even catch a falling cup without thinking, but was completely blind. Part of the brain could see. There was nothing wrong with the eye or the optic nerve or the motor cortex. But the bridge between those functions and the neocortex was cut. So the person was not consciously aware that he could see. Possibly the birth of the blind swordsmen legends?

And, of course, if you damage the brain you will change the personality. A lot or a little. In 1848 Phineas Gage was setting charges for a new railroad when a tamping bar was blown through his skull from top to bottom just behind his left eye. He didn't even lose consciousness (until blood loss and shock) and recovered, mostly. But his doctor reports that he wasn't the same afterwards. Less controlled, more arguing.

Going back to that long-ago Neuroanatomy prof: Once upon a time a young man decided to commit suicide with an electric drill. He gave up after nine holes. Only long-term effect seems to be that he cured his depression.

The brain is weird and fascinating. If you have dealt with stroke patients, use that experience.

We'll talk about lungshots in the chapter on dying. It is enough for here to say that if your breathing is compromised, your efficiency suffers. It doesn't matter how the breathing is compromised. If the throat is partially blocked whether from foreign object or swelling after a strike, less air is getting to the lungs. If the lungs are damaged or filling with fluids or being squeezed, less oxygen is getting to the blood. If less blood is pumping it doesn't matter whether the cause is a weakened heart or the fact that most of your blood is in a pool on the floor, the cells are not getting the oxygen they need. If the cells don't get the oxygen they need, they can't do their jobs. Hands don't work. The brain doesn't think efficiently. Things get bad.

If the digestive hollow organs (stomach, intestines, bladder, bowels) are perforated, they don't necessarily incapacitate immediately. Unlike the stomach muscles which are foundational to almost all movement, your character doesn't really *need* her stomach in any given second. It opens up two avenues for death, however. Septicemia and internal bleeding will be addressed in the next chapter. And it hurts. Gut wounds have a reputation for slow and agonizing death and the pain is enough to incapacitate most people. Imagine stomach acid vomited into a deep wound.

Bone: If the bullet shatters a bone, the character will lose structure and muscle attachments. Obvious again. Look at your body. When an author has a character say, "You took one in the shoulder but it went clean through, you'll be okay," look at your shoulder! How freaking obese would the character have to be for something to go clean through one of the most bone and tendon rich parts of the body (not to mention blood vessels and nerves) without shattering something?

Simple bone breaks are the one thing in the body that seems to heal stronger than the original. Not true for shattering wounds. There are little sharp chips everywhere and the broken ends don't know what needs to grow to what. Modern surgery is often necessary to regain anything approaching full use.

Joints. I won't stick strictly to bullet wounds here. Joints can be injured in a lot of ways. Strained, sprained, dislocated, shattered. A joint is a complex interplay of bone, cartilage, muscle, tendon and ligaments with a lot of nerves. Which means that a bullet tearing through will do an incredible amount of damage to a variety of different tissues, each of which heals differently.

If the muscles are torn, they will heal like other injuries. Bone in a joint injury may not. Fractures here tend to be complicated, with tiny chips. Left to themselves the bone chips will grow randomly and the limb will never be the same. Motion will be lost and it will always be painful. Bone chips in a joint require modern surgery or the equivalent to regain full use.

Tendons and ligaments (tendons hold muscle to bone, ligaments hold bone to bone) are not very vascular. Which means that they have very little blood running through them. Which means that once torn, they heal poorly if at all. Again, without modern surgery or the equivalent, ligament and tendon tears will mean an unstable and weak joint for the rest of the protagonist's life.

If the tendons and ligaments are stretched (without popping out, that's a *strain*), even if the joint pops out momentarily (momentary=sprain) they will heal over time, but they will be weak and sore for a long while. After my first shoulder dislocation I waited until the shoulder had been pain free for a month before I tested it ... and popped it right back out again. It never got back to full strength or stability.

If the joint is dislocated, tendons and ligaments will be stretched, there will be pain and swelling (generally, for whatever reason I almost never get edema, including with broken bones. No idea how common that is) and the limb is pretty much useless. Most people will cradle the arm if the elbow, shoulder or wrist is damaged. The dislocated parts of the limb can cut off blood flow or pinch off the nerves. That can cause you to lose the limb unless the dislocation is reduced, and an improper reduction can do even more damage to vessels and nerves.

Stabbed or slashed. Knives and swords. Most of what was said about bleeding out above applies, but that is one of the goals with a knife. That is why knife assaults are aimed at the vascular organs, especially the liver and kidney, and why the 'sewing machine' attack is preferred–multiple wounds bleed more and faster than single wounds.

Whereas a bullet might lacerate or nick an artery, knives are intended for that and so they often get more external bleeding and eviscerations than a bullet will cause.

Evisceration from a stab:

http://www.trauma.org/index.php/main/image/879/C13

Blade weapons are also more likely to sever a muscle completely than a bullet. A severed muscle is unusable. Your character takes a good slash to the hamstring, she can straighten the knee but not bend it. Her bicep gets slashed, she cannot bend her arm at the elbow. Sometimes minor wounds on the forearm will hamper function in part of the fingers.

Most light blades work on flesh and bounce off bone, but not swords. You've seen (or chosen to avoid) the machete pictures. I've used swords to butcher goats. A decent sword goes through hide, muscle and bone like air. It is easy. Lopping off an unarmored hand would be child's play.

Bigger bones would be harder, perhaps. Maybe in a few years we'll raise some cattle and I can let you know.

My EMT and military medic classes said that traumatic amputations sometimes don't bleed. The severed arteries and veins are retracted and the muscles around them tense, sealing them off. For a time.

Blunt weapons. I've known people who didn't realize they were cut and heard of some who didn't realize they were shot. I've never met or heard of anyone who didn't realize he was being hit with a baseball bat.

There are four basic injuries you get with a blunt weapon: bruises, fractures, concussions and special stuff.

Mild bruises fall under the pain category. You generally don't notice them until the adrenaline wears off. This is even true for deep bone bruising. The important part, for your character, is that when the adrenaline does wear off, the muscles seize up. You sometimes can't use the limb. Deep bruises can keep you from full activity for weeks. The limb just won't move to the full range, using the muscle hurts and it can be tender to touch.

That said, I find when adrenaline kicks in again, I don't notice it a bit.

Fractures are broken bones, and they are similar to what has already been described. Blunt weapons sometimes will split the skin over the bone even if the bone doesn't break. I was watching a forensic sciences show (fiction) on TV where they said authoritatively that the first blunt weapon strike to the head don't bleed. My scars know better. Maybe they meant that the first wound doesn't splash?

Concussions come from head trauma. There are a lot of different flavors of concussion. I don't believe in the Hollywood knockout where you get hit in the head, sleep for a little while and wake up fine. If that happened, the person fainted, they weren't knocked out (in my opinion, of course.)

The most common, I think, is the dizzy and nauseous concussion. My first was for three days. The second time I was also weirdly elated and uninhibited for a couple of days ... I think three again, but I don't remember. It was like being pleasantly drunk and happy but also sick and dizzy with a horrible headache.

The most painful concussion was because I decided to go snorkeling with the other concussion. Felt like a spike was being driven into my ear for hours afterwards. Never overpressure with head trauma.

The scariest concussion was one of the few times I've lost consciousness. It was in judo and I took a bad fall and everything went black just for a second. Then it happened again about ten minutes later. Then again an hour later. My brain tissue was swelling. First time I've ever been seen quickly at an HMO emergency room.

Basically, there aren't any freebies in head trauma. If a character gets hit hard enough to be put down, even temporarily, there will be other prices to pay. Paralysis, permanent or temporary. Memory loss (my deficit). Blindness is always on the table. Even at the best, the injured person will be clumsy and unsteady, usually for days. And if it gets worse, it means that they are dying as the brain swells.

The special strikes with a blunt weapon include things like smacking the throat, stunning, and rupturing organs.

A broken rib can lacerate liver, spleen, or lungs and, (very rarely) heart, causing internal bleeding. No outward injury except possibly a bruise. Symptoms of shock will come on, fast or slow depending on the damage.

The hollow organs, especially if full, can also be ruptured. Think the bladder. Though there will be internal bleeding, the big danger is from peritonitis as the icky fluids and solids infect the gut sack.

The throat can be collapsed. It will take, theoretically, about a minute to lose consciousness and four minutes to die. Few people fight, most grab at their throat with both hands like any other choking victim.

There are places you can hit, notable the sides of the neck, a flat slap to the ears, and the jaw hinge where you can get a stun. Not quite a knockout, more a momentary disorientation. Seems to work less reliably on crazy people and drugged-up people. With enough force, the jaw hinge strike can also break or dislocate the jaw and get a knockout. The ear slap can concuss and puncture eardrums

There have been survivors in more primitive times of the wounds listed here, but it is hard to say how and why luck smiled on that person, that day.

✧✦✧✦✧

TO RECAP:

- Different weapons have different mechanisms of injury
- Circulatory system, muscles, organs, bone, joints and brain can all be injured in different ways
- Bruises, cuts, fractures, dislocations, ruptures, and concussions
- There are no freebies with brain trauma

... 20 ...

HOW YOU DIE

Shock is "inadequate perfusion of tissues with blood and oxygen" and it is what causes organs and people to shut down, to die. This is the killer. This is vision fading and you don't know way because you were so adrenalized you didn't even know you've been stabbed. This is the world getting cold and dark and often thirsty. If you don't know what is going on, like carbon monoxide poisoning or hypothermia or an internal bleed you might just feel tired, sleepy.

If you do know what is going on it is often terrifying: in the midst of the pain, you realize your body is shutting down and each second you are becoming less able to do anything. As your need increases your ability decreases. This is the downward spiral.

Most of your characters after a fight will have to deal with hypovolemic shock, the effect of bleeding out. If the wound is external, they will probably know that they are bleeding, but not always. It's possible to have a serious wound and not realize it. Stabbed in the back the character thinks it is all over and he or she has won and can't figure out why their shoes feel full of warm water and things begin to fade.

The early symptoms of shock are psychological. The textbooks say anxiety or agitation. I find that people get a really bad idea and then fixate on it, e.g. "I can't go to the hospital and leave my house with all this blood on the floor" or a need to put away the tools carefully before binding a wound. Sometimes you physically have to fight a shocky person to help her.

The early obvious signs are cool clammy skin, pallor and sweating. The clinical signs would be a drop in blood pressure and a weak, rapid pulse.

Energy level goes down. Then you collapse, pass out, and die. If the last stages are anything like being strangled unconscious, you will hear a rushing sound in your ears, like the ocean. You will feel a warm and pleasant floating sensation. Then your eyes will start to go tunnel-vision, narrowing. In strangulation, sometimes the rim is black, sometimes red. I don't know why. My gut says that the rim when bleeding to death will be black. The very last thing, for me, is I hear a single, clear tone. That's probably angels singing.

That's bleeding to death.

The only thing that kills instantly (to my knowledge) is massive trauma to the brainstem. I talked about it briefly in the story about putting down Gazelle. By instant death, I mean that the subject goes completely limp. Most other forms of death, including truly massive brain trauma and decapitation involve involuntary clenching of certain muscles. In other words, even dead people can still pull triggers. They spasm and thrash and kick and try to breathe. "Bite the dust" was an ancient Greek observation (Samuel Butler's translation of Homer's "The Iliad") of this phenomenon.

This is where the 'sniper spot' comes in. Hostage rescue snipers are taught to aim, when they can, for the brainstem to prevent even involuntary fire from the threat. It is right at the top of the spine where it connects to the brain. The aim point from the front is the tip of the nose, from the sides the ear hole and from behind the first cervical vertebra or just above it.

Neck breaks above C4 (the fourth cervical vertebra, counting from the top) and including C4, require a ventilator. Without mechanical assistance the person will die of suffocation. Breaking the neck is not an immediate death. It may neutralize the threat immediately, but the threat will be conscious of his helplessness as he suffocates unconscious and then dies.

Sniper spot aside, the brain controls everything. Sufficient brain trauma will kill, but it won't be quick. As long as the brainstem is intact, there will be shuddering and spasming and agonal breathing and usually some seizure-like activity. That goes for many forms of death. It's not like going to sleep with a manly smile. There is thirst and pain and fear.

Never forget that heroes die screaming for their mothers. Just like everyone else.

Chest wounds frequently result in a pneumothorax or hemothorax. They can happen from internal injuries, such as a broken rib, or intrusive injuries (shootings and stabbings.) When air begins leaking into the space around the lung (the pleural sac) it can't normally escape. Each inhale traps more air and eventually squeezes both lungs until the person suffocates.

Hemothorax is the same thing but with leaking blood instead of air.

From the outside, breathing becomes labored. The bad sign is when the trachea actually starts to shift, being pushed to one side. If you listen, one lung is silent when the person inhales. With a little training and the right equipment, it is relatively easy to treat in the field.

If a character gets his trachea collapsed, he will suffocate. On one level it is like holding your breath until you pass out. You probably know, or can find out just by holding your breath what that feels like in your lungs. Maybe you have the will to keep it up until you panic or maybe you've come close enough to drowning to know that feeling. If not, it's hard to wrap your mind around exactly how terrifying and panicked the strongest, bravest or mellowest person can become.

But that leaves out a piece. The pain from a trachea strike is intense. It's left big men on their knees trying to scream. Then they panic more when it slowly registers that the scream is silent.

The next death that comes to mind comes in two flavors: Peritonitis and septicemia.

Before the invention of modern antibiotics, abdominal wounds had a very poor prognosis. If you know someone who has suffered a burst appendix, you know the basics of peritonitis: pain, fever. Without medical intervention, death.

The first symptom of peritonitis are often poor appetite and nausea. Then pain, starting as a dull ache that spreads and intensifies. The abdomen may become rigid and distended. Then fever, chills. It hurts, a lot, and you die.

Septicemia is sometimes called blood poisoning. It can be the result of infected wounds (for heaven's sake, if you have your characters do some escape from a castle that involves crawling through sewage, make the ones with open wounds die.)

The infection gets in the blood and spreads systemically. Blood pressure drops, fever increases. Early signs include a hot, sometimes pus-weeping wound and red lines moving up the veins. With modern treatment, severe septicemia has a mortality rate of 40-60%, patients who have suffered no severe organ compromise still die 15-30% of the time. I couldn't find a source on survival rates before the introduction of antibiotics, but mice with induced septicemia have a 23% survival rate at seven days.

Infection from a human bite:

http://pharmacityresearch.blogspot.com/2009/10/hand-infections.html

There is so much to dying. My lovely wife called me on this chapter. I distance myself by making it clinical. I go into medic mode. I can either do something or not. If not, walk away ....

This is personal. Dying is the starkest, realest thing. And the thing we most deny. If you have never seen the person fade from someone's eyes, the thing that makes a human a human, alive, this will be hard to understand.

We are meat when we die. You don't see that spark leave. You don't see it go elsewhere. It vanishes. And if you see enough, you know it is inevitable. The people all around you, in this time and place, almost all of your readers and writers seem oblivious to this. We have charities and institutions and policies for something that we all know to be a lie. You can't 'save the children.' You can't save anybody. You can just try to limit how they die and maybe when. But the world has a hundred percent mortality rate. It always has. It always will.

Humans don't do well with harsh inevitabilities. We want control. We want to cheat. We want something other than death and ending. Whatever world you write, there will be an element of this. There will be ritual and belief and customs.

We look for patterns. I mentioned earlier that without a disease theory, vampires, the dead reproducing made a certain amount of sense. Once we (I'm not identifying who this 'we' was) had eight deaths in two months. All suicides. I so badly wanted to find a skilled assassin or a supernatural cause, something that would make this tragedy into a pattern. Because we can manipulate patterns. We want a cause, we want something we can control.

The skin looks grey, especially at the edge of wounds. Yellowish when the blood has all pooled, except for the purplish places where the blood did pool and the white places that were in direct contact with the ground. If they are fresh and the stomach was mostly empty, the smell might not be that bad. Blood smells metallic, flesh like meat, as you would expect.

Sometimes when you move a body trapped air escapes through the throat and the corpse moans.

Immediately after death, the body is limp and very hard to move. So you get to the head end and lift it into a sitting position. Then you lift from the armpits and let it lean back so the knees lock. Once the knees lock you can push it to height and step around to the front and let it collapse over your shoulder so you can use a fireman's carry.

When the body goes into rigor mortis, it is stiff and easier to move but things may be sticking out at odd angles. I've been lucky and never had to fold a corpse in rigor. I don't know if the joints make noise.

After rigor passes, you are back to limp again. Then things get nasty as decomposition sets in and tissues and hollow organs swell with gasses.

Where there is a lot of death there will be flies and rats, feral dogs and the local scavenger birds. Lots of rats. Lots of flies.

TO RECAP:

- ✧ Shock is what causes death
- ✧ Internal bleeding is easily missed
- ✧ Brain trauma can kill slowly to quickly
- ✧ Seizure-like activity is usually associated with death
- ✧ Chest, throat and upper spine trauma tend to kill by suffocation
- ✧ Infections kill, slow and ugly
- ✧ You and your characters and their society must deal with inevitability

... 21 ...

RANDOM DETAILS

I've tried to organize the subjects in a semblance of logic and order, but in many ways violence is the soul of chaos and there are a bunch of things that don't fit in discrete areas. And these things are some of the details you might be able to mine to enrich your writing. So here goes, in no particular order:

An infighter is someone who prefers fighting at extremely close range, chest-to-chest, chest-to-shoulder, chest-to-back. I sometimes call it halitosis range. Most people feel safer the farther they are away from the threat, so you get punchers and kickers. Infighting finishes things fast and combines damage with controlling the body. It's more tactile than visual. Most people can be taken down by someone who fights closer.

Physically, that's because it is harder to stay away than it is to close. Mentally it is because there tends to be a fear reaction to things that fight closer than you. The farther away you can kill someone, the cleaner and more civilized it seems. When you run into someone who is willing to kill at biting range it is terrifying for most people.

If a woman is pushed to violence, her defaults will be to do damage and to use a tool. When a guy is pushed over the line, his default will be to do techniques that don't do much damage and to do so bare-handed.

There are cultural variations, of course, but even at the height of European dueling, a man would slap his opponent (empty hand, no damage) to signal the desire to duel. A samurai had a right to instantly cut down anyone who insulted him, *provided they were of a lower caste.* Within caste, tribe, or group men doing less damage and empty-handed is the norm. It is social violence.

Being the ambusher is a great advantage. As she is moving in she has time (if she knows what she is doing) to adjust her own adrenaline level to get closer to her peak, to the zone.

That's usually a combination of training and experience, but there are breathing exercises specifically for it (autogenic or 'warrior breathing'– in for a count of four, hold for a count of four, exhale for a count of four, hold empty for a count of four ... repeat. Takes too much time to use in a fight but can be used during the build-up or the approach.) Officers have time to do it when responding to calls.

There is also an advantage in that the bad guys will be somewhat adrenalized. Due to the tunnel vision and auditory exclusion effects it is very easy to sneak up on people who are already fighting and get in a great position.

Instant kills. Most take some time. The only instant kill on a human body is the brainstem, which is hard to reach with a knife. There are a lot of places that shut people down quickly, though. We are getting out of my direct experience here and what follows is stuff I have been trained (primarily military).

I have been told that kidney stabs make the victim go into shock almost instantly. You can hit the ascending aorta by stabbing down behind the collarbone and the person bleeds to unconsciousness in seconds (I'd guess ten, given that people with their heads cut off try to keep talking for about seven seconds ....) A neck break, especially an inward and upward strike with a tool against the first cervical vertebrae is probably the fastest and most reliable (death in a minute or less but paralysis instantly).

To clarify, when I mention brainstem as the only instant kill, it is the one place where the person goes dead *and* limp, as mentioned earlier.

There is a system to breaking a neck and it is to twist and bend (with a few exceptions, doing only one just strains the muscles) but the neck is both strong and flexible. The military systems to do a neck break usually involve full falling body weight or (and this is something that a lot of people for some reason forget) using a tool. A shovel or the edge of your own helmet will do damage to the c-spine (cervical spine, the neck) with a lot less effort and precision skill.

There is a group, Cane Masters, that both teach fighting with canes and make special hardwood versions with some extras. It's not something I've studied, but I have a friend near Victoria BC who teaches it:

http://defendyourself101.ca/

La canne is also taught in savate, and some hapkido instructors:

http://burrese.com/ teach it as well.

The hand is one of the primary targets in a sword fight. It is in range well before anything else (except sometimes the lead knee) and tends to stop the guy from fighting back when his fingers and sword drop to the ground (only one of my fingers and my thumbs haven't been broken yet in sword training). Bell guards make great punching tools and you can design the quillons to be blade catchers, which is pretty cool. The pommel can also be used as a weapon (where the word pummeling comes from). One detail is that the fancy pommels with dragon heads or wolves or whatever? Those little pretty bronze ears or horns tear the shit out of your forearm when you are practicing with the weapon.

Eye contact is way over-romanticized. There's a time for it, but staring in the eyes or glaring is what wannabes trying to look tough do. When you get the sensation of someone's eyes 'boring right through you' what you are picking up is that the eyes may be pointed at you but are out of focus. They are, in fact, focused to a point way behind you, where the horizon would be. This is the 'thousand yard stare' and it has nothing to do with shock or psychological damage. Focused vision, what you get with the center of your pupils, is great for picking up details but has the slowest reaction speed of any of the senses except, possibly, smell or taste. The thousand yard stare puts your hands, feet, shoulders and hips in the peripheral vision, which has much faster reaction time. It also helps break the tunnel vision problem.

Fighting or even sparring, I often deliberately look away. The threat is still in my peripheral vision, it reads as if I am unconcerned and it drastically improves my reaction time. Good benefits.

Infighting you can do with your eyes closed. In seminars, I usually get the students to try blindfolded infighting. The amount of information you can pick up by touch strikes most as amazing. Not only can you target precisely (with only a little practice most can accurately kick a knee just by the contact of a hand on the shoulder) but since almost any movement is preceded by a slight shift in weight, you can feel what the threat is about to do ... sort of a combative precognition.

Things you miss. This is part of my rant about fiction and movies. Here are a few of the things that people get wrong or don't realize.

1) The speed. I can empty two magazines (27 shots including a magazine change) in under five seconds. I can empty a 13 round magazine, fairly accurately, in a little over a second. That is much faster than you can really see or think or adapt to changing conditions.

Four people shooting–that can be about 50 shots a second (and that is just handguns, not including submachine guns).

2) It is hard to hit a moving target. It is hard for most people to hit a stationary target, but a lot is a matter of skill. I've been at the range when a federal agency was qualifying and one of their officers was missing the paper (2ft x 3ft) entirely at seven yards. On our side of the range we were expected to put two of two in a two-inch square. But we were training for hostage rescue and the feds were going through an administrative procedure to check off a box for a skill they never intended to use.

Even good shots, though, can't hit worth a damn once the adrenaline hits. And even the best have trouble hitting moving targets and even more trouble when trying to shoot and move simultaneously. Lots of elite teams do train for that, but training doesn't seem to help in your first fight.

There is not a lot of good science in this field. Adrenalized memories are notoriously unreliable. Many people have agendas or want to sell answers and even more want to buy them, so a lot of systems and training protocols have been created and are taught and many sound like they have scientific studies to back them up. And all of us, me included, like to have our perceptions/beliefs/memories backed up by the people in white coats.

But that doesn't make it science. A collection of interviews with survivors is a collection of anecdotes. There are patterns, we have all seen some weird things ... but it is not science. Looking for studies that seem to test something similar happens a lot—like using a cardiac stress test (running a treadmill) to replicate fear because both raise your heart rate.

Science requires experimentation. Without experimentation, you can show statistical correlation but you cannot show causation. It's been at least thirty years since any experiment on fear or battle stress had any chance of passing an American university's Ethics Review Board. Not only is there damn little hard science in this field, there won't be unless society changes drastically.

Suffice it to say that just telling the rookie to hit the zombie in the head will not help. That's a skill.

3) You can't see a damn thing. No one ever seems to have the basic politeness to shoot at you when you have good visibility and light and footing. Sometimes the bad guy is on you and it's so close that if you rely on your eyes all you will see is a boil on his neck or some nasty teeth.

In a military context, bad guys (and good guys, too) shoot from cover and concealment. Which makes it hard to see them well enough to aim. If there is dust and smoke, you can't see a thing and in the days of black powder all of the soldiers on a battlefield were effectively blind after a volley or two. The dust raised from marching in Roman times wasn't that different.

The snipers at Beslan couldn't see what was going on through the smoke and the FBI HRT snipers at Ruby Ridge were completely unprepared for how fast people/targets could move through a high-powered scope's field of vision (one of my examples of extreme training with limited experience.)

Which brings me to scopes. Scopes suck if you are on a moving platform. Try looking through binoculars and holding steady while a friend bounces you around.

4) Most of the time there isn't time to think. And your brain does some pretty damn weird things. On the defensive end, real violence happens really fast. You will go on instincts and training and if you take time to try to think or plan you will likely get clobbered. Fighting your way out of a hole is very much an animal thing, even with weapons, and the

human part of your brain tends to mess it up. Ferocity wins, or, in the words of US Marshall Jones: "Violence of action trumps technique."

Your brain will want to curl up in a ball. Or deny that this is happening. Or focus on some unbelievably trivial bullshit rather than face what is happening. It can be a pretty messed up headspace. Less so for people who have been there before, but these head games are one of the reasons why so few amateurs survive serious attacks.

5) You can't tell if you hit or not. People don't go flying through the air when shot and sometimes they don't even flinch. Unless you are using a rifle, and then only sometimes, there is no spray of blood from the exit wound or exploding heads or 'fine pink mist.'

A suicide. Real deal:

http://www.ebaumsworld.com/video/watch/312665/

Note that even though it is a contact shot from a large caliber handgun (.45 Colt) he doesn't get knocked off his chair, no brain matter gets blown into the wall.

Sometimes you can see dust puff from the threat's jacket. Sometimes, especially at long pistol range (20 yards is very long range for combat shooting with a handgun) and with a .45, you can hear the wet, meaty slap of the bullets hitting. But not usually. We've all been conditioned by TV what is supposed to happen when bullets meet flesh. None of it happens.

6) For that matter, silencers aren't silent. They aren't called silencers anyway, but 'sound suppressors.' Even if you could completely remove the sound of the explosives that fire the bullet, the weapon's action will still make a sound. Something like a sewing machine, but louder with an automatic weapon, like a submachine gun. And you'll hear the impact of the bullets. What do you think a lead ball hitting a skull at 1000 feet per second would sound like?

7) The sounds and the smells stay with you. Movies are very visual. Writing comes through your eyes, in words, and most writers are visual as well. The really visceral aspects of fighting don't come across visually.

People trying to scream through a collapsed throat make a high wheezing, not quite whistling noise. Someone dying does rattle, like an aborted snore.

In 2010 we had an excellent panel at Orycon, and I want to try to recap part of it here. The panel was Violence: What it Looks, Smells, Feels, Tastes and Sounds like.

The way we ran it was just as a huge series of throw-away details from me, Pat (A forensic scientist) Krista (A Somalia vet) and another lady added to the last panel at the last minute. I never got her name down.

The stuff I remember (and there was a ton more):

Looks:

-Bone newly exposed to air is very white.

-Venous blood is dark, arterial blood bright red. But, in bright sunlight, venous blood looks much brighter than most medics expect and they sometimes panic, thinking they have put an IV in an artery.

-The contrast, especially in dark-skinned people, between dark skin, yellowish fat, bright blood and white bone in a deep wound is striking.

-Brains splattered look just like fat.

Smells:

-The smell of human decomposition is sweetish, horrible, gagging and you can't tune it out. You never get used to it.

-In some way that couldn't be explained, life blood smells different than a non-lethal wound. One of my friends, who had to use a knife to kill in a war a long time ago says that life blood smells entirely different than blood from any other type of wound. He can't describe the difference, but it haunts him.

-Fresh brains smell like the freshest meat you've ever smelled and Ivory soap. It's appetizing. It is also possibly the slipperiest substance known to man.

-Sometimes, there is a slow internal bleed that has time to rot, and the bowel movements smell like shit mixed with rotten blood.

-Gut wounds smell like shit and puke and sharp and acidic.

-Gangrene has a horrible smell with a hint of vinegar. I haven't smelled gangrene, but the people who have get green just at the memory.

Feels:

-A tendon popping hurts, but a ligament just feels like the joint turned to water.

-Shock can be a warm and dreamy/floating feeling.

-Small bones and joints breaking, like fingers or ribs, are a sharp, sudden pain. Big bones can be, but sometimes it is much duller.

-In cold weather a fresh break can feel like a dull throb.

-Broken or dislocated fingers always hurt and are slow to heal because they keep catching on things.

-Broken ribs hurt when you move or breathe. Your core muscles are involved in everything and tug on the injured ribs constantly.

-You don't always feel cuts when the adrenaline is on and bullets can feel like slaps or punches.

-A broken tailbone is agony and the only position that doesn't hurt is prone, with a cushion. Every other position hurts constantly.

-When you poke on an exposed intestine it shrinks away from the touch. They hurt when they are stretched, not as much when pushed, but the guy was screaming continuously, so it was kind of hard to be sure.

Sounds:

-We didn't really get to this, but tendon snapping can sound like a pistol shot.

-Sometimes you can, with the right gun at the right distance, hear the bullet hit separate from the sound of the shot.

✧✦✧✦✧

... 22 ...

THE FINAL RANT

Let me go into lecture mode for a minute and talk about something I'm not qualified to talk about (writing) and something I am qualified to talk about (writing that makes me hate most fiction.)

Fiction is about the interplay between people. Or people and things, depending on your genre. And it all hinges on the people being different. As long as bees and ants have hive minds, no matter how far they will evolve, they will never tell real stories. If you actually have a story where two of the characters agree on everything, you can cut one of the characters completely and strengthen the work. Drama is in difference.

That's the part I'm not qualified to talk about. Here's the other part.

The last seventy years in the western world have been a bizarre little bubble. Relative peace. A surplus of food that would be unimaginable in most places in history or many places in the world today. And a stable enough rule of law that violence and crime are a somewhat risky strategy. This is all *new*, and it has allowed us a level of compassion and a freedom to develop sympathies and take chances that would have been dangerous, maybe even suicidal, at other times in history.

Has there ever been, or could there ever be, a society that suffered 10% starvation deaths each winter who merely imprisoned criminals, keeping the criminals fed and warm? How valuable is negotiation when the greatest threats to life aren't people? Before the advent of serious trade (mercantilism) was there a better strategy for expanding wealth and power than war? And before you think that expanding wealth and power don't need to be primary goals, remember that EVERYONE needs to agree on that belief for it to work. Otherwise one group that does concentrate on power can kill or enslave the other groups.

Don't get me wrong. I love this world, I want my family to live and be safe and that is achievable here and now more than any place or time in history. But I am aware that it is a profoundly unnatural state of affairs, maintained by will and technology. A slightly lesser degree in the will to maintain it or a medium loss of technology and we are a short step away from New Orleans after Katrina.

It is unnatural. And historically rare. And likely unsustainable, though I hope otherwise. Those of us raised in it find it normal and common sense. It is not.

One of the most infuriating things that fantasy and historical fiction authors do is take the beliefs of this bizarre bubble of time, beliefs that would have been dangerous and even pathological for most of history, and just assume they are normal. People ambushing travelers because they need food can't be challenged to not be cowards and come out and fight like men of honor. Someone who has buried most of her own family (the odds, until relatively recently, of any given child surviving to adulthood was very, very low) really doesn't go into a blue funk at a senseless death. All death was senseless. People raised tribally appear to have absolutely no PTSD associated with hacking outsiders up with machetes. When you or your family was victimized, until the late 1700s (and many places even now) you choices were vengeance or victimhood. There was no abstract justice. No one would investigate or prosecute or punish unless you or your family did.

Rights were things taken by force of arms, written into a treaty and only extant as long as force could keep them. Those without the leisure time and wealth to get skill at arms (which means all the peasants, farmers and merchants) were helpless meat to anyone raised with a sword.

Someone attempting to use modern ethics and principles would simply die. Gandhi was successful against the British. He was too smart to try it in South Africa and if there was a Gandhi in ancient Rome or Soviet Russia or Pol Pot's Cambodia or Iraq under Saddam he (and likely his family) simply disappeared. We saw how well the modern idea of peaceful resistance worked in Tiananmen Square.

As authors of almost anything except modern relationship talking heads, we need to be able to get under the skin of other people. Here's the deal: unless you can not only write things like the mass slaughter at Halabja, but write from a point of view where slaughtering Kurdish men, women and children to test chemical weapons just made sense, your fiction will always be missing something. It will always be two-dimensional.

That's the big picture and the underlying source of what I am about to write. The things that often bug me in fiction are the details.

The heroes fight people that no one would fight for reasons that are pitiful to funny to unbelievable. Then when they do fight, they fight stupid and the more bad-ass the character is, the stupider he fights, almost the opposite of the real world. Characters in fiction avoid weapons and ambushes and those are how real fighters get the job done and stay alive.

The inexperienced person that hires them says, "I'm coming along and you can't stop me." Trust me, if you hired me to kill ten people I can sure as hell stop you from following. Or I can slap the shit out of you for being a whiney amateur who will get the person I'm supposed to rescue killed because of your combination of stupidity and arrogance. Or I can just refuse the job. I don't want to die and/or fail because of a stupid, arrogant employer.

Our common culture presents passion and the passionate amateur as super-powers. Perhaps because so many of the readers and (dare I say) writers are themselves passionate amateurs. So the concerned parent with no skills insists on coming on the raid and saves the day. The untrained everyman who happens to fall into a relationship with a spy or a team of criminals becomes the lynchpin.

Really? It works about as well as amateur surgery. Amateurs are amateurs because they do not know what to do. And that gets people killed. And passionate people, amateur or professionals, make mistakes. If you are passionate, if you are emotional, the limbic system, not the neocortex, is operating. In other words, passionate people, emotional people are incapable of using the parts of their brains that make good decisions. And that gets people killed.

And authors play up guns like they are easy to use (as if just telling someone to shoot the zombies in the head will suddenly make a high school kid pull off something that Olympic medalists have failed to do under stress) and then either play up the damage (people getting knocked down from handgun bullets) or play down the damage, ("It went right through, I'll be fine.")

I haven't used much bad language yet, but the willful ignorance in those scenes makes me want to puke.

They approach fighting as if it was a sport–do a training montage and get in shape and you can hold your own. Experienced sport fighters get blown over and blindsided when it's for real because they have no idea what to expect. That's assuming they don't just get shot, like champion Alex Gong.

I freakin' hate the 'knockout' where you get hit in the head and go to sleep for a little bit and are just fine, as opposed to the days of dizziness and puking and giddiness and the bad coordination and the very real possibility of going blind and all that from a shot that wasn't hard enough to make me lose consciousness.

And I hate, hate, hate when an author uses the same level of emotional power for a life-threatening situation that they use for an emotional issue. "Does he really love me?" Is bullshit angst. "Will I live to see my children again?" Is fear. An author who doesn't know the difference gets my absolute, undying and total contempt.

Authors and script writers try to take something that, at its heart, is a dirty and dangerous job and try to make it noble. It has a lot more in common with driving a garbage truck than it does with riding a white horse.

Anyone see "Jail Break" the TV series? T-Bag is the average criminal. Yep. Clearly the writer's worse nightmare but he would barely blip my radar. The only reason they don't get away with as much in a real prison or jail is because almost the entire pool of potential victims is just exactly the same. So they got one detail right, and made it seem special, an aberration.

There's more, but that should be enough of a rant for now. That's why I need to remind you that I'm not your target audience. And I'll throw in a non-rant: You write for your readers. Not for me. Use anything in this book, any detail that makes your writing better. If people really wanted complete authenticity, they'd be out in the trenches.

✧✦✧✦✧

BIBLIOGRAPHY

These are the books mentioned in the text. Most are good, a few are great, some, well .... Read carefully. Always double-check with your own experience. Try to differentiate between your experience and what you want to believe. That's hard. You're a writer. Be a reader, too.

Anderson, Elijah. *Code of the Streets: Decency, Violence and the Moral Life of the Inner City*. New York: W. W. Norton & Company, 2000

Artwohl, Alexis. "Perceptual and Memory Distortions in Officer-Involved Shootings." FBI Law Enforcement Bulletin, October, 2002

Artwohl, Alexis. "No Recall of Weapons Discharge" Journal of the Law Enforcement Executive Forum, May, 2003

Artwohl, Alexis and Christensen, Loren. *Deadly Force Encounters*. Boulder, CO: Paladin Press, 1997

Ayoob, Massad. *Ayoob Files: The Book*. Police Bookshelf, 2004

Beck, Tobi. *The Armored Rose*. Beckenhall Publications 1999

Brison, Susan. *Aftermath: Violence and the Remaking of a Self*. Princeton, NJ: Princeton University Press, 2003

Caroline, Nancy L. *Emergency Care in the Streets*.

(There are a number of editions of this and it was my EMT textbook. It looks like the latest versions are running nearly $200. If you can find a used one for research, it might help. But you should really, at minimum, take a good first aid class.)

DeBecker, Gavin. *The Gift of Fear*. Boston: Little, Brown and Company, 1997

Giduck, John. *Terror at Beslan: A Russian Tragedy with Lessons for America's Schools*. Golden, CO: Archangel Group, 2005

Hatzfeld, Jean. *Machete Season: The Killers in Rwanda Speak*. New York: Farrar, Straus and Giroux. English translation 2005

Johnson, Jeffry L. "Use of Force and the Hollywood Factor" AELE Mo. L. J. 501 Special articles section April, 2007

Katz, David S. "The Selection and Testing of Soft Body Armor" for http://www.globalsecuritygroup.com

Keegan, John. *The Face of Battle: A Study of Agincourt, Waterloo and the Somme*. New York: Penguin Group (USA), 1978

Liddell-Hart, Sir Basil Henry. Strategy.London: Faber & Faber, Ltd. 1954

Miller, Rory. *Meditations on Violence: A Comparison of Martial Arts Training and Real World Violence*. Wolfeboro, NH: YMAA Publication Center, 2008

Miller, Rory. *Facing Violence: Preparing for the Unexpected*. Wolfeboro, NH: YMAA Publication Center, 2011

Miller, Rory. *Force Decisions, A Citizen's Guide: Understanding How Police determine Appropriate Use of Force*. Wolfeboro, NH: YMAA Publication Center, 2012

Miller, Rory (Editor). *Campfire Tales From Hell: Musings on Martial Arts, Survival, Bouncing and Other Thug Stuff*. Marc MacYoung, 2012

Miller, Rory and Kane, Lawrence. *Scaling Force: Dynamic Decision-Making Under Threat of Violence*. Wolfeboro, NH: YMAA Publication Center, 2012

Plutarch. *Lives of the Noble Greeks and Romans*. Numerous translations.

Shay, Jonathon. *Achilles in Vietnam: Combat Trauma and the Undoing of Character*. New York: Simon and Schuster, 1995

Siddle, Bruce. *Sharpening the Warrior's Edge: The Psychology and Science of Training*. PPCT Research Publications 1995

Strong, Sanford. *Strong on defense: Survival Rules for You and Your Family's Protection Against Crime*. New York: Atria Books, 1997

Tueller, Dennis. "How Close is too Close/" SWAT magazine, March 1983

The United States Marine Corps. *Warfighting*. New York: Bantam Doubleday Dell Publishing Group, 1994

U.S. Supreme Court Graham v. Connor, 490 U.S. 386 (1989)

Whitcomb, Christopher. *Cold Zero: Inside the FBI Hostage Rescue Team*. New York: Warner Books, Inc. 2001

Wiesel, Elie. *Night*. New York: Hill and Wang 1958

Zupan, Mark. *Gimp*. New York: HarperEntertainment 2006

WEBSITES

Kevlar© Survivor's Club
http://iacp.dupont.com/SurvivorClub/Search?

Cornered Cat
http://www.corneredcat.com/

Box o' Truth
http://www.theboxotruth.com/

My Online Recommended reading list
http://chirontraining.com/Site/Reading.html

A suggestion from Guy Letourneau, my historical gun Subject Matter Expert (SME)
http://www.sirwilliamhope.org/Library/DDLR/renaud.php

chirontraining.blogspot.com

chirontraining.com

Horrible Stories
I Told My Children
R. A. Ellis

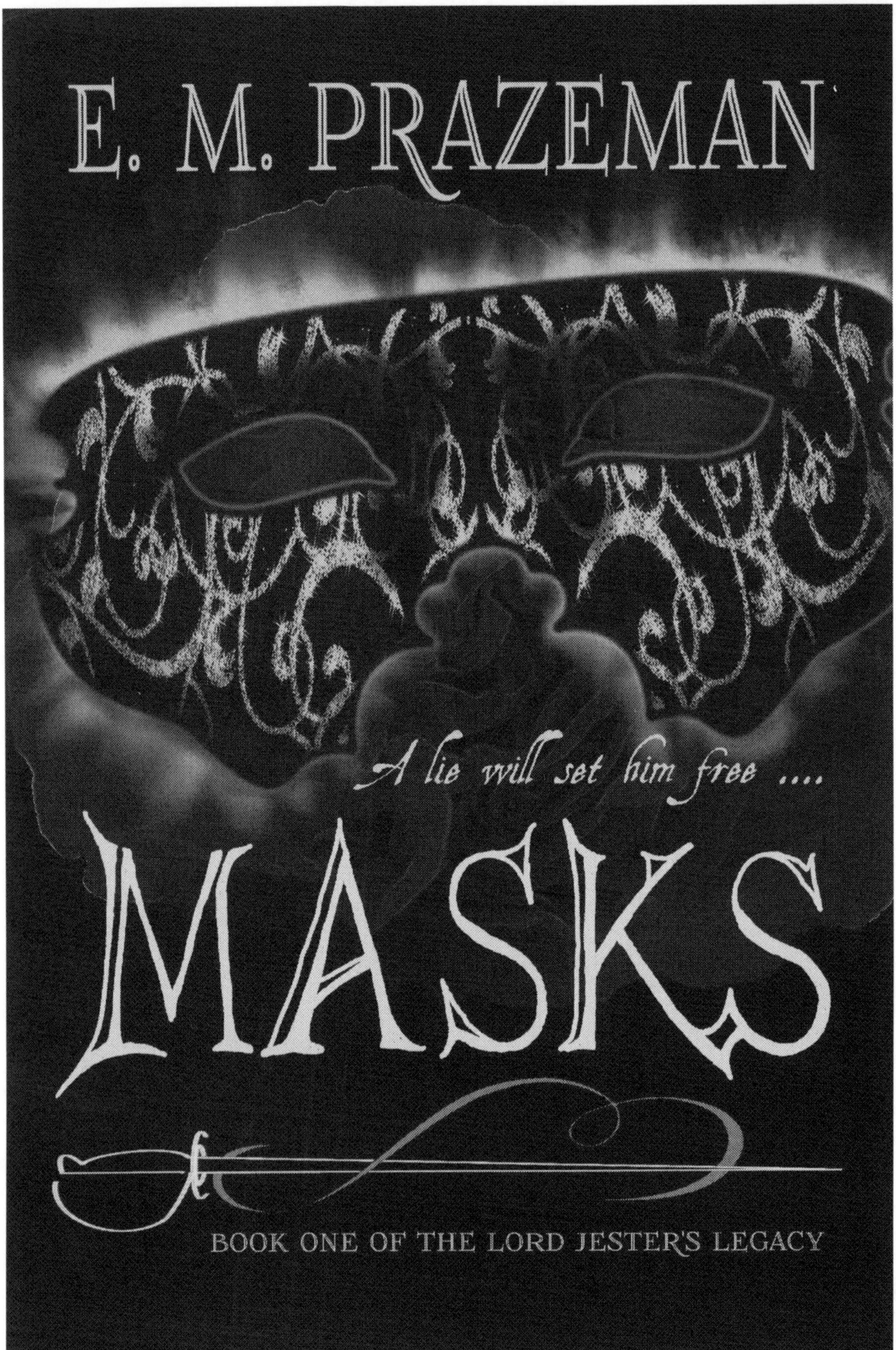

A young man tries to escape a life of servitude and deadly intrigues, only to weave his heart and soul among the threads of a sinister conspiracy that threatens a young democracy.

6x9 trade paperback, 350 pages

9568028R00159

Printed in Great Britain
by Amazon.co.uk, Ltd.,
Marston Gate.